Global Vietnam: Across Time, Space and Community

Series Editors

Phan Le Ha🆔, Sultan Hassanal Bolkiah Institute of Education, Universiti Brunei Darussalam, Brunei-Muara, Brunei Darussalam

Liam C. Kelley🆔, Institute of Asian Studies, Universiti Brunei Darussalam, Brunei-Muara, Brunei Darussalam

This book series is committed to advancing scholarship on Vietnam and Vietnam-related issues and to nurturing a new generation of Vietnam scholars in arts, humanities, education and social sciences, and interdisciplinary studies. It engages with Vietnam in global contexts and with global Vietnam across time, space and community. It features new writings and understandings that reflect nuances, complexities and dynamic that Vietnam in all of its possible meanings and constructs has inspired, generated and pushed. It recognises the ever expanding circles of Vietnam scholars around the world whose scholarship can be seen as the products of a new era when knowledge production has become increasingly globalized and decentralized. All of these have been reflected and in motion in the well-established over-a-decade-long Engaging With Vietnam conference series, of which this book series is an offspring. For more, visit: https://engagingwithvietnam.org/global-vietnam-book-series/

Quang Dai Tuyen

Heritage Conservation and Tourism Development at Cham Sacred Sites in Vietnam

Living Heritage Has A Heart

 Springer

Quang Dai Tuyen
Faculty of Tourism
Nguyen Tat Thanh University
Ho Chi Minh City, Vietnam

ISSN 2731-7552 ISSN 2731-7560 (electronic)
Global Vietnam: Across Time, Space and Community
ISBN 978-981-99-3349-5 ISBN 978-981-99-3350-1 (eBook)
https://doi.org/10.1007/978-981-99-3350-1

© The Editor(s) (if applicable) and The Author(s) 2023. This book is an open access publication.

Open Access This book is licensed under the terms of the Creative Commons Attribution 4.0 International License (http://creativecommons.org/licenses/by/4.0/), which permits use, sharing, adaptation, distribution and reproduction in any medium or format, as long as you give appropriate credit to the original author(s) and the source, provide a link to the Creative Commons license and indicate if changes were made.
The images or other third party material in this book are included in the book's Creative Commons license, unless indicated otherwise in a credit line to the material. If material is not included in the book's Creative Commons license and your intended use is not permitted by statutory regulation or exceeds the permitted use, you will need to obtain permission directly from the copyright holder.
The use of general descriptive names, registered names, trademarks, service marks, etc. in this publication does not imply, even in the absence of a specific statement, that such names are exempt from the relevant protective laws and regulations and therefore free for general use.
The publisher, the authors, and the editors are safe to assume that the advice and information in this book are believed to be true and accurate at the date of publication. Neither the publisher nor the authors or the editors give a warranty, expressed or implied, with respect to the material contained herein or for any errors or omissions that may have been made. The publisher remains neutral with regard to jurisdictional claims in published maps and institutional affiliations.

This Springer imprint is published by the registered company Springer Nature Singapore Pte Ltd.
The registered company address is: 152 Beach Road, #21-01/04 Gateway East, Singapore 189721, Singapore

This book is dedicated to my Cham community and my fellow scholars in the field of Cham Studies.

For their care, endless love, support, and engagement, I am eternally grateful.

Acknowledgments

I am deeply grateful for the support of the International Postgraduate Research Scholarship (IPRS) and UQ Centennial Scholarship (UQCent) in enabling me to pursue my studies at the University of Queensland, Brisbane, Australia. This research would not have been possible without the guidance and support of many individuals who have played a crucial role in its development.

Firstly, I would like to express my sincere gratitude to my supervisors, Prof. Ian Lilley and Associate Prof. Annie Ross, for their unwavering support, encouragement, and guidance throughout my research and writing journey. Their invaluable feedback and insightful comments have been instrumental in shaping the final outcome of this book. I am also grateful to a former book committee member, Dr. Andrew Sneddon, for his early encouragement and helpful comments. Additionally, I extend my thanks to the administrative staff of the School of Social Sciences at the University of Queensland for their support and assistance throughout my studies.

I would also like to extend my heartfelt thanks to my former advisor at the University of Hawaii, Manoa, Prof. Miriam Stark, who always encouraged me to think critically and complete this research. Furthermore, my appreciation extends to Prof. Phan Le Ha and Liam Kelley at the University of Hawaii, Manoa, who have provided valuable insights and meaningful conversations that have been instrumental in my personal and academic development.

I am grateful for the many friends and colleagues I have met throughout my academic journey, who share a passion for Cham culture. I would like to single out David Griffiths Sox (aka. Cei Sah Bingu), who has been a special friend and mentor, engaging in meaningful and stimulating discussions about Cham terminology and translation, and generously sharing his vast collection of documents on Cham culture. I am also thankful to the members of the Cham studies team, especially Dave Paulson and William Noseworthy, who have been integral to my journey of promoting and preserving Cham culture. Through my interactions with Dr. Lawrence Ross, who works on Cham traditional music, and Ph.D. candidate Mai Bùi Diệu Linh, who focuses on Cham religion, I have been reminded of the rich heritage and cultural legacy of my Cham community. I am deeply appreciative of their contributions to editing this book.

I would also like to express my gratitude to my family and Cham community in the United States, Cham scholars, my friends and colleagues in Vietnam, and my office mates at the University of Queensland, as well as fellow researchers, for their encouragement and support throughout my studies. I extend my heartfelt thanks to all my interviewees and the Cham Ahier priests who have been patient and kind in answering my questions and sharing their experiences.

I would like to extend my gratitude to Nguyen Tat Thanh University for their support in this research endeavor. Their support has been invaluable in allowing me to carry out my study and I am grateful for their recognition of the importance of this work. Their support has greatly contributed to the success of this project and has enabled me to achieve my research goals. I am truly grateful for their support and am proud to have been associated with such a renowned institution.

Finally, I would like to express my heartfelt thanks to the members of my Cham community who have been an integral part of my life and have contributed significantly to my growth and understanding of Cham culture. Their voices and perspectives have become the soul of this book, and I am proud to be a part of such a rich and vibrant community. This book is a tribute to my community, whose nurturing and support have shaped who I am today. *Dhar phuel!*

Contents

Abbreviations

AHD	Authorzsed Heritage Discourse
ASEANCOCI	The ASEAN Committee for Culture and Information
CSICH	Convention for the Safeguarding of the Intangible Cultural Heritage
EFEO	The École française d'Extrême-Orient
HAPs	Hoi An Protocols for the Best Conservation Practice in Asia
ICCROM	International Centre for the Study of the Preservation and Restoration of Cultural Property
ICOMOS	International Council on Monuments and Sites
IUCN	The International Union for Conservation of Nature
SEAMEO SPAFA	Regional Centre for Archaeology and Fine Arts
UNESCO	The United Nations Educational, Scientific and Cultural Organization
UNWTO	World Trade Organization

List of Figures

List of Tables

Chapter 1
Introduction—Jalan Nao

A culture survives when it has enough confidence in its past and enough say in its future to maintain its spirit and essence through all changes it will inevitably undergo. —Wade Davis, "The Way finders: Why Ancient Wisdom Matters in the Modern World".

Jalan Nao: A Personal Journey—Reflecting on My Experience with My Cham Community and Temples

I still recall my first visit to the Po Rome temple during the Katé festival 32 years ago. As a child, my grandfather, who was well-versed in history, folk stories, and oral traditions, often regaled me and my friends with tales of the Cham people, their kings, and temples. I remember seeing the temple on top of the hill from our village and feeling its sacredness, a sentiment shared by my parents and community. Although I was too young to fully appreciate it, my family did not take me to the temple for spiritual worship during any ceremonies or festivals.

In junior high school, I and some friends decided to attend the Katé festival at the Po Rome temple. I was filled with excitement and eagerness and couldn't sleep the night before. I wondered about the Cham people, the Champā kingdom, and how the Cham temples were built (my grandfather had said that the construction of Cham temples was still a mystery). In the early morning, some friends suggested that we walk instead of cycling, as it was supposed to be "near." But my understanding of the term "near" was as immature as I was at the time. In my later years, I came to realize that people always say that the temples are "near" us, referring to the gods who watch over us from the hills. The two-hour walk was tiring, but the temple was, and always will be, "near." Upon arrival, we were exhausted and dehydrated, but people from nearby villages offered us water before we visited the sacred space. The temple was magnificent, and my awe and inspiration overcame any sense of fatigue. I saw Ahier priests and members of the Cham community preparing offerings for worship, and it was the first time I had witnessed the Katé festival at a Cham temple.

© The Author(s) 2023
Q. D. Tuyen, *Heritage Conservation and Tourism Development at Cham Sacred Sites in Vietnam*, Global Vietnam: Across Time, Space and Community,
https://doi.org/10.1007/978-981-99-3350-1_1

I walked around the temple and came across some collapsed remains close to the main tower. I touched the bricks and felt the ancients, with my grandfather's words and the stories of our ancestors present. I could sense the talent and ingenuity of generations that made these monuments possible. I watched as other people prayed for the safety and prosperity of their families and community. Despite my young age, it was a deeply moving experience that helped me understand the significance of the Po Rome temple as a living sacred site. I felt the heartbeat of heritage and the rhythm of the collective Cham communities visiting the temple for prayer and worship.

After the festival, we visited a Cham village about a kilometer away to see my uncle, who had married a woman from the village and, following our matriarchal traditions, had relocated there with his wife's family. I sat with my family and friends and realized that I had learned so much more about Cham culture that day. The temple brought the Cham people together, and I felt the presence of my ancestors in my senses. This experience inspired me to pursue my current path as a researcher of Cham culture and an advocate for my community and traditions.

I became one of the first students in a new generation of anthropologists in Vietnam, where ethnology had been the dominant field of study until the early 2000s. I studied in Ho Chi Minh City for my undergraduate degree and worked at the Cham Cultural Research Center in Ninh Thuan Province, combining my education with the inspiration of my grandfather's life. During my time at the Cham Center, I visited many Cham villages and traditional ceremonies throughout Vietnam and learned about the diversity and interconnectedness of Cham culture with everyday life. These experiences reinforced the importance of our temples as symbols of our people, connecting all Cham communities despite the loss of our civilization.

The survival of the Cham people after the fall of the Champā kingdom is a poignant tale of perseverance and determination. During a recent visit to Binh Thuan Province, I had the privilege of learning about the struggles and sacrifices of our ancestors as they sought to preserve their rich cultural heritage.

One particularly moving account came in the form of an Ariya, an ancient Cham poem, that tells the story of the Cham people being hunted down and killed by Vietnamese Minh Mang's King forces. Many were forced to flee their homes and take refuge in the wilderness, living in hiding during the day and using the light of the moon and the white sand along the coast to guide their way. Despite the dangers and difficulties they faced, the Cham people never gave up their traditions. Even as they journeyed to safety, they made sure to pass down their script, the Cham Akhar Thrah, by writing letters in the sand. Each night, before departing, they would erase the markings to avoid detection by their enemies.

This is a story of resilience, of a people who refused to let their heritage be erased by adversity. It is a reminder of the strength and courage of the Cham ancestors, and the importance of preserving our cultural heritage for future generations.

The Cham people have a rich and storied history, passed down through generations in the form of folk tales, hymns, and songs. One such story is the tale of how Cham history and traditions were transformed into sacred hymns, which today remain an integral part of Cham religious ceremonies and rituals.

When I visited Binh Thuan, I had the opportunity to witness the power of these hymns firsthand, as I listened to the haunting melodies of the Kadhar and Maduen singing the anthems of the Champā kings. Through the music, the Cham people have ensured that their history and traditions are not lost to time. This connection to their heritage is felt deeply by the Cham community, who view their cultural heritage as sacred and protected. Encroachments on this sacredness, such as violations of the temple, are met with deep sadness and a physical manifestation of grief. It is this unbreakable bond to their heritage that drives the Cham people to preserve their traditions and culture, no matter what challenges they may face. This devotion to their heritage is what has kept the Cham community strong and vibrant for generations, and it is what will continue to keep it alive for generations to come.

My experience at the Po Dam temple was a turning point for me in my work to preserve Cham cultural heritage. Despite the fact that the temple was under the care of conservationists, the exclusion of the Cham community from the preservation efforts left me feeling frustrated and heartbroken. The Cham priests with whom I was traveling were equally upset, as they had not received any information or consultation from the heritage authorities about the conservation works being carried out at the temple. This experience highlighted a larger issue in the conservation of cultural heritage, particularly when it comes to sites that hold spiritual significance for marginalized communities. The Po Dam temple, like many other Champā temples in Vietnam, holds deep spiritual significance for the Cham people, who have been the custodians of these sites for generations. The exclusion of the Cham community from the conservation process raises questions about who the cultural heritage belongs to and who has the right to preserve and protect it.

I was concerned about the potential for the conservationists to make changes to the temple that would be inconsistent with Cham cultural heritage and spirituality. The Cham community's anger and frustration at being excluded from the preservation process were completely understandable. They felt that their heritage was being taken away from them, and they were left with no say in how it was being preserved.

In my work, I strive to ensure that ethnic communities like the Cham are included in the conservation and preservation of their cultural heritage. It is essential to involve these communities in the decision-making process and to ensure that their perspectives and cultural values are taken into account in any conservation efforts. Only through collaboration between the community, conservationists, and heritage authorities can we ensure that cultural heritage sites are preserved in a manner that is respectful and consistent with the cultural heritage and spirituality of the community. Such "approaches" have been used at the other Champā temples in Central Vietnam, as well as in Binh Thuan and Ninh Thuan provinces where the Cham communities still practice their spirituality. I felt that the conservationists looked upon us as a threat to their conservation efforts. The Cham priests were surprised about the conservation works at Po Dam temple, as they had not received any information from the heritage authorities. The priests told the archaeologists that we Cham needed to know what the "conservationists" were doing and why the Cham were excluded from the preservation of a temple they have been looking after for many generations. What would happen if the conservationists changed something and reconstructed the temple incorrectly and inappropriately to the Cham temple? Whose cultural heritage does the site belong to? The Cham custodians who follow a long tradition of caring for the temple through many generations were annoyed by the behavior of these "conservationists" and disapproved of these kinds of conservation approaches.

As a researcher, I have come to understand that the preservation of cultural heritage is a complex process that involves not just the physical conservation of sites, but also the preservation of cultural traditions, rituals, and values that are associated with these sites. The exclusion of the Cham community from the conservation efforts at Po Dam temple highlights the larger issues surrounding the marginalization of Indigenous communities in the field of heritage management. These communities often possess valuable knowledge about their ancestral heritage and cultural practices, and their involvement in the conservation process can greatly enhance the authenticity and effectiveness of conservation efforts.

Through my work, I strive to promote the idea of community-led conservation, where the voices and perspectives of Indigenous communities are valued and integrated into the decision-making process. This approach can ensure that the heritage sites are conserved in a manner that is consistent with the cultural values and traditions of the community, and that the community remains connected to its ancestral heritage. It is my hope that by highlighting the experiences of the Cham community, I can contribute to the wider discourse on heritage conservation and help promote more inclusive and equitable practices in the field. By working together, we can create a world where the living heritage of all cultures is respected and valued, and where Indigenous communities have a prominent role in the preservation of their ancestral heritage.

Exploring the Evolution of Issues in Living Heritage Conservation and Tourism Development: A Gateway

For more than a decade, the concept of living heritage has been acknowledged as a central component in the definition of heritage. Smith (2006) defines heritage as a process of engagement, communication, and making meaning in the present and for the future, based on shared experiences and memories with one's community. This definition recognizes the interconnection between objects, places, and practices in the past and present across socio-cultural landscapes.

Smith (2006) argues that heritage cannot be defined solely by objects or "things". Instead, heritage is constructed through various cultural and social activities, which give value and meaning to the "things". Only after this value and meaning have been assigned, do the "things" become heritage. Similarly, Harrington (2004) views heritage as not just about the past, but as a connection between the present and a distant time and/or place, with intangible components at its core. UNESCO (2003) also recognizes the significance of intangible cultural heritage in maintaining cultural diversity.

The importance of living heritage lies not only in its manifestation but also in its ability to pass knowledge and skills through generations. Scholars such as Bauer et al., (2017) emphasize that intangible cultural heritage represents the traditions, customs, practices, and knowledge recognized by communities, while the term "living heritage" conveys the connection between these intangible cultures, monuments, and sacred sites that have been continuously used for rituals and social interaction (Bauer et al., 2017, p. 96).

International organizations have recognized the importance of considering the full range of spiritual and social values embodied in heritage places since at least the 1990s. The Nara Document on Authenticity (ICOMOS, 1994) highlights the importance of respecting all values, both tangible and intangible, that shape a heritage place. The World Heritage Committee (ICOMOS, 1995) adopted three categories of cultural landscapes to list on the World Heritage List, including "clearly defined landscapes designed and created intentionally by humanity," "organically evolved landscapes," and "associative cultural landscapes," where natural landscapes are invested largely or entirely with intangible cultural values.

The associative cultural landscape is defined to include "the powerful religious, artistic, or cultural associations of natural elements rather than only material cultural features" (WHC, 2019). This category recognizes the significance of intangible dimensions of places and the heritage of local communities and Indigenous people (Brown et al., 2005; Buggey, 1999; Rössler, 2005). This shift in heritage management approaches from a focus on tangible aspects to one that includes intangible dimensions (UNESCO, 2013) highlights the importance of the intangible heritage values embedded in the cultural landscapes and physical geographies to which Indigenous peoples give meaning (Buggey, 1999).

The research highlights the need for intangible aspects of heritage to occupy more prominent spaces in legislative language and ruling. Although it is possible to bring intangible values under Criterion VI, they remain apart from this legislation and need to be more prominently recognized. In 1987, the Uluru-Kata Tjuta National Park in Central Australia received recognition as a World Heritage site for its outstanding natural heritage values. However, in 1994, its status was expanded to encompass both its natural and cultural values, reflecting the close connections between nature and humanity in the area. This cultural landscape holds a wealth of religious, artistic, and cultural meanings, shaped by the interactions between local communities and the natural environment, as well as by Indigenous ownership, knowledge, and traditional land management practices. The World Heritage Convention acknowledges both cultural and natural forms of heritage, but the protection of living heritage was not explicitly addressed until the adoption of the 2003 Convention for the Safeguarding of Intangible Cultural Heritage (CSICH). The CSICH recognizes the need to preserve cultural heritage that is not tied to a specific place, including oral traditions, performing arts, social practices, knowledge about nature and the universe, and traditional craftsmanship. This intangible cultural heritage is constantly passed down and reinterpreted by communities and groups, and it provides a sense of identity and continuity while also promoting respect for cultural diversity and human creativity (UNESCO, 2003).

Living heritage is deeply rooted in the cultural traditions and beliefs of Indigenous and local communities. The 2003 Convention emphasizes the importance of these communities in the protection and management of intangible cultural heritage, and it supports cultural practitioners, who are the masters of local traditions, as the primary stewards of these practices. Indigenous leaders working to maintain their traditions are helped to develop a sense of socio-cultural identity, which depends on the sustained interaction between local people and the natural environment (Harrington, 2004, p. 56).

The recognition of the importance of the cultural dimensions of heritage sites is increasingly gaining attention. In 2005, the IUCN and UNESCO conference emphasized that the preservation of sacred sites, cultural landscapes, and traditional agricultural systems cannot be achieved without considering the cultures that have shaped and continue to shape them. Indigenous people, as custodians of sacred sites and holders of traditional knowledge, play a critical role in maintaining both biological and cultural diversity. In the same year, ICCROM defined heritage sites as living spaces where the community is engaged with the place and its significance. Cultural heritage management should not only focus on preserving the material elements of a site, but also consider the local community's values and social issues (ICCROM, 2005).

Kong (2008) conducted a study on the social impacts of conservation and tourism development in two traditional living communities in China and Japan. The results showed that conservation efforts have often been focused on physical elements of heritage sites and ignore their effects on the social well-being of local communities (Kong, 2008). Top-down and expert-based conservation approaches have largely neglected the perspectives of these communities, resulting in a lack of understanding of local cosmologies and cultural perspectives related to heritage preservation. This has led to economic instability and degradation of daily life among local communities (Kong, 2008). Hence, the conservation and management of living heritage sites should be inclusive of local perspectives and enriched by the communities who live and make meaning with such locations (Kong, 2008).

Southeast Asia was the first region where ICCROM launched its Heritage Site Programme in 2003. This program focused on conserving the living dimensions of cultural heritage and involved several countries in the region. The core aim of the program was to establish strong connections between local communities and heritage sites, and it has been successful in highlighting the essential role of the "living" aspects of heritage conservation. Local communities have been involved in the conservation process across Southeast Asia through this program, and critical issues and features of conservation have been explored (Tunprawat, 2009; Wijesuriya, 2008). The program has also presented the living heritage approach as the most practical and efficient solution to the challenges faced in heritage conservation (Tunprawat, 2009).

The undervaluation and marginalization of living heritage, particularly Indigenous living heritage, is a widespread issue in the field of cultural heritage management. Despite its significant social, cultural, and economic values, living heritage is often ignored or even demonized in both local and international systems of heritage management (Bwasiri, 2009; Byrne, 2012, 2014; Karlström, 2005; Kwanda, 2010; Miura, 2005). On the other hand, community involvement is considered to be an essential aspect of the preservation of living heritage (Renault & Collange, 2008; Smith, 2012; UNESCO, 2003).

Efforts like the Heritage Site Programme launched by ICCROM in Southeast Asia in 2003 have emphasized the importance of involving local communities in the conservation process and have proven to be effective in highlighting the critical significance of the "living" dimensions of heritage conservation (Tunprawat, 2009; Wijesuriya, 2008). By understanding the features of living heritage, it is possible to foster mutual respect for social, cultural, and human rights and promote the appreciation of cultural diversity (Huong, 2015; Lenzerini, 2011; Logan, 2012; Wijesuriya, 2008; Wijesuriya et al., 2006).

The recognition of the importance of intangible cultural heritage and the role it plays in national development and historical preservation in Vietnam has led to various initiatives aimed at safeguarding and promoting this type of heritage. One of the key initiatives has been the establishment of the National Intangible Cultural Heritage Centre (NICHC) in 2007. The NICHC is responsible for conducting research and collecting data on intangible cultural heritage, as well as organizing activities to promote and preserve this heritage. The Centre has also collaborated with various local and international organizations to raise awareness about the importance of intangible cultural heritage and to develop strategies for its preservation.

Another important initiative has been the establishment of the National List of Intangible Cultural Heritage, which aims to document and recognize the significant contributions made by Vietnam's intangible cultural heritage to the country's rich cultural heritage. The List is updated regularly and contains a wide range of intangible cultural heritage items, such as traditional music, dance, oral traditions, and craftsmanship, among others.

In sum, the recognition of the importance of intangible cultural heritage and the role it plays in national development and historical preservation in Vietnam has led to various initiatives aimed at safeguarding and promoting this type of heritage. These initiatives have contributed to the recognition and preservation of the unique cultural heritage of Vietnam and will continue to play an important role in ensuring the survival of these traditions and cultural practices for future generations.

As specified by the Law on Cultural Heritage in Vietnam, all policies aimed at preserving cultural heritage must have a positive impact on the nation's economic and social development (Lask & Herold, 2004). However, the Law does not address the issue of cultural tourism and the strategies necessary to mitigate its negative impact on cultural heritage sites or provide guidelines for sustainable use and maintenance of heritage for future generations (Council of Europe, Committee of Ministers, 1996, as cited in Lask & Herold, 2004). To address this, numerous projects have been initiated under the National Target Program to study, document, and collect Vietnamese cultural heritage (Binh, 2001; Van, 2001). In 2009, the 2001 Law was revised to effectively manage intangible cultural heritage in accordance with international standards and practices, and its definition was updated to match the 2003 UNESCO Convention. In this Law, intangible cultural heritage is considered a cultural practice carried on by individuals, groups, or communities known as "cultural carriers" (Salemink, 2012). Thus, the protection and preservation of cultural heritage should be primarily focused on these "cultural carriers" (Salemink, 2012).

In the Vietnamese Law on Cultural Heritage, the term "community" is not explicitly mentioned in the definition of intangible cultural heritage (Giang, 2015). Additionally, this law fails to acknowledge the rights of individuals and communities to participate in discussions and decisions concerning the cultural heritage that they own or preserve (Giang, 2015). Nevertheless, as heritage experts suggest, this type of legislation should not diminish the role of bearers or holders of intangible cultural heritage, as they are the rightful owners of that heritage (Hong, 2015, p. 617).

To effectively identify and classify living heritage that can be protected and maintained by local communities, several criteria need to be considered. These criteria include:

1. The heritage is an integral part of the local community's cultural fabric and daily life;
2. The cultural practices and functions of the heritage are passed down from generation to generation within the local community;
3. The local community plays a role in defining the heritage and it forms part of their ethnic identity;
4. The heritage reflects the cultural diversity and mutual respect between different communities and groups (Hong, 2015, p. 617).

In the field of tourism, sustainable development has been a widely discussed topic since the 1990s as a way to mitigate negative impacts and enhance positive outcomes from tourism activities on society, cultural heritage, and the environment (Bramwell & Lane, 1993, 2012; Buckley, 2012; Sharpley, 2000). Cultural heritage has been recognized as a significant source of economic growth in Vietnam, leading to increased interest from the state in preserving and promoting these resources (Thien, 2017). The concept of sustainable development has been explored from a range of perspectives, including economics, the environment, and local communities (Dat & Huu, 2015; Logan, 1998; Tran & Walter, 2014; Truong et al., 2014). Despite this focus on sustainability, scholars have noted a common issue with a lack of community involvement in the strategic planning process for sustainable development and heritage management (Gilbert et al., 1998; Jansen-Verbeke & Go, 1995; Logan, 1998, 2015; Haley & Haley, 1998). Heritage management experts in Vietnam argue that sustainable development is only achievable when there is a balance of rights and interests among stakeholders, including the local community, who should benefit from the economic and cultural value of their cultural heritage (Larsen, 2015; Logan, 2015). However, in practice, local communities are often not given the opportunity to participate in heritage management activities due to restrictions in heritage management legislation or the traditional customs of their community (Larsen, 2017).

Despite the recognition of the cultural heritage as a potential source of economic development in Vietnam, the impact of conservation policies and regulations on the local communities has been a matter of concern. The concept of "community" is often mentioned in heritage management, but the actual voices and participation of the community are often neglected in the planning and conservation process (Larsen, 2018). Indigenous groups, in particular, are frequently unaware of their rights, and their traditional livelihoods, beliefs, and customs are often disrupted by conservation measures.

Furthermore, government documents and plans for local heritage rarely consider the role of community participation in heritage management. This is exemplified by the forced displacement of local communities from protected heritage areas, where their livelihoods and practices, passed down through generations, were deemed a threat to the heritage values of the sites (Dung, 2015). This lack of consideration for community perspectives highlights the need for more inclusive and participatory approaches in heritage management, which take into account the needs and rights of local communities and their relationship with their cultural heritage.

It is crucial for the government to recognize the relationship between cultural heritage and the communities that practice and preserve it. The absence of community participation in the decision-making process has led to the marginalization of local people and the disregard for their cultural practices, livelihoods, and beliefs (Giang, 2015). The failure to incorporate community perspectives in heritage management has resulted in the loss of important cultural traditions and livelihoods, which is against the principles of sustainable heritage development (Larsen, 2018). Therefore, it is imperative for the government to revise its cultural heritage laws and policies to ensure that the community is adequately represented and has a voice in decisions concerning their cultural heritage. The legislation must be revised to reflect the rights and interests of the communities and to ensure their active participation in the heritage management process. It is essential to establish a legal framework that upholds these rights and creates a balance between heritage conservation and the rights of local communities (Logan, 2015). The implementation of these policies can lead to the sustainable preservation and promotion of cultural heritage, which will benefit not only the communities but also the country as a whole.

These challenges highlight the need for a more comprehensive and inclusive approach to heritage conservation in Vietnam that considers the perspectives, needs, and rights of local communities. The involvement of communities in the decision-making process and the allocation of benefits from heritage tourism should be prioritized in order to ensure that heritage conservation not only protects cultural assets, but also contributes to sustainable development and the well-being of local communities. To achieve this, there is a need for a shift in the current approach to heritage conservation, from a top-down, state-centered approach to a participatory and community-led approach that recognizes the rights of local communities to their cultural heritage and the resources that it provides. The government and other stakeholders should work together to create a policy and legal framework that recognizes and protects the rights of local communities and ensures their participation in decision-making processes related to heritage conservation. This can be achieved through consultations with local communities, the development of participatory planning processes, and the establishment of clear mechanisms for the distribution of benefits from heritage tourism.

The community's participation in cultural practices associated with heritage sites in Vietnam has been facing a number of challenges, as evidenced by multiple studies (Giang, 2015; Kong, 2008; Larsen, 2015, 2017; Logan, 2015; Spenceley et al., 2017). Despite the recognition of human rights to livelihood in legal documents relating to heritage sites, there is a lack of protection for human rights to participate in planning and decision-making or to have access to justice and development (Larsen, 2017). The Cultural Heritage Law does not sufficiently link heritage to human beings, which exacerbates these issues.

Furthermore, scholars have pointed out that the economic benefits generated from tourism are not equitably shared with cultural owners of heritage, leading to unequal community rights related to their heritage (Hoa, 2005; Kong, 2008; Lask & Herold, 2004; Le, 2015; Logan, 2015; Spenceley et al., 2017; Tran & Walter, 2014). The authorities may claim that they are providing benefits for local communities, but the ways in which those benefits are shared are often unclear and not based on specific objectives or mechanisms for implementation. The Heritage Management Board has not established clear management mechanisms to ensure community representation in decision-making, and many cases in Vietnam, such as the Phong Nha World Heritage Site, have shown that the majority of the income generated from tourism is used for staff salaries and contributions to the federal and provincial budget, with only a small portion being invested in local communities (Larsen, 2015, 2017).

The literature highlights that ignoring community participation and economic benefits in the conservation of cultural heritage can lead to the loss of cultural rights, livelihoods, and traditional habitats for local communities (Logan, 2015). There is a lack of understanding among heritage practitioners and government officials in Vietnam about different definitions and conceptualizations of heritage conservation, which has resulted in a uniform strategy being applied to preserve and manage diverse heritage sites with absolute authority in the hands of the state officials (Phuong, 2006). This approach marginalizes and excludes local communities and in some cases denies them access to their own heritage sites, causing negative impacts on their cultural heritage (Huong, 2015). Thus, it can be argued that such heartless approaches to heritage management, which aim to protect Indigenous culture or heritage, often do so at the exclusion or detriment of the very communities they purport to serve.

In Ninh Thuan Province, economic development is a priority in legislative planning, often taking precedence over cultural preservation initiatives. The province's tourism industry plays a significant role in its economic development, with Cham cultural heritage serving as a major tourist attraction (Anh, 2012; Dop et al., 2014; Phan An, 2015; Sakaya, 2003; Thuy, 2012). Local authorities aim to preserve and promote Cham cultural heritage to attract more tourists, which has brought some economic benefits to the Cham community through Cham handicraft villages (Tuyen, 2014). However, the focus on increasing the number of tourists to the province (from 2.1 million in 2015 to 3.5 million by 2030) fails to take into consideration the well-being of the local communities who contribute to sustainable development (Quynh Trang, 2013). This development also risks negatively impacting the Cham Indigenous community, potentially leading to cultural changes and commercialization, without appropriate policies in place to mitigate these impacts (Hoa, 2005).

As the Cham community holds its Indigenous heritage and cultural values close to its temples and villages, local cultural heritage management in the region is viewed as a form of "living culture" (Sakaya, 2001). Given this context in Vietnam, my central research question seeks to examine how heritage management recognizes the values of living heritage for cultural sites. *(1) How does heritage management balance the conservation and tourism development of the living sacred sites, such as the Po Klaong Girai temple, in Vietnam with the preservation of authenticity and cultural pride of the Cham community, and (2) how can heritage management better recognize and address the values of living heritage as perceived by the Cham community in the context of cultural heritage preservation in Southeast Asia?*

Understanding Living Heritage: The Interplay Between Community, Culture, and Place

Heritage is often referred to as "living" when it is closely tied to the cultural practices of a community and is passed down from generation to generation. Living heritage is centered around the community who created it and is a crucial aspect of cultural preservation (Weise, 2013). This type of heritage helps foster a sense of belonging and often plays a vital role in the social, cultural, and economic lives of community members (Wijesuriya et al., 2006).

However, when traditions are imposed from outside, they can stand in opposition to this locally sourced type of heritage (Weise, 2013). This highlights the importance of considering community input in the conservation of living heritage sites, as they are the ones who understand the meaning behind these traditions (Renault & Collange, 2008) and play a significant role in determining their future (Miura, 2005; Wijesuriya et al., 2006).

The concept of "living heritage" has emerged, stating that "Heritage is all about culture and has been created by people, and it has been created for people" (Sarah & Wijesuriya, 2014). This encompasses all expressions resulting from the interaction between people and nature, including both tangible and intangible elements. These expressions have evolved and been reinterpreted over time, reflecting changes in society, and communities continue to benefit from them (Wijesuriya et al., 2006).

Heritage management that is centered around the community is known as the "living heritage" approach. This approach recognizes that heritage belongs to the members of society whose values are reflected in its definition and that the most effective means of caring for heritage are through their active involvement (ICCROM, 2003 cited from: Stovel et al., 2003). The concept of continuity is key in characterizing the connection between living heritage sites and traditional communities (Tunprawat, 2009).

Poulios (2014a) categorizes different types of associations between heritage sites and communities, including those between a site and a local, dwelling, or evolving community, or a site that has a special connection with a community. All of these associations have their strengths, but communities often play a role in heritage management under the control of heritage authorities (Poulios, 2014a).

To address this issue, Poulios (2014b) has proposed a set of criteria for identifying and managing living heritage, including: the continuity of the heritage site's original function, the continuity of the community's connection with the site, the continuity of the site's expressions, and the continuity of community care for the site through management systems and traditional knowledge. This framework views heritage as an integral part of the current community's life (Poulios, 2014b; Sarah & Wijesuriya, 2014; Wijesuriya, 2007).

The continuity between the past and the present is a critical aspect of cultural traditions (Poulios, 2014b; Tunprawat, 2009; Wijesuriya, 2007). Living heritage is deeply rooted in the past but also embraces change, adapting continuously to contemporary conditions. Andrews and Buggey (2008) assert that heritage may be created in the past, but its meaning is produced and given in the present. Maintaining heritage is an ongoing process that involves embracing change to respond to contemporary political, economic, historical, and social environments (Poulios, 2014b; Tunprawat, 2009; Wijesuriya, 2007). However, neglecting local participation and continuity in the management of cultural heritage can negatively impact its significance to local communities and result in disastrous consequences (Weise, 2013; Wijesuriya, 2014). Positive change must be recognized as a natural process, but it must unfold according to local culture and as defined by local communities (Ayoubi, 2015).

Unfortunately, traditional cultural heritage management often overlooks the significance of living heritage, such as local beliefs, social practices, and traditional ways of life among local communities (Byrne, 2012; Karlström, 2005, 2013; Miura, 2005). For example, in the case of Maori heritage, Whiting (2005, p. 180) points out that "technical conservation knowledge is not enough to deal with the complexities of recognizing and maintaining the cultural and spiritual values of a site or place." Byrne (2014, pp. 2–3) refers to "counter-heritage" as a more democratic heritage practice, one that respects the existence of other ways of relating to old things. Heritage conservation should consider objects as dynamic, embedded in social practices rather than as static physical materials related to the conservation project (Byrne, 2004).

In recent years, the focus of heritage research has shifted from the preservation and interpretation of material-based heritage to the role of living heritage (Bwasiri, 2008; Miura, 2005; Pearson & Gorman, 2010; Pearson & Sullivan, 1995). This shift in perspective recognizes the importance of understanding and managing heritage sites and objects that are connected to core communities, who play a crucial role in the preservation of living heritage (Poulios, 2014b).

Traditionally, conservation efforts as outlined in foundational texts such as the Venice Charter have ignored the role of core communities, with heritage professionals taking a dominant role in heritage conservation. However, there has been a growing recognition of the significance of the core community as a key stakeholder in heritage conservation, with a shift towards giving the core community more agency in the decision-making process (Kong, 2008; Poulios, 2014b; Wijesuriya, 2014). This approach can be seen in recent developments in Australia's Burra Charter and the Asian-focused Hoi An Protocols. In this view, heritage professionals serve a

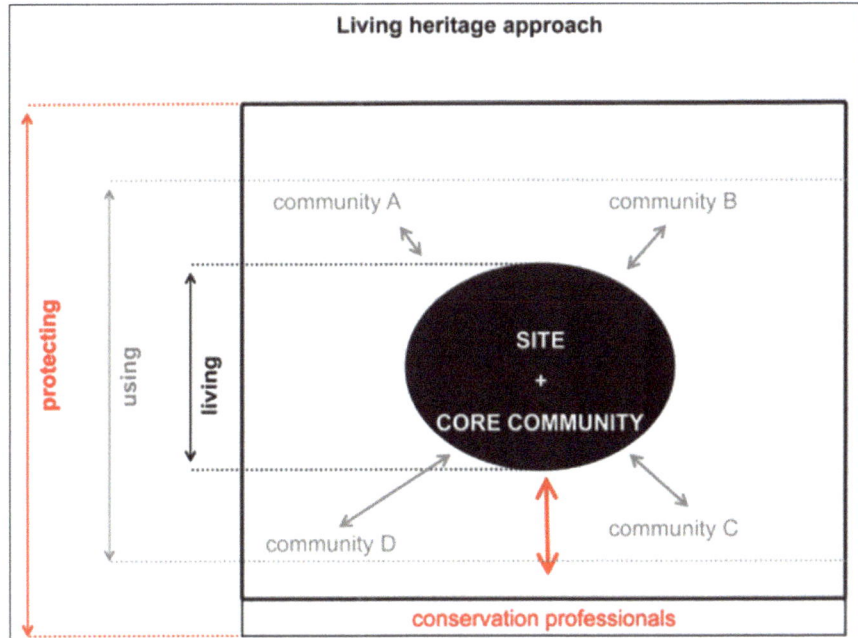

Fig. 1.1 Core community and heritage site: An intrinsic connection in living heritage (Poulios, 2014b, p. 130)

supportive and advisory role, assisting the core community in their conservation efforts (Figure 9).

As illustrated in Fig. 1.1 of Poulios (2014b), the close connection between a heritage site and the core community, who maintains its values and continuity, is crucial to the preservation of living heritage. Scholars emphasize the importance of respecting and prioritizing the culture, values, and feelings of the core community, who are the traditional owners of their cultural heritage (Kong, 2008; Poulios, 2014b; Wijesuriya, 2014).

Living heritage engages the core community in the long-term conservation of the heritage site, with a focus on connecting heritage and community through managing continuity and change in use patterns, livelihood, and mutual well-being (Wijesuriya, 2014, p. 33). This approach, which places the community at the center of heritage conservation, creates a framework for sustainability (Ayoubi, 2015; Poulios, 2014b; Sarah & Wijesuriya, 2014; Wijesuriya et al., 2006).

Arkarapotiwong (2015) recognizes the importance of considering both the emphasis of conservation experts on man-made heritage and the demands of local communities for the development of their living heritage space in achieving equality in managing living heritage sites. The author advocates for a collaborative network between the private sector and local communities and suggests that power should be balanced among all stakeholders to ensure sustainable management. However, this perspective overlooks the distinction between the core community, who are the traditional owners and stewards of their cultural heritage, and other local communities who may reside near the heritage sites. In the author's research, the Cham people are identified as the core community, while other stakeholders, such as the Kinh community living near the temple, the Raglai community ritually tied to certain heritage sites, heritage practitioners, and business sectors, also play a role in the management and conservation of the heritage sites.

The Basis Behind: Rationale

In this study, the Po Klaong Girai temple in Vietnam serves as a case to explore the Cham community's perspectives on heritage management and to develop modifications for the effective management of their cultural heritage. The research takes into account the diverse approaches to heritage assessment within the Cham community, particularly their emphasis on intangible heritage, which encompasses traditions and living expressions passed down from ancestors to descendants, and living heritage, which encompasses cultural expressions and practices that provide meaning and continuity to social life across generations of individuals, social groups, and communities (UNESCO, 2003).

In Southeast Asia, heritage conservation responsibilities have typically been assumed by government authorities and heritage professionals, who may not accurately reflect the views of ethnic minority communities. This has led to a disconnection between heritage sites and minority communities, and has resulted in poor outcomes for heritage preservation (Arkarapotiwong, 2015; Byrne, 1991, 2012; Karlström, 2005; Lewis & Rose, 2013; Alexopoulos, 2013; Ayoubi, 2015; Kong, 2008; Poulios, 2014a; Tunprawat, 2009). The lack of community participation in conservation regimes has been identified as a key factor reducing the effectiveness of these efforts (Balen & Vandesande, 2015; Waterton, 2015), and more inclusive approaches to heritage management are necessary (Poulios, 2014a). The case study of Po Klaong Girai temple will challenge this lack of recognition and explore the values of living heritage for cultural sites within the Cham community.

The study will focus on the significance of festivals, temple usage, and the role of the temple in Cham lives, as central to the creation and maintenance of cultural heritage for the Cham community. The heritage assessment of the Cham community will be considered, and the emphasis placed on intangible heritage, which includes traditions and living expressions passed down from ancestors to descendants, and living heritage, which encompasses cultural expressions and practices that form a body of knowledge and provide continuity, dynamism, and meaning to generations of people as individuals, social groups, and communities (UNESCO, 2003). This research will contribute to the development of more inclusive approaches to heritage management and promote a better understanding of the role of living heritage in preserving cultural identity and promoting sustainable tourism practices.

Cham cultural heritage plays a crucial role in both the cultural diversity and economic development of Vietnam. The coastal plains of Central Vietnam are home to several Cham heritage sites that serve as popular tourist destinations, generating substantial income for the surrounding provinces. One such example is the My Son sanctuary, which was declared a UNESCO World Cultural Heritage site in 1999 (UNESCO, 1999). It is widely known as one of the most sacred places of the Cham civilization and has had a positive impact on the country's economy, especially for the ethnic Kinh majority.

However, while these heritage sites are an important source of revenue, they are often viewed by outsiders as "dead monuments" that are disconnected from the contemporary Cham community. In reality, many of these sites are still actively used for spiritual purposes and are considered living heritage sites by the Cham people. This raises the question of how to properly protect, preserve, and promote these living heritage sites, both for the Cham community and as a form of conservation.

The aim of this research is to examine the various heritage sites and conservation strategies to highlight the significance of living heritage. The study will also seek to identify what is appropriate for the Cham community, ensuring that the cultural and spiritual values of these sites are properly recognized and respected.

The Cham people have a rich cultural heritage that significantly contributes to the diversity and economic growth of Vietnam. Despite the recognition of their traditions and practices by the government in 2012, their role in the management and preservation of their sacred sites remains marginal. The increasing influx of tourists, who visit the sites for both religious and recreational purposes, has generated substantial benefits for a small portion of the Cham community who are involved in the tourism industry. However, the Cham Ahier priests and the wider Cham community have not yet reaped the benefits of their heritage in the tourism development process.

My research aims to examine the social and cultural concerns of the Cham custodians and community members in relation to heritage conservation, and to identify ways in which their participation in the protection and management of their ancestral sites can be effectively promoted. The study will also delve into the policies that govern Cham heritage management and uncover the problems that arise from the lack of insider knowledge among government authorities, who are responsible for managing the living heritage sites. This lack of knowledge could potentially lead to the commodification of Cham heritage sites, rather than the preservation and respect of their traditional and religious significance.

Tourism is seen as a major factor in Vietnam's progress towards becoming a developed nation (Saltiel, 2014). Within this framework, the cultural heritage of ethnic minorities plays a crucial role in tourism and its preservation is therefore vital (Lask & Herold, 2004; Salemink, 2013; Saltiel, 2014; Truong, 2016). The province of Ninh Thuan is relying heavily on tourism as a means of driving economic growth, and local authorities are promoting Cham temples as popular tourist destinations while claiming to preserve them. However, the manner in which tourism has been used to exploit these sacred places disregards local perspectives, creating challenges for preserving their authenticity and sacredness among local communities. The book delves into the role of living heritage and community participation in conservation and tourism development at living heritage sites in Vietnam.

Additionally, this research also aims to identify the ways in which the government can better support and collaborate with the Cham community in preserving their ancestral heritage sites. The study highlights the importance of considering the cultural, social, and religious values attached to living heritage sites, and the role of the community in their preservation and management. By taking into account the needs and perspectives of the Cham community, the research aims to promote a more equitable and sustainable approach to heritage management and tourism development in Vietnam. The findings of this research can serve as a valuable resource for policymakers, heritage professionals, and communities looking to engage in heritage preservation and cultural tourism initiatives.

Additionally, the following objectives are also a part of this study:

1. To understand the relationships between the Cham community and the government in terms of the conservation and management of their ancestral heritage sites.
2. To evaluate the policies and regulations related to the preservation and promotion of Cham cultural heritage and determine their effectiveness.
3. To identify best practices for community-based cultural heritage preservation and tourism development.
4. To provide recommendations for the preservation of the authenticity and sacredness of the Cham cultural heritage sites in the face of tourism and commercial exploitation.

By addressing these objectives, this research will contribute to the existing knowledge on the relationship between cultural heritage, tourism development, and community-based preservation, and provide valuable insights for the preservation and promotion of Cham cultural heritage in Vietnam and similar contexts.

To ensure that the focus of this research is clear, some limitations have been established. These include:

5. This study specifically concentrates on the views and perspectives of the Cham community and heritage authorities involved in the management of Po Klaong Girai temple, without considering other stakeholders such as private companies, the local Kinh community, and tourists.
6. This research is not solely centered on the agreement or disagreement among members of the Cham community, but primarily delves into the underlying meanings and perceptions surrounding the management of cultural heritage.
7. The collaboration between the Cham and government authorities in managing Cham cultural heritage will not be extensively discussed, as these issues will be touched upon in the findings of each theme in the study.

The Role of the Researcher

As a researcher, it is important to understand the role that one plays in the community being studied and to consider how interactions with participants may have affected that role. This requires an active participation and self-examination to determine the necessary triangulation (Creswell, 2014; Merriam, 2002; Stake, 1995). To achieve a complete understanding of a culture, it is important to have both insider (emic) and outsider (etic) perspectives. The emic perspective involves subjective investigation from the native's point of view and allows for an understanding of a culture as the people of that culture understand it (Malinowski, 1992). On the other hand, the etic perspective uses an objective, external viewpoint to generate theories and analyze culture through theoretical applications (Haskell et al., 1992; Sinha, 2004). However, the etic perspective alone may not grasp the nuances and richness of a culture, and it is important to consider both perspectives in order to gain a holistic view of the study (Morris et al., 1999).

In conducting field research, it is essential for the researcher to have both insider and outsider perspectives in order to gain a holistic understanding of the culture being studied (Morris et al., 1999). As an anthropologist, one must be involved in active participation and self-reflection to understand how their role in the community may have been impacted by interactions with participants and to determine the type of triangulation needed (Creswell, 2014; Merriam, 2002; Stake, 1995).

In this study, the author's role as a researcher is both as an insider and as an outsider. As a former researcher at the Cham Cultural Research Center and a member of the Cham community, the author has a deep understanding of Cham culture and history, which gives them an insider's perspective. This long-standing relationship with the Cham community and experience working in the cultural heritage sector also allows the author to have a strong rapport with Cham priests, intellectuals, and community members. However, since the author left the Cham Cultural Research Center and started their Ph.D. studies, they recognize that they have become somewhat of an outsider in terms of their familiarity with recent developments in the cultural heritage sector. Nevertheless, the author's extensive experience as a researcher for the Cham Cultural Research Center and their commitment to the well-being and development of Cham traditions and Indigenous heritage provide them with some advantages in approaching Cham people and asking them to share their thoughts on issues of culture.

The author's ability to emotionally detach themselves from their culture and provide an objective, outsider's perspective also allows them to explore trans-historical generalizations and compare cultures (Morris et al., 1999). This combination of insider and outsider perspectives is necessary for gaining a comprehensive understanding of Cham culture.

Overall, the author's unique combination of insider and outsider perspectives, along with their extensive experience and strong relationships within the Cham community, make them well positioned to conduct field research on Cham culture and heritage.

My post-graduate education has been primarily in Western academic institutions in the United States and Australia, and as a result, my research draws on the standard Western methodological traditions of interviews, group discussions, and observations (Menzies, 2004). However, I am mindful of the need to incorporate Indigenous and decolonizing perspectives in my research design (Smith, 1999). Smith (1999) argues that research on Indigenous people has historically perpetuated imposed Western paradigms, which often neglect the needs and perspectives of the local communities being studied. To address this issue, I aim to establish a collaborative research relationship that prioritizes the needs and perspectives of the Cham community being studied and considers the practical outcomes of the research (Menzies, 2004). This will be achieved through incorporating an Indigenous methodological perspective and through proposing practical recommendations for heritage practitioners, researchers, and the Cham communities to consider when cultural programs are implemented at Cham heritage sites. The ultimate goal of this research is to benefit the Cham community and the local authorities through providing actionable policy recommendations that can be used to protect and preserve Cham cultural heritage.

This study represents a pioneering effort in the field of cultural heritage management among the Cham people in Vietnam. To the best of our knowledge, there has been a lack of research that has specifically focused on the direct engagement of stakeholders in issues related to Cham heritage management. This presented some unique challenges as it was the first time that heritage authorities were asked to openly discuss and share their experiences and challenges in managing Cham cultural heritage. Additionally, many of the participants were not familiar with being interviewed and were especially cautious when speaking to a researcher, particularly when it came to sensitive topics related to government employees involved in Cham heritage management. Despite these difficulties, I was gratified to receive positive feedback from my informants and valuable insights on my research questions from various members of the Cham community.

As noted by Menzies (2004), the research relationship should meet the needs of both the researcher and the researched community, and aim to bring about practical benefits for the latter. The same author also highlights the importance of being accountable to the community in order to establish a trustworthy and collaborative relationship. In the case of this study, which focuses on cultural heritage management among the Cham people in Vietnam, the challenge of gaining access to sensitive cultural information can be compounded by the fact that Cham people are an ethnic minority who have historically faced challenges in expressing their views freely.

To overcome these challenges, I leveraged my personal connections and professional experience. As a former researcher at the Cham Cultural Research Center and a current supporter of the Council of Cham Brahman Dignitaries, I have built a rapport with many Cham priests and intellectuals. These relationships allowed me to approach members of the Cham community and gain their trust, which in turn facilitated access to their deeply held and personal thoughts on cultural issues. The importance of trust-building in research is emphasized by Smith (1999), who notes that research with Indigenous communities must take into account the history of imposed Western paradigms and prioritize the benefits that the community will realize from the research.

This approach to research aligns with the Indigenous methodology perspective, where the researcher and the community are seen as equal partners in the research process. It is crucial for the researcher to develop a relationship of trust with the community and to approach the research in a respectful and ethical manner. This not only leads to more meaningful and accurate results, but it also helps to promote the self-determination and empowerment of the Indigenous community being studied (Smith, 1999). As Porsanger (2004) highlights, conducting research in a way that is seen as respectful, ethical, correct, sympathetic, useful, and beneficial to Indigenous peoples is vital. This is especially important in my research, where I am studying the cultural heritage management of the Cham people in Vietnam. By taking this approach, I hope to gain a deeper understanding of the issues and challenges faced by the Cham community and to provide practical recommendations for heritage practitioners, researchers, and the Cham community to consider when implementing cultural programs at Cham heritage sites.

The task of obtaining interviews from the local authorities in Ninh Thuan proved to be a significant challenge for me, especially when I revealed the nature of my research on the conservation of Cham heritage sites in the province. Despite my previous experience as a cultural specialist in this field, which had allowed me to build strong relationships with heritage officers, many of their responses during the interviews seemed to avoid the most pressing and relevant issues. Only a handful of these individuals sought my advice on how to resolve current problems in cultural heritage management and how to improve the management of Cham cultural heritage. These officials often shied away from open and honest discussions to address issues and find solutions, and tended to evade any mention of individual responsibility. However, when I approached members of the Cham Monument Management Unit (re-established in 2017), some heritage officers declined to participate in interviews due to concerns about misrepresenting sensitive information that their agency may not allow them to disclose. In an effort to alleviate these concerns, I attempted to emphasize to these officials that the aim of my research was to uncover current challenges and find ways to improve the management of Cham heritage sites, rather than causing conflicts among stakeholders. In response, the Unit referred me to a representative who was responsible for public relations and could best answer my research questions.

When I engaged with the Cham Cultural Research Center, I discovered that the researchers there had a wealth of knowledge and insights that could significantly enhance the management of Cham cultural heritage and foster cooperation among relevant parties. Despite the fact that these researchers possess extensive expertise in Cham culture, the Provincial Department of Culture, Sports and Tourism seems to be disinterested in seeking their consultation when developing projects related to Cham cultural heritage in Ninh Thuan. By disregarding the expertise of these specialists, the heritage management and heritage departments risk repeated mistakes and negative outcomes in their conservation efforts, as they lack a complete understanding of Cham culture. This neglect of Cham experts not only represents a missed opportunity, but it also goes against the objective of the Cham Cultural Research Center to serve as a consultative resource for local authorities on Cham cultural policies in Ninh Thuan. Despite multiple attempts to arrange meetings with heritage authorities at higher levels, such as the Ministry of Culture, Sports and Tourism, I encountered difficulties in scheduling appointments with them. Nevertheless, I was fortunate enough to have productive and informative discussions with some members of the Council of National Cultural Heritage.

Organizing the Content: Navigating Through the Book's Framework

This book is divided into ten chapters, each serving a specific purpose in presenting the research.

Chapter 1: Introduction—Jalan nao: In this chapter, the structure and purpose of the book are outlined. The problem statement, research questions, rationale, research design, and narrative of the research are explained. The chapter concludes with a reflection on the use of observant participation and the importance of considering both etic and emic perspectives in the case study.

Chapter 2: The Cham Civilization and Its People—An Overview of Bhum Cham: This chapter provides a comprehensive view of the research field, focusing on ethnic minorities in Vietnam and the Cham people specifically. It covers their environment, geography, history, cultural heritage, and the background of cultural heritage management in Vietnam. The chapter highlights the importance of the Cham traditional management system and the changes that have taken place to demonstrate the community's involvement in preserving their cultural heritage.

Chapter 3: Cham Culture and Traditions: Understanding Their Worldview Through Custodianship and Philosophy: This chapter explores the religion, beliefs, traditional philosophies, and taboos of the Cham people and how they relate to the dissatisfaction with tourism development at their sacred spaces. The chapter provides insights into how religion, tradition, and philosophy are closely linked and preserved by the Cham community, particularly under the guidance of religious dignitaries.

Chapter 4: The Conservation of Cham Cultural Heritage in Vietnam: This chapter reviews and assesses heritage conservation in Vietnam through different periods and policies, with a focus on heritage conservation for ethnic minorities. The chapter also explores the conservation approaches of Cham cultural heritage in Vietnam, particularly in Ninh Thuan Province, and highlights the efforts of state authorities and conservationists to preserve it.

Chapter 5: Living Heritage in The Everyday: Roles of Po Klaong Girai Temple in The Cham Community: This chapter examines the role of Cham temples in the contemporary life of Cham people. The chapter demonstrates that the Po Klaong Girai temple plays a crucial role in the community for spiritual practice and cultural identification. Inappropriate conservation and development efforts that do not align with Cham cultural traditions will likely be rejected by the Cham community, which seeks to preserve the temple's significance for religion, ritual practice, heritage, history, and cultural identity.

Chapter 6: Examining Overlooked Living Traditions: An Analysis of the Conservation of Sacred Places in the Cham Culture of Vietnam: This chapter examines the heritage conservation of Cham living heritage sites and the perceptions of the Cham community in Vietnam. It demonstrates that heritage conservation has focused primarily on tangible forms of heritage and has not considered the local cultural meanings related to the Cham temples. The chapter also highlights the negative effects of a new pathway, which was constructed to facilitate access for visitors but is perceived as an offense to the Cham worldview and spiritual practice.

Chapter 7: Balancing Authenticity and Tourism Development: The Challenge of Incense at Cham Temples: This chapter explores the perception of authenticity in the Cham community, focusing on the issue of joss-stick incense as an external imposition. The chapter asks how Cham community members perceive and respond to assertions of authenticity and what can be learned from these perceptions. The chapter also highlights the importance of understanding the broader history of threats to both living and tangible forms of Cham cultural heritage in Vietnam.

Chapter 8: Staging Culture, Selling Authenticity: The Commodification of the Cham Community's Traditions: This chapter examines the relationship between the Cham community's perception of the commodification of their sacred spaces and culture and the practices of Vietnamese heritage authorities. The chapter highlights the criticism from the Cham community regarding tourism development that deviates from their expectations and creates misunderstandings about their cultural traditions. It also explores the negative impact of such misunderstandings on youth community members' knowledge of Cham culture and visitors' understanding.

Chapter 9: Navigating the Balance Between Revenue Generation and Conservation at a Cham Living Sacred Heritage Site: Priestly Views and Challenges: This chapter explores the perspectives of Cham community members on economic benefits and revenue sharing from cultural tourism at sacred living heritage sites. It highlights the economic pressure on Cham Ahier priests and the tension between the community and government over these issues.

Chapter Conclusion: Towards a Sustainable Future: Navigating the Cham Living Heritage in Tourism's Landscape: The focus is on summarizing the main findings of the research and discussing their implications and impact. The chapter provides an overview of how the study contributes to the field and discusses the potential impact of the policy recommendations made. The author also acknowledges any limitations of the study, including any gaps in data, research design, or methodology that may have impacted the results. Additionally, the chapter outlines potential areas for future research to continue exploring the intricate relationship between the Cham community, their cultural heritage, and the development of tourism in Vietnam. Overall, this chapter serves as a conclusion and reflection on the study's insights, highlighting the significance of the Cham cultural heritage and the importance of preserving it for future generations.

References

Alexopoulos, G. (2013). Management of living religious heritage: Who sets the agenda? The case of the Monastic Community of Mount Athos. *Conservation and Management of Archaeological Sites, 15*(1), 59–75. https://doi.org/10.1179/1350503313Z.00000000047

Andrews, T., & Buggey, S. (2008). Authenticity in Aboriginal Cultural Landscapes. *APT Bulletin, 39*(2), 63–71.

An, P. (2015). Phát huy giá trị văn hóa Chăm để phát triển du lịch tỉnh Ninh Thuận. *Phát Triển Kinh Tế-Xã Hội, 62*, 22–26.

Anh, P. Q. (2012). Văn hóa Chăm v´ới phát triển du lịch ở Ninh Thuận [Cham culture with the development of tourism in Ninh Thuan]. In Bảo tồn, phát triển văn hóa dân tộc Chăm trong bối cảnh công nghiệp hóa, hiện đại hóa và hội nhập quốc tế (pp. 11–20). Phan Rang- Thap Cham: Bộ VHTTDL.

Arkarapotiwong, P. (2015). *The investigation of living heritage attributes in living heritage sites Case study: Nan, Thailand and Luang Prabang.* The Bauhaus-Universität Weimar.

Ayoubi, A. (2015). Community-based conservation of the sacred living heritage at the Bauddhanath Monument Zone, Kathmandu Valley World Heritage Site, Nepal. Retrieved April 27, 2016, from http://iflaonline.org/2015/06/community-based-conservation-of-the-sacred-living-heritage-at-the-bauddhanath-monument-zone-kathmandu-valley-world-heritage-site-nepal/

Balen, K. Van, & Vandesande, A. (2015). Community involvement in heritage management (Reflections on Cultural Heritage Theories and Practices). Organization of World Heritage Cities (Vol. 10). Garant Uitgevers nv.

Bauer, B., Sinha, N., Trimarchi, M., & Vincenzo, Z. (2017). Tourism community involvement strategy for the living world heritage site of Hampi, India. A case study. In B. Laurent, G.-B. Maria, & R. Mike (Eds.), *World heritage sites and tourism : Global and local relations* (pp. 94–104). Routledge, Taylor & Francis Group.

Binh, T. Q. (2001). The protection and enhancement of cultural property in Vietnam. In A. Galla (Ed.), *Protection of cultural heritage in Southeast Asia* (pp. 63–65). Asia Pacific Organisation of the International Council of Museums in partnership with the Vietnam Ministry of Culture and Information.

Bramwell, B., & Lane, B. (1993). Sustainable tourism: An evolving global approach. *Journal of Sustainable Tourism, 1*(1), 1–5. https://doi.org/10.1080/09669589309514792

Bramwell, B., & Lane, B. (2012). Towards innovation in sustainable tourism research? *Journal of Sustainable Tourism, 20*(1), 1–7. https://doi.org/10.1080/09669582.2011.641559

Brown, J., Mitchell, N. J., & Beresford, M. (2005). *The protected landscape approach: Linking nature.* IUCN.

Buckley, R. (2012). Sustainable tourism: Research and reality. *Annals of Tourism Research.* https://doi.org/10.1016/j.annals.2012.02.003

Buggey, S. (1999). An Approach to Aboriginal Cultural Landscapes. Historic Sites and Monuments Board of Canada.

Bwasiri, E. (2008). *The management of indigenous living heritage in archaeological World Heritage Sites: A case study of Mongomi wa Kolo Rock painting site, central Tanzania.* The South African Archaeological Bulletin, 1–115.

Bwasiri, E. (2009). *The management of indigenous living heritage in archaeological World Heritage Sites: A case study of Mongomi wa Kolo Rock painting site.* Central Tanzania. Unpublished.

Byrne, D. (1991). Western hegemony in archaeological heritage management. *History and Anthropology, 5*(2), 269–276. https://doi.org/10.1080/02757206.1991.9960815

Byrne, D. (2004). Chartering Heritage in Asia's Postmodern World. *The Getty Conservation Institute Newsletter, 19*(2), 16–19.

Byrne, D. (2012). Buddhist stupas and Thai Social Practice. In S. Sullivan & R. Mackay (Eds.), *Archaeological sites : Conservation and management* (pp. 572–587). Getty Conservation Institute.

Byrne, D. (2014). Counterheritage: Critical perspectives on heritage conservation in Asia. Rougtledge.

Creswell, J. W. (2014). *Research design qualitative quantitative and mixed methods approaches* (p. 398).

Dat, T. T. H., & Huu, T. T. (2015). Integrated potential assessment of community—Based ecotourism in A Luoi District, Thua Thien Hue Province. *Vietnam Journal of Earth Sciences, 36*(3), 271–280. https://doi.org/10.15625/0866-7187/36/3/5910

Dop, P. Van, Anh, P. Q., & Thu, N. T. (2014). Văn hóa phi vật thể ngư ời Chăm Ninh Thuận [Intangible cultural heritage of the Cham people in Ninh Thuan]. Ho Chi Minh: NXB Nông Nghiệp TP.HCM. http://chamstudies.net/2016/02/18/van-hoa-phi-vat-the-cua-nguoi-cham-ninh-thuan/

Dung, P. T. (2015). *Heritage sites neglect community needs.* Retrieved August 25, 2017, from http://vietnamnews.vn/sunday/features/280226/heritage-sites-neglect-community-needs.html

Giang, N. L. (2015). Legal analysis: Current framework, challenges and opportunities. In understanding rights practices in the world heritage system: Lessons from the Asia Pacific (p. 16). The Viet Nam Academy of Social Sciences & Ha Noi UNNESCO Office.

Gilbert, A. L., Hoa, N. T. M., & Vu, T. B. (1998). A strategic model for using information technology in developing sustainable tourism. *The Journal of Viet Nam Studies, 1*(1), 1–17.

Haley, U., & Haley, G. (1998). Investing in sustainable tourism in Vietnam: Implications for governmental policy. *The Journal of Viet Nam Studies, 1*(1), 8–32.

Harrington, J. T. (2004). *Being here: Heritage, belonging and place making—A stduy of community and identity formation at Avebury (England), Magnetic Island (Australia) and Ayuthaya (Thailand).* James Cook University.

Haskell, G. H., Headland, T. N., Pike, K. L., & Harris, M. (1992). Emics and Etics: The Insider/Outsider Debate. *The Journal of American Folklore, 105*(418), 489. https://doi.org/10.2307/541632

Hoa, D. N. (2005). The impact of tourism on people's heritage: A case study of the Cham in Vietnam. Ateneo de Manila University.

Hong, N. V. (2015). Conservation of cultural heritage from cultural stakeholders. In Universidad Complutense de Madrid (Ed.), *Proceedings of the II Internacional Conference on Best Practices in World Heritage: People and Communities* (pp. 614–625). Servicio. https://doi.org/978-84-606-9264-5

Huong, P. T. T. (2015). Living heritage, community participation and sustainability: Redefining development strategies in Hoi an ancient town world heritage property, Vietnam. In W. L. Sophia Labadi (Ed.), *Urban heritage, development and sustainability International frameworks, national and local governance* (pp. 274–290). Rougtledge.

ICOMOS. (1994). The Nara Document on Authenticity. *Nara Conference. Doi, 10*(1063/1), 4748569.

ICOMOS. (1995, April). *Asia-Pacific workshop on associative cultural landscapes.* http://whc.unesco.org/archive/cullan95.htm

Jansen-Verbeke, M., & Go, F. (1995). Tourism development in Vietnam. *Tourism Management, 16*(4), 315–321. https://doi.org/10.1016/0261-5177(95)97356-U

Karlström, A. (2005). Spiritual materiality: Heritage preservation in a Buddhist world? *Journal of Social Archaeology.* https://doi.org/10.1177/1469605305057571

Karlström, A. (2013). Local heritage and the problem with conservation. In S. Brockwell, S. O'Connor, & D. Byrne (Eds.), *Transcending the culture-nature divide in cultural heritage: Views from the Asia-Pacific region* (pp. 141–156). Australian National University E-Press.

Kong, P. (2008). Social quality in the conservation process of living heritage sites. Berlageweg 1, 2628 CR Delft The Netherlands: International Forum on Urbanism (IFoU).

Kwanda, T. (2010). Tradition of conservation: Redefining authenticity in Javanese architectural conservation. *International Conference on Heritage and Sustainable Development.*

Larsen, P. B. (2015). Some preliminary issues and lessons from Phong Nha Ke Bang, Vietnam. In understanding community participation and rights-based approaches in world heritage (p. 13). The Viet Nam Academy of Social Sciences & Ha Noi UNNESCO Office.

Larsen, P. B. (2017). *World Heritage and human rights: Lessons from the Asia-Pacific and global arena.* Routledge. https://www.routledge.com/World-Heritage-and-Human-Rights-Les sons-from-the-Asia-Pacific-and-global/Larsen/p/book/9781138224223

Larsen, P. B. (2018). World Heritage and Ethnic minority rights in Phong Nha Ke Bang, Vietnam: Cosmopolitan Assemblages in Neoliberal Times. In P. B. Larsen (Ed.), *World heritage and human rights lessons from the Asia-Pacific and global arena.* Rougtledge.

Lask, T., & Herold, S. (2004). An observation station for culture and tourism in Vietnam: A forum for World Heritage and public participation. *Current Issues in Tourism, 7*(4–5), 399–411.

Le, L. T. T. (2015). Representation of Cham's ethnic identity through a cultural festival organized by the state. In interdisciplinary study in social sciences and humanities. Vietnam National University. https://doi.org/10.13140

Lenzerini, F. (2011). Intangible cultural heritage: The living culture of peoples. *European Journal of International Law, 22*(1), 101–120. https://doi.org/10.1093/ejil/chr006

Lewis, D., & Rose, D. (2013). The shape of the dreaming: The cultural significance of Victoria River rock art. In R. Mackay & S. Sullivan (Eds.), *Archaeological sites: Conservation and management* (pp. 607–614). Getty Conservation Institute.

Logan, W. (1998). Sustainable cultural heritage tourism in Vietnamese cities: The case of Hanoi. *The Journal of Viet Nam Studies, 1*(1), 32–40.

Logan, W. (2012). Cultural diversity, cultural heritage and human rights: Towards heritage management as human rights-based cultural practice. *International Journal of Heritage Studies, 18*(3), 231–244. https://doi.org/10.1080/13527258.2011.637573

Logan, W. (2015). Community participation in World Heritage sites in Australia and Vietnam. In understanding community participation and rights-based approaches in world heritage. The Vietnam Academy of Social Sciences & Ha Noi UNNESCO Office.

Malinowski, B. (1992). *Argonauts of the Western pacific. An account of native entrepise and adventure in the archipelagoes of Malensian New Guinea.* LOWE AND BRYDONE. https://ia802706. us.archive.org/3/items/argonautsofweste00mali/argonautsofweste00mali.pdf

Menzies, C. R. (2004). Putting words into action: Negotiating collaborative research in Gitxaala. *Canadian Journal of Native Education, 64*(1), 15–32.

Merriam, S. B. (2002). *Qualitative research in practice: Examples for discussion and analysis.* The JosseyBass higher and adult education series (Vol. 44). https://doi.org/10.1177/074171360426 3057

Miura, K. (2005). Conservation of a 'living heritage site' A contradiction in terms? A case study of Angkor World Heritage Site. *Conservation and Management of Archaeological Sites, 7*(1), 3–18. https://doi.org/10.1179/135050305793137602

Morris, M. W., Leung, K., Ames, D., & Lickel, B. (1999). Views from inside and outside: Integrating emic and etic insights about culture and justice judgment. *Academy of Management Review, 24*(4), 781–796. https://doi.org/10.5465/AMR.1999.2553253

Pearson, M., & Gorman, T. (2010). Managing the landscapes of the Australian Northern Territory for sustainability: Visions, issues and strategies for successful planning. *Futures, 42*(7), 711–722. https://doi.org/10.1016/j.futures.2010.04.008

Pearson, M., & Sullivan, S. (1995). *Looking after heritage places: The basics of heritage planning for managers.* Melbourne University Press.

Phuong, T. K. (2006). *Cultural resource and heritage issues of historic Champa States: Champa origins, reconfirmed nomenclatures and preservation of sites.* SSRN Electronic Journal. https://doi.org/10.2139/ssrn.1317157

Porsanger, J. (2004). An essay about Indigenous methodology. *Nordlit, 8*(1), 105–120. http://sep tentrio.uit.no/index.php/nordlit/article/view/1910

Poulios, I. (2014a). Discussing strategy in heritage conservation: Living heritage approach as an example of strategic innovation. *Journal of Cultural Heritage Management and Sustainable Development, 4*(1), 16–34. https://doi.org/10.1108/JCHMSD-10-2012-0048

Poulios, I. (2014b). *The past in the present: A living heritage approach—Meteora.* Ubiquity Press. https://doi.org/10.5334/bak

Quynh Trang. (2013). Quy hoạch phát triển ngành Du lịch tỉnh Ninh Thuận đến năm 2020 và tầm nhìn 2030. Retrieved May 23, 2017, from http://www.ninhthuan.gov.vn/News/Pages/Quy-hoach-phat-trien-nganh-Du-lich-tinh-Ninh-Thuan-den-nam-2020-va-tam-nhin-2030.aspx

Renault, M., & Collange, P. (2008). *Tell me about living heritage.* UNESCO Publishing.

Rössler, M. (2005). World Heritage cultural landscapes: A global perspective. In J. Brown, N. J. Mitchell, & M. Beresford (Eds.), *The protected landscape approach: Linking nature, culture and community.* IUCN--The World Conservation Union. https://portals.iucn.org/library/efiles/html/PA-protected-landscape-approach/PartI-section3.html

Sakaya. (2001). The Cham forklores in tourism development [Văn hóa dân gian ngư ời Chăm v ́ới vấn đề phát triển du lịch Ninh Thuận]. *Văn Hóa Nghệ Thuật Ninh Thuận, 9,* 19–23.

Sakaya. (2003). The festivals of the Cham people [Lễ hội của ngư ời Chăm]. Ha Noi: NXB Van Hoa Dan Toc.

Salemink, O. (2012). "Di sản hóa" văn hóa Việt Nam: Di sản văn hóa phi vật thể gi ̃ưa các cộng đồng, Nhà nư ́ớc và thị trư ̀ờng [The 'heritagization' of culture in Vietnam: Intangible cultural heritage between communities, state and market]. In *The 4th International Conference on Vietnamese Studies: Vietnam on the Road to integration and sustainable development* (pp. 243–291). Vietnam Academy of Social Sciences.

Salemink, O. (2013). Appropriating culture: The politics of intangible cultural heritage in Vietnam. In H.-T. H. T. M. Sidel (Ed.), *State, society and the market in contemporary Vietnam: Property, power and values* (pp. 158–180). Routledge. https://doi.org/10.4324/9780203098318

Saltiel, L. (2014). Cultural governance and development in Vietnam. *University of Pennsylvania Journal of International Law, 35*(3), 893–915. https://scholarship.law.upenn.edu/jil/vol35/iss3/6

Sarah, C., & Wijesuriya, G. (2014). *People-centred approaches to the conservation of cultural heritage: Living heritage.* Italy. https://www.iccrom.org/publication/people-centred-approaches-conservation-cultural-heritage-living-heritage

Sharpley, R. (2000). Tourism and sustainable development: exploring the theoretical divide. *Journal of Sustainable Tourism, 8*(1), 1–19. https://doi.org/10.1080/09669580008667346

Sinha, J. B. P. (2004). Etic and emic approaches to Asian management research. In S. Kwok Leung, White (Ed.), *Handbook of Asian Finance* (Vol. 2, pp. 19–50). Kluwer Academic. https://doi.org/10.1016/B978-0-12-800982-6.00016-0

Smith, L. (2012). *Discourses of heritage: Implications for archaeological community practice.* Nuevo Mundo Mundos Nuevos. http://nuevomundo.revues.org/64148

Smith, L. T. (1999). Decolonizing methodologies. https://doi.org/10.1097/NAQ.0b013e318258ba14

Smith, L. (2006). *Uses of heritage.* Routledge. https://doi.org/10.4324/9780203602263

Stovel, H., Stanley-Price, N., Killick. (2003). *Conservation of living religious heritage: Papers from the ICCROM forum on living religious Heritage: Conserving the sacred* (pp. 1–11). ICCROM.

Spenceley, A., Snyman, S., & Rylance, A. (2017). Revenue sharing from tourism in terrestrial African protected areas. *Journal of Sustainable Tourism.* https://doi.org/10.1080/09669582.2017.1401632

Stake, R. (1995). *The art of case study research.* Sage Publications. https://doi.org/10.1108/eb024859

Thien, N. N. (2017). Linking preservation of intangible cultural heritage with socio-economic development in Vietnam today. *Communist Review,* (892). \http://english.tapchicongsan.org.vn/Home/Culture-Society/2017/1032/Linking-preservation-of-intangible-cultural-heritage-with-socioeconomic-development-in-Vietnam-today.aspx

Thuy, N. T. T. (2012). Bảo tồn và phát huy giá trị hệ thống đền tháp Bà La Môn giáo của ngư ời Chăm qua các hoạt động du lịch văn hóa. In Bảo tồn, phát triển văn hóa dân tộc Chăm trong bối cảnh công nghiệp hóa, hiện đại hóa và hội nhập quốc tế (pp. 305–313). Phan Rang- Thap Cham: Bộ VHTTDL.

Tran, L., & Walter, P. (2014). Ecotourism, gender and development in northern Vietnam. *Annals of Tourism Research, 44*(1), 116–130. https://doi.org/10.1016/j.annals.2013.09.005

Truong, V. D. (2016). Tourism policy development in Vietnam: A pro- poor perspective tourism policy development in Vietnam: A pro-poor perspective. *Journal of Policy Research in Tourism, 5*(1), 28–45. https://doi.org/10.1080/19407963.2012.760224

Truong, V. D., Hall, C. M., & Garry, T. (2014). Tourism and poverty alleviation: Perceptions and experiences of poor people in Sapa. *Vietnam. Journal of Sustainable Tourism, 22*(7), 1071–1089. https://doi.org/10.1080/09669582.2013.871019

Tunprawat, P. (2009). Managing living heritage sites in Mainland Southeast Asia. Sipakorn University.

Tuyen, Q. D. (2014). Nhìn lại các chính sách phát triển tại một làng nghề truyền thống người Chăm, qua cái nhìn từ bên trong cộng đồng Chăm [Implementing Development projects at a Cham handicraft village, Ninh Thuan Province: A view from the Cham indigenous community]. In Nghiên cứu cùng cộng đồng: Ứng dụng nhân học trong phát triển ở vùng dân tộc thiểu số Việt Nam (pp. 163–177). ISEE.

UNESCO. (1999). My Son Sanctuary—UNESCO World Heritage Centre. Retrieved February 23, 2016, from http://whc.unesco.org/en/list/949

UNESCO. (2003). Convention for the safeguarding of the intangible Cultural heritage. Retrieved November 15, 2017, from http://unesdoc.unesco.org/images/0013/001325/132540e.pdf

UNESCO. (2013). Operational guidelines for the implementation of the world heritage convention. Operational guidelines for the implementation of the world heritage convention.

Van, D. N. (2001). Preservation and development of the cultural heritage. In O. Salemink (Ed.), *Viet Nam's cultural diversity: Approaches to preservation* (pp. 33–62). UNESCO.

Waterton, E. (2015). Heritage and community engagement. In *The ethics of cultural heritage* (pp. 53–67). https://doi.org/10.1007/978-1-4939-1649-8_4

Weise, K. (2013). Discourse. In K. Weise (Ed.), *Revisiting Kathmandu safeguarding living urban heritage* (pp. 1–52). UNESCO. Kathmandu Office. https://publik.tuwien.ac.at/files/publik_229 747.pdf

WHC. (2019). Operational guidelines for the implementation of the world heritage convention. Paris15: UNESCO World Heritage Centre.

Whiting, D. (2005). Conserving marae buildings. In S.-P. & K. Stovel (Ed.), *Conservation of living religious heritage (ICCROM Conservation Studies 3)*. ICCROM.

Wijesuriya, G., Nishi, K., & Joe, K. (2006). Living heritage sites workshop: Empowering the community. *ICCROM Newsletter*. http://www.iccrom.org/ifrcdn/pdf/ICCROM_newsl32-2006_en.pdf

Wijesuriya, G. (2007). Conserving living Taonga: The concept of continuity. In D. Sully (Ed.), *Decolonizing conservation: Caring for Maori meeting houses outside New Zealand (Critical Cultural Heritage Series)* (pp. 59–69). Left Coast Press Inc.

Wijesuriya, G. (2008). Values of the Heritage in the Religious and Cultural Traditions of Southern Asia. In A. Tomaszewski (Ed.), *Values and criteria in heritage conservation:Proceedings of the International Conference of ICOMOS*, ICCROM, Fondazione Romulado Del Bianco: Florence, March 2nd–4th 2007 (pp. 72–78). David Brown Book Company.

Wijesuriya, G. (2014). Introducing people-centred approach to conservation and management of Hani Rice Terraces. In ICOMOS China (Ed.), *International workshop on the sustainable development of Honghe Hani Terraces* (pp. 23–34). Mengzi.

Open Access This chapter is licensed under the terms of the Creative Commons Attribution 4.0 International License (http://creativecommons.org/licenses/by/4.0/), which permits use, sharing, adaptation, distribution and reproduction in any medium or format, as long as you give appropriate credit to the original author(s) and the source, provide a link to the Creative Commons license and indicate if changes were made.

The images or other third party material in this chapter are included in the chapter's Creative Commons license, unless indicated otherwise in a credit line to the material. If material is not included in the chapter's Creative Commons license and your intended use is not permitted by statutory regulation or exceeds the permitted use, you will need to obtain permission directly from the copyright holder.

Chapter 2
The Cham Civilization and Its People—An Overview of Bhum Cham

Introduction

Vietnam is a culturally diverse country, bordered by Cambodia to the southwest, the Lao Peoples Democratic Republic (PDR) to the northwest, and China to the north. According to the General Statistics Office (2019), the Vietnamese population was 85.8 million in 2009 and is made up of 54 ethnic groups. These groups are classified by language, with three main language families: Sino-Tibetan, Austroasiatic, and Austronesian (Malayo-Polynesian) (General Statistics Office, 2019). The Kinh people, the largest ethnic group, make up 85.7% of the population while the other 53 ethnic groups together account for 14.3% of the total population (General Statistics Office, 2019). The Kinh, Hoa (Chinese), Khmer, and Cham predominantly live in the lowlands, while the other ethnic groups reside in the highlands stretching north to south throughout the entire western part of the country. A significant number of Kinh people now also reside in the highlands of certain provinces. This chapter focuses on the Cham community, and their civilization. Each ethnic group contributes to the cultural diversity of Vietnam and plays an important role in shaping the country's cultural landscape.

The Cham People and the Civilization of Champā

Clarifying the Terminology: Understanding the Concept of Indigenous People in Different Contexts

Indigenous peoples are known by various names across different countries, such as tribes, first peoples, aborigines, ethnic groups, or ethnic minorities. In some Asian nations, despite the use of the term "Indigenous" by the groups themselves, state

© The Author(s) 2023
Q. D. Tuyen, *Heritage Conservation and Tourism Development at Cham Sacred Sites in Vietnam*, Global Vietnam: Across Time, Space and Community,
https://doi.org/10.1007/978-981-99-3350-1_2

authorities prefer to use the terms "ethnic groups" or "ethnic minorities" (Corntassel, 2003; Merlan, 2009).

In Vietnam, the term "Indigenous" is not officially recognized by the government. Instead, the Vietnamese government prefers to refer to Indigenous peoples as "ethnic minorities" (dân tộc thiểu số or dân tộc ít ngư ời) (IWGIA, 2012). The use of the term "Indigenous peoples" (ngư ời bản địa) is not widely accepted in official documents and public discourse. However, the government is considering the use of the term "tộc ngư ời tại chỗ," which has a similar meaning to "Indigenous," but does not fully encompass the concept of "Indigeneity." The government defines Indigenous groups as those individuals who have Vietnamese nationality and live in the country, but do not share the same language, culture, or identity as the majority group, the Kinh (IWGIA, 2012). As a result, the Kinh are considered the majority group, while the other 53 cultural and ethnic groups in the country are considered ethnic minorities.

Despite the fact that many Indigenous communities in Vietnam acknowledge their ancestral connections to their lands, their understanding and reference to the international discourse on Indigenous identity and related definitions is limited, due to a lack of access to this information (IWGIA, 2012).

Despite this, however, the use of the term "Indigenous" by international organizations and researchers is not necessarily recognized by the Vietnamese government. According to the government's definition, Indigenous groups are defined as those who have Vietnamese nationality and do not share the same characteristics as the Kinh majority group in terms of language, culture, and identity (IWGIA, 2012). This means that the term "Indigenous" as used by international organizations and scholars may not be in line with the official stance of the Vietnamese government.

Furthermore, while some Indigenous groups in Vietnam have been able to access the international discourse on Indigenousness, the majority of these groups have not yet been exposed to these definitions and discussions (IWGIA, 2012). This lack of exposure means that the use of the term "Indigenous" by international organizations and scholars may not be fully understood or appreciated by the Indigenous groups themselves.

In conclusion, the use of the term "Indigenous" in Vietnam is a complex issue that is influenced by a range of factors including the views of international organizations and scholars, the stance of the Vietnamese government, and the level of exposure of Indigenous groups to the international discourse on Indigenousness.

In this study, the author has analyzed and acknowledged the policies and initiatives of the Vietnamese government aimed at preserving and promoting the cultural heritage of the country's 54 ethnic groups. The term "Indigenous peoples" used in this study does not carry any political implications or connotations, but rather highlights the long-standing existence of communities that have created, maintained, and passed down cultural heritage from generation to generation. This longevity of cultural tradition highlights the element of living heritage that is being sustained by the community as cultural bearers.

Throughout the study, the term "Indigenous people" is used to align with the terminology used by contemporary scholars of Vietnam, as well as to align the case study of heritage preservation in Vietnam with other Indigenous communities around the world. However, the term may also be used interchangeably with "ethnic minority" at times.

The Civilization of Champā

The civilization of Champā had a significant impact on the history of Vietnam. The Chamic-speaking peoples are believed to have migrated from Borneo to Central Vietnam between 2,000 and 3,000 years ago and mixed with the local Indigenous population along the coast and highlands, eventually settling in the region and establishing the foundations of the civilization of Champā (Dharma, 1999). This civilization covered an area that stretched from south of the Ngang Pass (currently Quang Binh Province) to the Dong Nai River, including both the coastal plains and the interior highlands of Central Vietnam (Fig. 2.1) (LaFont, 2014; Momoki, 1999).

Historic Champā was comprised of five polities, which changed status from principalities to independent kingdoms, depending on the historical period (Dharma, 1978; Lafont, 2014). These polities were Indrapura, Amaravati, Vijaya, Kauthara, and Panduranga, each with its own autonomous political institution and the ability to secede from the federal kingdom and become a separate independent kingdom (Dharma, 1999; LaFont, 2014; Momoki, 2011).

In the tenth century, Champā faced challenges from the Dai Viet state, leading to the eventual decline of the civilization's political prominence (Brossard, 1901; Li, 1998; Phat, 1970; Taylor, 1983). The Dai Viet state, which had gained independence from China, was focused on reconstructing and organizing its economy and society and saw the conquest of Champā as a means to increase its power. In 1832, after centuries of struggle, the last Champā kingdom, Panduranga, fell and became a part of the Dai Viet state, which later became what is now known as Vietnam (Dharma, 1999, p. 31; Lafont, 2014, p. 210).

This map showcases the shifting borders of the Champā civilization over time and provides a visual representation of the different polities that existed within its confines, including Indrapura, Amaravati, Vijaya, Kauthara, and Panduranga. The map provides valuable insight into the evolution and geographical extent of the Champā civilization, helping to better understand its rich cultural heritage and historical significance.

Over the course of the last eighteen centuries, the Cham community has established a distinct cultural identity by creatively incorporating elements of Hinduism and Islam into their preexisting religious and cultural traditions. This process of localization and selective adaptation has resulted in a unique fusion of different beliefs and practices (Biên et al., 1991; Lafont, 2014; Mus, 1934; Sakaya, 2003).

Fig. 2.1 Map of the historical frontiers of Champā, showcasing its principalities and kingdoms in uppercase (Po Dharma, 2001)

Peoples and Languages of Champā

The Champā civilization was composed of two language family groups: Austronesian and Austroasiatic (Dharma, 1999; Lafont, 2014; Lockhart, 2011; Thurgood, 1999). According to Cham folklore, the kingdom of Champā was ruled by two clans: the Areca Clan, also known as the Pinang clan in the Cham language, who descended from mountain people (Atuw Cek) and held control over the northern region, and the Coconut Clan, referred to as the Li-u clan in the Cham language, who descended from sea people (Atuw Tasik) and governed the southern region (Maspero, 1928, p. 23; Phuong, 2008, p. 6).

The Cham people are widely distributed throughout Southern Vietnam, with a population of around 160,000 (General Statistics Office, 2019). They are grouped into three main communities based on their location in Vietnam:

1. Central Vietnam Cham—This community shows cultural similarities to the cultures of ethnic minorities in the uplands of Vietnam, as well as many cultural features that were once present in the lowlands of Champā (Lafont, 2014).
2. Southern Central Cham—This is the largest Cham community in Vietnam and is concentrated in southern central regions (General Statistics Office, 2019).
3. South-western Vietnam Cham—This community, largely made up of followers of Islam, is the last major Cham community in South Vietnam, with similar origins to the Panduranga Cham (Biên, et al., 1991; Lafont, 2014; Mus, 1934; Sakaya, 2003).

These communities have maintained a distinct cultural identity despite centuries of southern expansion by the Vietnamese, and they continue to preserve their traditions, beliefs, and language (Dharma, 1999; Lockhart, 2011; Thurgood, 1999).

The Champā civilization had early contact with South Asian civilizations, and as a result, became familiar with South Asian languages, literature, and cultural elements from an early time (Lafont, 2014; Phan, 2012). This is evident in the characteristic use of Champā stone inscriptions to narrate events from the dynasty and to praise the gods and the kings' predecessors. From the fifteenth century onwards, the Cham people began to increasingly use other materials, such as paper, bamboo, cloth, leather, and palm leaves, to write in the Akhar Thrah writing system (Phan, 2012; Sakaya, 2016a).

Despite the rich cultural heritage of the Cham people, younger generations struggle to express themselves in their mother tongue or to write in Cham script (Hao, 2015; Phan, 2012). This highlights the significance of preserving physical heritage sites as a means to connect to the past. To address this issue, the Committee for Drafting School Textbooks in the Cham Language (Ban Biên Soạn Sách Chʼư Chăm) was established with the goal of creating textbooks and overseeing education for Cham children in primary schools. The committee currently supervises over 150 primary schools and more than 5,000 Cham children (Dharma, 2001). After a decade of operation, the committee has published five textbooks for students from Classes 1 to 5, as well as for Po Klaong Girai High School. This initiative has helped Cham children learn to read and write in their native language.

The committee has received support from both national and international institutions, including the Centre d'Histoire et Civilisations de la Péninsule Indochinoise (CHCPI), which is part of the École Pratique des Hautes Études (Sorbonne, Paris, 4th Section). The CHCPI has provided technical support, including software in Cham characters, to help publish additional textbooks on Cham stories, legends, history, culture, and customs (Dharma, 2001). Despite these efforts, many challenges still remain, primarily due to a lack of financial support (Dharma, 2001). Nevertheless, the state and local authorities continue to work towards preserving and promoting the intangible cultural heritage of the Cham people.

Preserving the Legacy: Ancient Monuments of the Champā Civilization

The remnants of the Champā civilization, scattered throughout the central plains and uplands of Vietnam, demonstrate the wealth, power, and sophistication that once characterized the civilization (Hubert, 2012; Tieu et al., 2000; Momoki, 1999; Phuong, 2009; Shigeeda, 1994; Sox, 1972; Stern, 1942). In this research, the focus is on the Champā temples, particularly those that continue to hold significance for the contemporary Cham population.

Temples and temple-tower complexes: The 19 standing temple groups, ranging from Quang Tri Province to Binh Thuan Province in central coast and uplands of Vietnam, are estimated to have been built from the 7th to the sixteenth centuries (Doanh, 2006; Luu Tran Tieu et al., 2000). Henri Parmentier's early 20th-century French documentation of Cham ruins is the earliest known international academic source on Cham heritage sites (Hardy et al., 2009). Parmentier's study found that the Champā people constructed numerous Hindu and Buddhist temples that displayed sophisticated architectural techniques. Some of the notable surviving Cham temples in the region include Mỹ Sơn, Đồng Dương, Po Inâ Nâgar, Dương Long, and Yang Praong, in addition to numerous isolated sculptures made of sandstone and metal alloys (Fig. 2.2).

The Cham Community in Ninh Thuan Province

The Cham community in Ninh Thuan Province represents a significant concentration of Cham people who have maintained strong connections to their cultural heritage and the legacy of Champā. This section provides an overview of the region, including its geography and history, as well as a detailed description of the Cham population in Ninh Thuan Province and their unique cultural heritage.

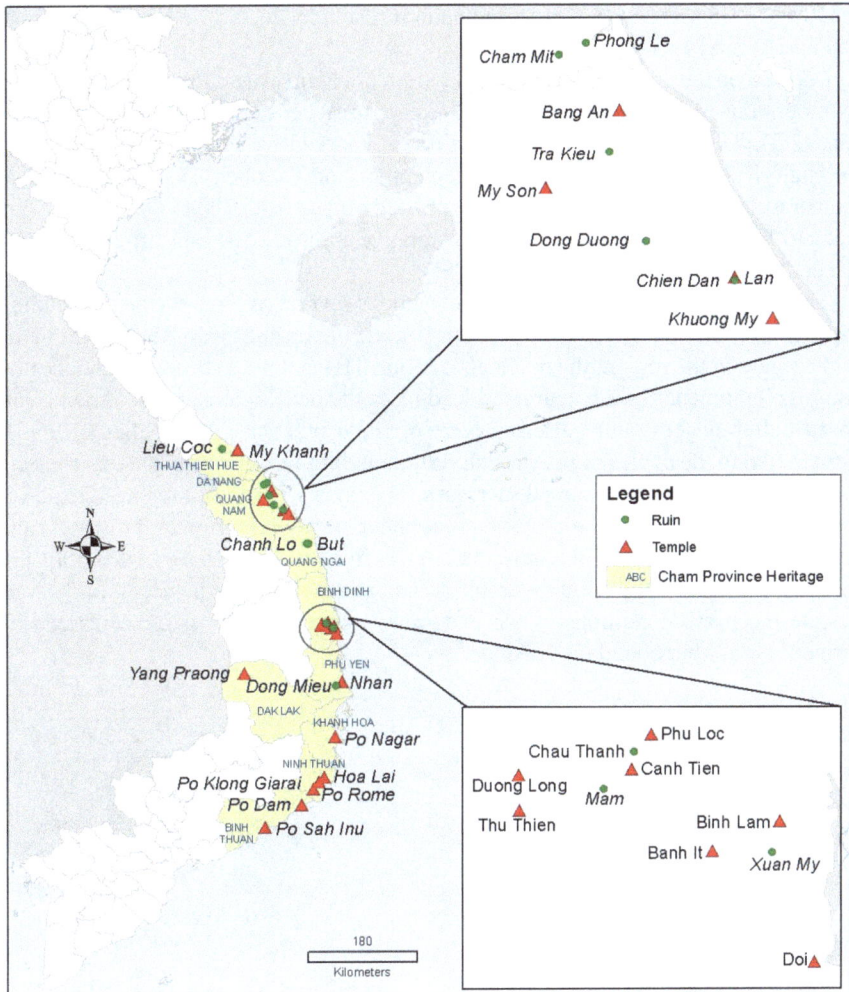

Fig. 2.2 The distribution of Champā remains in Vietnam

The Geography of Ninh Thuan Province

Ninh Thuan Province is situated in the South Central Coast region of Vietnam and is bordered by the South China Sea to the east, Binh Thuan Province to the south, Khanh Hoa Province to the southeast, and Binh Dinh Province to the northwest. The province covers an area of approximately 8,000 square kilometers and has a population of around 800,000 inhabitants. The geography of Ninh Thuan Province is diverse, featuring mountainous terrain, sandy beaches, and fertile plains. It is renowned for its abundant and varied natural resources including forests, minerals, and agricultural land.

Located on the coast of South-Central Vietnam, Ninh Thuan Province is protected by mountains and sheltered from wind, except for its eastern part that faces the sea (Fig. 2.3). The region has a tropical climate, marked by monsoon seasons, with the majority of rainfall occurring in September and October. The average annual temperature is 26–27 °C, while average rainfall ranges from 700 to 800 mm in Phan Rang to 1,100 mm in the mountains, with relative humidity hovering around 75–77% (General Statistics Office, 2019, p. 7).

The ecology of Ninh Thuan Province includes several riverine systems, including the Cai River or Dinh River and its tributaries, and the La and Quao Rivers. Due to the arid climate in the region, the residents of Ninh Thuan have a strong dependence on natural phenomena for their survival, leading to the development of an agricultural-based belief system with intricate layers of ritual practices. This belief system is closely tied to the cycles of the rice harvest, including fertility rites, prayers for rain, the opening of dams, and animal sacrifices. The gods are believed to have the power to control the success of the crops, natural phenomena such as natural disasters and enemy-inflicted disasters, and thus, the farmers in Ninh Thuan believe that prayer to these natural gods will bring favorable weather conditions for a successful harvest despite the harsh conditions of the Panduranga region, which is characterized by limited rainfall but abundant sunshine.

Fig. 2.3 Map of Ninh Thuan Province and the location of Po Klaong Girai temple

Champā in Ninh Thuan Province

Ninh Thuan Province is situated in the northern half of the ancient kingdom of Champā, specifically in the Panduranga region. This area is considered an ideal location for studying Cham history and society due to its preservation of numerous Cham manuscripts, knowledgeable Cham intellectuals, and traditional Cham cultural practices (Dharma, 1987, 1999; Abdul, 2013, p. 13).

Although records of Panduranga are scarce, it has been mentioned in several historical documents from the sixteenth century, including in a dispute between two factions of the Nguyen and Trinh clans of the Viet/Kinh people (Khoang, 1969; Kim, 1986; T. Li, 1998). This demonstrates the significance of Panduranga in Cham history and its relevance to the broader Southeast Asian region.

The Cham in this region were followers of Le Van Duyet, who battled against Minh Mang and the Nguyen Dynasty. In 1832, after the death of Le Van Duyet, Minh Mang took back the land and punished those who had followed him, leading to the brutal slaughter of many Cham people. Despite subsequent attempts at independence, including the Islamic movement of Katip Sumat (1833–1834) and the revolt of Ja Thak Wa (1834–1835), all efforts failed and the kingdom of Champā was eventually conquered by the Nguyen Dynasty (Dharma, 1987, 1999). Today, Ninh Thuan remains the greatest repository of evidence about the last kingdom of Champā and its rich history, with a wealth of cultural heritage still evident in its ancient architecture, inscriptions, and religious practices (Bien et al., 1989; Bien et al., 1991; Doanh, 1998; Dop et al., 2014).

Cham Heritage in Ninh Thuan: Living Cultural Landscapes

The Cham in Ninh Thuan Province retain a distinct cultural identity through the preservation of traditional practices such as arts, rituals, festivals, ceremonies, religion, customary law, language, and literature (Dop et al., 2014; Phan, 1996). The Cham communities, known as palei, are organized around a matrilocal kinship network, where ancestor veneration is emphasized on the mother's side of the family and property inheritance is passed down through the youngest daughter. Women hold significant power within the family, with the oldest female serving as the head of the household. Men, on the other hand, primarily work as laborers and hold little power within the family. Historically, only priests and clerics held significant influence, but the intelligentsia has gained power since the mid-twentieth century (Noseworthy, 2017).

The Cham people in Ninh Thuan Province practice a diverse array of religious beliefs, with two major denominations being the Ahier, an Indigenous form of Hinduism, and the Awal, an Indigenous form of Islam. While a small number of Awal have been converted to traditional Islam, other beliefs such as polytheism and

Christianity (mainly Protestantism) are present in smaller numbers (Noseworthy, 2017).

Interestingly, Buddhism, which was once an influential religion in the region and demonstrated a crucial center for Buddhist studies in Southeast Asia since the seventh century, is no longer practiced by the Cham community (Phu, 2012; Schweyer, 2009; Van Son, 2014). Nevertheless, several architectural arts from the Champā era, indicative of its important role in Buddhist studies, still remain in Central Vietnam.

In addition, the Cham community also holds a strong tradition of oral storytelling, passed down through generations, which is used to preserve the history and culture of their people (Phan, 1996). This oral tradition is an important part of the Cham cultural heritage and is still highly valued and practiced today. Furthermore, the Cham people have a rich tradition of traditional festivals and ceremonies, such as the Kate Festival, the Cambun Festival, and the Rija Nagar Festival, which are celebrated annually to commemorate important events in Cham history, to pray for good health and prosperity, and to mark the changing of the seasons (Phan, 2010; Sakaya, 2003). These festivals and ceremonies provide a platform for the Cham to express their cultural identity, to preserve their traditions, and to maintain their spiritual connection to their ancestors and their cultural heritage.

The Cham community in Ninh Thuan and Binh Thuan retains its traditional classes of Halau Janâng (the system of priests) and Gihéh (the laity), despite the significant changes that the community has experienced throughout history (Phan, 2010). The Cham people have established rich cultural arts, including sculpture, architecture, music, and dance, that reflect their unique identity and express their thoughts, emotions, and aesthetic views (Bien et al., 1991; Dop et al., 2014; Sakaya, 2003). Their folklore across various genres and myths also showcases their distinct cultural heritage. Although influences from South and other Southeast Asian cultures can be seen, the Cham have managed to preserve their own identity (Phan, 1996).

Religious communities in the Cham community usually reside in separate palei, but some may live together in the same village (Hieu, 2013; Phan, 1996). The two major religious groups among the Cham are the Ahier (an indigenized form of Hinduism) and the Awal (an indigenized form of Islam), with a small number of Awal having been converted to traditional Islam. Other denominations, such as polytheism and Christianity (mainly Protestantism), are in the minority (Phan, 1996).

The Cham custodians play an important role in managing natural resources, religion, and culture. They provide direct management and protection of sacred sites, such as temples, shrines, and Kut graves, or support for those who do (Phan, 1996). The preservation of the Cham community's heritage is also supported by the matrilocal kinship network, where the youngest daughter inherits property, the oldest female in each generation is the head of the household, and the duty to preserve religious sites is passed down along matrilineal lines (Noseworthy, 2017).

Cham communities have two main types of custodians derived from within the community: priests and knowledgeable elders. The priests directly perform ceremonies and manage sacred sites and natural resources, while the elders assist in carrying out ceremonies and providing guidance to the community (Phan, 1996). These two groups are critical in maintaining the spiritual and cultural heritage of the

Cham people. The rituals that take place in the temples are for the wider membership of the communities, while those in the village palei are more focused on individual families or clans (Hieu, 2013). Hence, both the priests and all social classes in the Cham community are responsible for preserving and protecting their natural resources and sacred sites, which are essential for their daily lives and spiritual practices.

The Cham people's rich history and culture have often been viewed by Vietnamese officials as distinct and more advanced compared to other minority groups in the country. However, there is a need to further explore and understand the Cham community, including their cultural beliefs, practices, and misunderstandings.

In conclusion, this chapter highlights the cultural, religious, and social aspects of the Cham people in Ninh Thuan and Binh Thuan Provinces in Vietnam. The Cham have a distinct identity that is reflected in their traditional practices, arts, and culture. They have two major religious groups, Ahier and Awal, with influences from South and Southeast Asian cultures visible in their folklore, music, dance, and sculpture. Despite the changes that the Cham have experienced in their history, the basic classes of traditional society still exist in the Cham communities, with custodians playing a significant role in managing natural resources, religion, and culture. The ceremonies in the temples are for the wider community while those in the village palei are for each family or clan. The development of the Cham kingdoms and people is viewed as advanced by Vietnamese officials, but this view may not be entirely accurate.

References

Abdul, M. E. (2013). *Nager Cam and the Priests of Prowess: A history of resilience.* University of Hawaii at Manoa, USA.

Dharma, P. (1999). The Contribution to Understanding the History of Champa [Góp phần tìm hiểu lịch sử Champa]. Nghiên Cứu Lịch Sử Văn Minh Champa (Champaka), 1.

Bien, P. X., An, P., & Dop, P. Van. (1989). The Cham people in Thuan Hai Province [Người Chăm ở Thuận Hải]. Phan Rang Thap Cham: Văn hoá Thông tin Thuận Hải.

Bien, P. X., An, P., & Dop, P. Van. (1991). The Cham culture [Văn hoá Chăm]. Ho Chi Minh: KHXH.

Brossard, C. (1901). Géographie Pittoresque Et Monumentale De La France Et De Ses Colonie. Flammarion. http://gallica.bnf.fr/ark:/12148/bpt6k5834316w/f2.image.texteImage

Corntassel, J. (2003). Who is indigenous? Peoplehood'and ethnonationalist approaches to rearticulating indigenous identity. Nationalism and Ethnic Politics. http://www.tandfonline.com/doi/abs/10.1080/13537110412331301365

Dharma, P. (1978). Chroniques du Panduranga. EPHE-Sorbonne.

Dharma, P. (1987). Le Paθurajga (Campa) 1802–1835. Bulletin de l'Ecole Française d'Extrême-Orient—BEFEO, 1–2.

Dharma, P. (2001). The intangible cultural heritage of two provinces of central Vietnam—Ninh Thuan and Binh Thuan. In O. Salemink (Ed.), *Viet Nam's cultural diversity: Approaches to preservation* (pp. 265–270). UNESCO.

Doanh, N. Van. (1998). The Rija Nagar festival of the Cham [Lễ hội Rija Nưgar của người Chăm]. Ha Noi: Văn Hoá Dân Tộc.

Doanh, N. Van. (2006). *Champa: Ancient towers, reality & legend (2nd ed.).* The Gioi.

Dop, P. Van, Anh, P. Q., & Thu, N. T. (2014). Văn hóa phi vật thể người Chăm Ninh Thuận [Intangible cultural heritage of the Cham people in Ninh Thuan]. Ho Chi Minh: NXB Nông Nghiệp TP.HCM. http://chamstudies.net/2016/02/18/van-hoa-phi-vat-the-cua-nguoi-cham-ninh-thuan/

General Statistics Office. (2019). *Results of the entire 2019 Census* [Kết quả toàn bộ Tổng điều tra dân số 19/12/2019. Trung tâm Tư liệu và Dịch vụ Thống kê, Tổng cục Thống kê]. General Statistics Office of Vietnam.

Hao, P. (2015). Cham manuscripts, the endangered cultural heritage from a lost Kingdom. *Restaurator, 36*(2), 101–120. https://doi.org/10.1515/res-2014-0019

Hardy, A., Cucarzi, M., & Zolese, P. (2009). Champa and the archaeology of Mỹ Sơn (Vietnam). NUS Press.

Hieu, L. T. (2013). Các làng Chăm Ninh Thuận: Nghiên cứu địa danh học [The village of Cham in Ninh Thuan: A toponymy]. *Tạp Chí Xửa Và Nay, 443*, 34–37.

Hubert, J.-F. (2012). *The art of Champa*. Parkstone International.

IWGIA. (2012). The Indigenous World 2012—(C. Mikkelsen, Ed.), IWGIA. Copenhagen, Denmark: IWGIA. http://www.iwgia.org/publications/search-pubs?publication_id=573

Khoang, P. (1969). Việt sử xứ Đàng Trong (Cuộc Nam Tiến của dân tộc Việt Nam) 1558-1777. Khai Tri Press.

Kim, T. T. (1986). Việt Nam sử lược. Glendale, Đại Nam.

Lafont, P. B. (2014). *The kingdom of Champa: Geography, population, history*. International Office of the Champa.

Li, T. (1998). *Nguyen Cochinchina, Southern Vietnam in the Seventeenth and Eighteenth Centuries*. Southeast Asia Program Publications.

Lockhart, B. (2011). Colonial and post-colonial constructions of "Champa." In B. L. Tran Ky Phuong (Ed.), *The Cham of Vietnam: History, society and art* (pp. 1–53). NUS Press.

Maspero, G. (1928). Le Royaume de Champa [The Champa kingdom—The history of an extinct Vietnamese culture]. Retrieved January 6, 2016, from http://www.amazon.com/Le-Royaume-de-Champa/dp/2855395437

Merlan, F. (2009). Indigeneity: Global and local. *Current Anthropology*. https://doi.org/10.1086/597667

Momoki, S. (1999). A short introduction to Champa studies. In F. Hayao (Ed.), *The dry areas in Southeast Asia: Harsh or benign environment* (pp. 65–74). Center for Southeast Asian Studies. Kyoto University.

Momoki, S. (2011). Mandala Champa seen from Chinese sources'. In T. K. P. and B. M. Lockhart (Ed.), *The Cham in Vietnam: History, society and art* (pp. 120–137). NUS Press.

Mus, P. (1934). *India Seen from the East: Indian and Indigenous Cults in Champa*. Monash Asia Institute.

Noseworthy, W. (2017). *Khik Agama Cam: Caring for Cham Religions in Mainland Southeast Asia, 1651–1969*. University of Wiscosin-Madison.

Phan, T. (1996). Religious organizations and traditional soceity of the Cham people in Phan Rang region [Tổ chức tôn giáo và xã hội truyền thống của người Chăm ở vùng Phan Rang]. Tap San Khoa Hoc [Đại Học Tổng Hợp Tp. HCM], 1(1), 165–172.

Phan, T. (2010). Some research issues related to traditional beliefs and religions of the Cham people in Vietnam today [Một số vấn đề nghiên cứu liên quan đến tín ngưỡng - tôn giáo truyền thống của người Chăm hiện nay ở Việt Nam]. In P. T. Y. T. Lương Văn Hy, Ngô Văn Lệ, Nguyễn Văn Tiệp (Ed.), Hiện đại và động thái của Truyền thống ở Việt Nam: Những cách tiếp cận Nhân học (tập 2) (pp. 215–227). HCM National University.

Phan, T. (2012). Language and hand writing documents of the Cham indigenous people in Vietnam in the study of cultural anthropology [Tiếng nói và văn bản viết tay của dân tộc bản địa ở Việt Nam trong Nghiên cứu Nhân học văn hóa]. In The Annual Conference of the Association for Asian Studies (AAS). http://www.asian-studies.org/Conferences/AAS

Phat, T. B. (1970). Lịch Sử Cuộc Nam Tiến Của Dân Tộc Việt Nam [History of Southern Expansions of Vietnam]. *Sử Địa [historical Geography]*, 19–20, 125–128.

Phu, B. T. (2012). Phật Giáo Champa. http://baotanglichsuvn.com/phat-giao-cha-mpa-ts-ba-trung-phu-98.html

Phuong, T. K. (2008). Vestiges of Champa Civilisation. Thế Giới Publishers.

Phuong, T. K. (2009). The Architecture of the Temples of Ancient Champa. In Andrew Hardy, Mauro Cucarzi and Patrizia Zolese (Ed.), *Champa and the archaeology of my son (Vietnam)* (pp. 155–186). NUS Press.

Sakaya. (2003). The festivals of the Cham people [Lễ hội của người Chăm]. NXB Van Hoa Dan Toc.

Sakaya. (2016a). An approach to palm leaf manuscript heritage (Agal Bac) as a cultural Treasure of Cham People in Vietnam. *Studies on Asia Series V, 1*(2). https://chamstudies.files.wordpress.com/2016/04/sakaya-palm-leaf.pdf

Schweyer, A.-V. (2009). Buddhism in Čampā. *Moussons.* https://doi.org/10.4000/moussons.810

Shigeeda, Y. et al. (1994). Artifacts and culture of the Champa Kingdom (Exhibition Catalogue).

Son, Q. Van. (2014). Phật Giáo Champa từ tư liệu lịch sử đến nhận thức[The Budhsim in Champa kingdom from historical document to cognition]. *Nghiên Cứu Tôn Giáo, 6*(132), 46–57. https://thuvienhoasen.org/images/file/Dk2Ms_co1QgQAHVR/phat-giao-champa-tu-tu-lieu-den-nhan-thuc.pdf

Sox, D. G. (1972). Rescoure—Use system of ancient Champa [Master's thesis]. University of Hawaii at Manoa.

Stern, P. (1942). The art of Champa (formerly Annam) and its evolution [L'art du Champa et son evolution]. Publication du Musee Guimet.

Taylor, K. (1983). *The birth of Vietnam.* University of California Press.

Thurgood, G. (1999). *From ancient Cham to modern dialects: Two thousand years of language contact and change. Pragmatics (Vol. 10).* University of Hawai'i Press. https://doi.org/10.1353/ol.2000.0014

Tieu, L. T., Doanh, N. Van, & Hung, N. Q. (2000). Giữ gìn những kiệt tác kiến trúc trong nền văn hóa Chăm [Preservation of the architectural masterpiece of the Cham culture]. Nxb Văn hóa Dân tộc.

Open Access This chapter is licensed under the terms of the Creative Commons Attribution 4.0 International License (http://creativecommons.org/licenses/by/4.0/), which permits use, sharing, adaptation, distribution and reproduction in any medium or format, as long as you give appropriate credit to the original author(s) and the source, provide a link to the Creative Commons license and indicate if changes were made.

The images or other third party material in this chapter are included in the chapter's Creative Commons license, unless indicated otherwise in a credit line to the material. If material is not included in the chapter's Creative Commons license and your intended use is not permitted by statutory regulation or exceeds the permitted use, you will need to obtain permission directly from the copyright holder.

Chapter 3
Cham Culture and Traditions: Understanding Their Worldview Through Custodianship and Philosophy

Introduction

The Cham people have a rich history and culture that has been shaped by various events and changes throughout time. Despite the changes, the basic social classes of traditional Cham society still persist in the communities of Ninh Thuan and Binh Thuan, particularly the Halau Janâng and the civilian population (Phan, 2010). This traditional society is responsible for managing and preserving the natural resources, religion, and culture of the Cham people. In addition, in the Cham community, there are two types of custodians who are responsible for managing and protecting sacred sites and natural resources. These custodians include the dignitaries, who directly perform ceremonies and manage sacred sites, and the knowledgeable elders who assist the dignitaries. The rituals performed in temples serve the larger community, while those performed in village palei are specific to each family or clan. This study aims to shed light on the traditional management systems of the Cham people, including their agricultural and religious systems, with a focus on the religious folk and Ahier religious priest systems. These systems are essential in preserving the natural resources, religion, and culture of the Cham people and are carried out by key custodians of the temples.

Religion and Culture in Cham Society: A Deep-Rooted Connection

Religion holds a vital place in the lives of the Cham people, shaping their spiritual beliefs, daily practices, and cultural identity. The interweaving of religion and culture in Cham society is so close that many individuals find it difficult to distinguish between the two. For the Cham, practicing spirituality is also a way of preserving their cultural traditions.

© The Author(s) 2023
Q. D. Tuyen, *Heritage Conservation and Tourism Development at Cham Sacred Sites in Vietnam*, Global Vietnam: Across Time, Space and Community,
https://doi.org/10.1007/978-981-99-3350-1_3

The Cham people, like other Southeast Asian communities, have a strong Indigenous agricultural tradition, particularly in the practice of wet rice farming. This matriarchal system has dominated all aspects of Cham society and serves as a guiding principle in their religious beliefs and ceremonies. The original folk beliefs of the Cham people are similar to those of other ethnic groups, with Brahmanism playing a significant role in shaping the Cham cultural identity.

The Cham temples, considered as a legacy of Hindu-related culture, were present in Champā as early as the fourth century. Hinduism was highly respected and dominant in the region from the seventh century to the twelfth century. However, the practice of this religion declined after the defeat of Champā in 1471. The nobility in the southern region of Champā embraced a syncretistic religion that incorporated several forms of worship practiced by the local community (Sharma, 1992, p. 32). Overall, religion has played a vital role in shaping the Cham culture and continues to be deeply intertwined with their daily lives and spiritual beliefs.

The Cham people have a rich and diverse religious history, which has played an integral role in their spiritual life, daily life, and culture. When Brahmin religion was first introduced into Champā, the Cham people built temples to worship Hindu gods such as Shiva, Brahma, and Vishnu. The influence of Shivaism was particularly profound, and ancient Cham temples in Central Vietnam today still bear symbols of this god.

Alongside the development of Brahmanism, Buddhism also played a role in Cham religious history. During the ninth century, King Indravarman II built a monastery in Indrapura to practice Mahayana Buddhism, which intersected with Brahmanism. However, Buddhism faded out in the tenth century, and the Cham people returned to Hinduism.

In the tenth century, Islam also began to spread among the Cham people. At first, this new religion was met with resistance, but from the 11th to the seventeenth centuries, it continued to grow. This resulted in conflicts between the Brahmin and Islamic religions, which led to the concept of "dualism" introduced by King Po Rome in the mid-seventeenth century. This concept allowed the two religious communities to live and work together as "two but one," expressed in rituals such as weddings and funerals and the dress of the priests of both religions. In short, the religious history of the Cham people reflects the diversity and complexity of their culture, and the ways in which religion and spirituality have shaped their daily lives.

The unique blending of Brahman and Islam in Cham history has resulted in the creation of two local religions, Ahier and Awal. The Ahier followers worship both Hindu gods as well as Allah, while the Awal worship both Allah and the Hindu gods of the Cham Ahier. The Cham Ahier and Awal communities have found a way to coexist and reconcile their religious differences through the concept of "duality." This concept is reflected in various aspects of Cham culture, including rituals, dress, and religious practices. The creation of Ahier and Awal has also led to the development of different systems of priests that serve the spiritual needs of the Cham community. In this research, the focus will be on the systems of folk and Ahier beliefs and their connection to the temples. These two religions have become a distinct part of

Vietnam's religious heritage and continue to be practiced by the Cham people to this day.

Traditional Cham culture, which encompasses the traditional culture of Southeast Asian wet rice, has undergone a process of localization and has merged with other religions to form the common culture of the Cham people. Despite the changes in doctrines and the divine system, the worship of the Cham people remains strong, including the system of ceremonies and religious and folk priests (Anh, 2004).

Cham communities have maintained over one hundred ceremonies held throughout the year (Sakaya, 2003). The ritual system is both rich and complex, and religious and folk dignitaries play a significant role. The folk ritual system of the Cham people is diverse and is a mixture of folk and religious ceremonies (Bien et al., 1991; Sakaya, 2003). As a result, the system of ceremonies can sometimes be difficult to distinguish, with folk dignitaries attending several religious ceremonies and religious dignitaries participating in some folk rituals.

Agricultural Management System in Traditional Cham Culture

The Agricultural Management System of the Cham people is responsible for over-seeing and serving the community in regard to their agricultural activities. This system includes three key figures: On Banak, who manages irrigation systems; On Hamu Aia, who manages water systems; and Po Pariya Hamu, who presides over agricultural ceremonies.

Po Pariya Hamu is in charge of conducting rituals and ceremonies related to the folk beliefs and agricultural production. To become a Po Pariya Hamu, one must receive knowledge and training from a teacher. On Banak is responsible for the maintenance of dams and the regulation of water sources to rice fields. He also organizes the village to repair irrigation systems and resolves disputes concerning irrigation. On Hamu Aia, appointed by On Banak, assists in the mobilization of workers for irrigation and collects compensation from those who do not participate.

While On Banak and On Hamu Aia focus on the technical aspects of irrigation management, Po Pariya Hamu offers a spiritual perspective, performing rituals to ensure the stability of the dams and protect them from evil spirits. However, since 1975, the agricultural ritual system and its dignitaries have disappeared.

Management Systems in Relation to Religious Practices

The Civilian Class (Gihéh)

The civilian class is a key group that operates outside the religious hierarchy, serving as a support for dignitaries who organize rituals and festivals for communities, villages, clans, and families. They assist in collecting funds to build or renovate religious sites and participate in the conduct of religious rituals. Civil society is composed of two groups: intellectuals and farmers, who have distinct backgrounds and roles in their collaboration with religious priests (Phan, 2010).

The intellectuals, who are often retired state employees, farmers, or researchers, play a crucial role in supporting the dignitaries and adapting religious regulations to modern Cham social life. They are nominated to the Village Custom Committee and the Council of Religious Dignitaries, serving as the closest connection between village members and the religious activities. They inform village members about religious activities, mobilize funds, and prepare for ceremonies.

Meanwhile, ordinary people contribute to the spiritual activities of the Cham community by helping to prepare offerings and tools for ceremonies. They do not seek personal gain, but rather contribute out of a sense of duty and responsibility as "sons" of Cham after a period of working in state agencies. According to Cham intellectuals, participation in community spiritual activities brings blessings from the Yang gods, as well as opportunities to learn about Cham culture and religion and connect with others in the community.

Both the Cham Ahier and Awal communities have this civilian class to support their spiritual activities, and their role is greatly valued and respected by the Cham communities.

The Folk Dignitaries

The Cham people, following polytheistic beliefs, formed the folk dignitaries to conduct various folk ceremonies. These dignitaries play a crucial role in both the Cham Ahier and Awal communities, contributing greatly to the preservation of Cham cultural heritage. They are responsible for performing ceremonies not only at temples but also for crucial rituals such as Rija, agricultural, and Kut ceremonies, among others.

The distinction between Cham Ahier and Awal religions is blurred among the folk dignitaries, as they share the same traditional beliefs. They work closely with both Ahier and Awal dignitaries to conduct these ceremonies. The folk dignitaries have many parts as follows:

On Kadhar priest and *Muk Pajuw*: They are two important folk dignitaries in Cham communities. They participate in various rituals and ceremonies related to Cham folk beliefs, including those performed at temples, family gatherings, and the Kut, Ngap puis, and Ngap Chwa ceremonies. The Kadhar is a skilled musician who provides musical accompaniment on a traditional instrument called the kanyi and is responsible for singing hymns in praise of the gods during these rituals.

Muk Pajuw is a female medium who invites the gods to be worshipped (Mâliéng yang) and prepares offerings for ceremonies and dances to celebrate their success. As a priestess or prophetess, *Pajuw* is often believed to be the one who communicates with the spirits during ceremonies and rituals. To maintain the purity of their spiritual connection, Muk Pajuw follows a strict diet, avoiding certain foods such as beef, eel, catfish, dead animals, and fruits such as seeded bananas and figs (Fig. 3.1).

The positions of Ong Kadhar and Muk Pajuw are traditionally passed down through hereditary lines, with Ong Kadhar being passed from father to son, and Muk Pajuw from mother to daughter. However, at present, there are no longer any women assuming the role of Muk Pajuw at the Po Rómé temple. This is a cause for concern as it means that a crucial part of the Cham community's role in conducting ceremonies at temples and families may be lost. To mitigate this, families near the Po Rómé temple often invite Muk Pajuw from other areas to help with ceremonies in collaboration with Ong Kadhar.

| *Muk Pajuw* | *Ong Kadhar* | *On Camnei* |
| *Muk Rija* | *Ong Ka-ing* | *Gru Urang* |

Fig. 3.1 The folk dignitaries (Courtesy of the author, 2017)

To become officially recognized as folk dignitaries and to be appointed as the chief of Cham rituals, Ong Kadhar and Muk Pajuw must undergo ordination rituals, including the "*Paoh bangâh tagok Gru*" and "*kakuak ndaw.*" After these important ceremonies, *Ong Kadhar* is officially referred to as "Ong Kadhar Gru." Additionally, both Ong Kadhar and *Muk Pajuw* must participate in the Panoja ceremony to purify their minds and bodies. *On Camnei,* the temple guard, is responsible for the upkeep of temples and acts as the protector of sacred objects. He ensures the offerings for the gods are safe and assists Po Adhia, the Head of Ahier priest, in conducting ceremonies at the temples. His role is crucial in maintaining and safeguarding the tangible aspects of the temples. The *On Kadhar, Muk Pajuw,* and *On Camnei* priests have close ties with the Balamon or Ahier priests as they work together in conducting various Cham rituals at the temples and villages. They are members of the Council of Cham Brahmanism Religion. *On Maduen* serves as an officiant for important Cham ceremonies such as the Rija ceremony at the family and village levels, but has no affiliation with Hindu temples (Fig. 3.2).

The Muk Rija is a shamanic figure who serves as a vessel for the spirits of Cham deities during possession ceremonies. While she does not play a direct role in guiding or supporting ceremonies at the temples, she does offer offerings to the gods on behalf of her family and community during various rituals.

Fig. 3.2 The Maduen priest (Courtesy of the author, 2014)

The Ong Ka-ing is a male dancer and a member of the lower religious elite in the Cham hierarchy. He is only involved in Rija Harei and Rija Nagar ceremonies, which take place within villages and families.

The Gru Urang is a magician, while the Gru Tiap Bhut is a necromancer. Neither of these figures play an important role in temple rituals, but they are members of the Cham communities and may practice their craft in the temples. There are also several other folk priests who work in Cham ceremonies today, but they do not play a significant role in the temples.

The Awal Religious System

The Awal religion is a form of localized Islam that has been modified to reconcile with the Cham culture in Vietnam. According to Manguin (2001), Islam was introduced to Champā in the tenth century. However, the Cham Awal/Bani in Vietnam embraced many local factors (Phu, 2005). The Cham Awal do not identify themselves as orthodox Muslims and do not follow the same daily worship practices as traditional Muslims (Phu, 2008; Yasuko, 2012). The role of the Acar priests is to safeguard the religion from corruption and to lead the community in prayer (Phu, 2008).

In Ninh Thuan Province, there are seven Awal mosques, also known as "sang magik," located in seven villages: Rem, Cuah Patih, Katuh, Cang, Aboah Hadeng, Pabmblap Klak, and Pamblap Biruw. Each mosque is managed by the Acar class, who play a crucial role in maintaining the religious and cultural activities of the Cham Awal community (Ba Trung Phan, 2010; Phu, 2008). The Awal religion is divided into four hierarchical levels, including Acar (the lowest level), Madin, Katip, Imâm, and Po Gru, who holds the highest position in the Awal religion (Phan, 2010) (Fig. 3.3).

- *Acar*: The Acar class is made up of newly ordained priests in the Bani clergy. Based on their experience and ability to memorize sutras, they are further divided into four levels: Jamâak, Talavi, Po Sit, and Po Praong. The promotion ceremony takes place during the month of Ramâwan.
- *Mâdin*: Mâdins are responsible for announcing the date and time of religious ceremonies for dignitaries in the mosque (Sang magik). They are in charge of opening and closing the ceremony at the mosque.
- *Katip*: The dignitary at this level is authorized to perform certain rituals inside and outside the mosque. They give lectures on doctrine and report on religious matters.
- *Imâm*: An Imâm is a priest who has dedicated at least 15 years to the practice of the religion, has memorized all the Kuraan scriptures, and is capable of conducting all religious rituals.
- *Po Gru*: Po Gru is the highest and only position in a Bani Islam village or mosque. They are responsible for making decisions on religious and life issues, and they alone set the date for religious ceremonies.

Fig. 3.3 Dignitaries of the Awal/Bani community performing a ritual in Ninh Thuan Province. *Source* Author, 2017

Each Sang Magik is led by Awal religious priests and highly respected members of the community who are elected to manage the religious affairs and serve the needs of the Awal community in the village. The mosque leadership's responsibility is to convey the directions of Po Gru, the highest authority in the Bani Islam, to the believers and to receive and address their feedback, suggestions, and concerns. The leadership board is composed of Madin, Katip Tan, and Imâm Tan, selected through an objective and democratic process for a term of three to five years (Anh, 2004).

The Awal religious system works in collaboration with the Ahier religious priests to coordinate the dates of religious rituals according to the Cham sakawi calendar. This involves adjusting the dates of both the Awal and Ahier rituals and ceremonies, including the times for the Cham festivals. These changes also have an impact on the ceremonial days at Cham temples. However, the focus of this study is mainly on the Ahier religious system.

The Cham Brahman Religious System

The introduction of Brahma into Cham society was localized by the rich and ancient traditional culture, resulting in the formation of Cham culture that influenced Brahma religion, but maintained a strong cultural identity (Bien et al., 1991). The Cham architectural works in the central part of the Champā Dynasty were originally built for the worship of Brahma, Vishnu, and Shiva gods, with a focus on Shiva worship

(Bien et al., 1991). Over time, the Cham honored new deities identified with Shiva as Po Klaong Girai, Po Rome, and Po Inâ Nâgar, with the Motherland being identified with the goddess Uma (Bien et al., 1991). However, the Brahma religion in the Cham community is believed by many researchers to no longer embrace enough of the elements of an orthodox religion, such as the catechesis system, canon law, and a clear system of followers and believers (Bien et al., 1991; Phan, 1996, 2010). The Cham people refer to themselves as Ahier, rather than Brahmins. Despite their strong localization, the dignitaries, clergymen, and their missions are still systematically maintained in the Cham Ahier community.

Each type of cremation ritual has a different level of importance and reflects the social status and prestige of the deceased and their family. The presence of more dignitaries at the cremation ceremony is considered a symbol of honor and respect for the deceased. The role of the Brahmin priests in the cremation ritual is to lead the ritual, perform religious rites and prayers, and guide the family of the deceased through the process. The exact details of the cremation ceremony may vary among different villages and communities within the Cham Ahier society. Nevertheless, the significance of the caste hierarchy in the cremation ritual highlights the enduring influence of the ancient Brahmin culture and beliefs in the Cham Ahier community today.

In Brahmanism, the Brahmin class is considered the highest class and is believed to have been born from the mouth of Sanura (Manu) (Xuyen, 1999). The Brahmin class is also considered the god of the earth, responsible for presiding over worships and the manipulation of ancient spiritual life (Xuyen, 1999, p. 193). Today, the Brahman priests continue to hold an important role in the Cham Ahier community, despite the fading of the caste system (Anh, 2004; Bien et al., 1991).

Even though the caste system has faded, it still exists through the cremation ritual of the Ahier community, which is regulated by the hierarchy of clans (Anh, 2004). The highest level in this hierarchy is still held by the Brahman priests (Anh, 2004).

In my observation of Cham Ahier cremation, I have identified three types of cremation rituals: (1) the cremation ritual with four Basaih dignitaries officiating, (2) the cremation ritual with two Basaih dignitaries, and (3) the cremation ritual with only one Basaih priest (Fig. 3.4).

The number of priests in the Cham Ahier cremation ritual reflects the deceased's, the host family's, or clan's status and class in the Cham society, both in the past and today. The process of this ritual is intricate, with the simplest version involving two officiates of Basaih and being simpler than the version with four Basaih dignitaries. The latter requires three types of musical instruments: four kanyi players, one Hagar, and one Seng player. Other cremation rituals only require two kanyi players. The distinction in the number of priests during the cremation ritual symbolizes the class distinction of Cham Ahier people in the past and one that their descendants still maintain today. The author noticed that the cremation rituals for members of their family always involved four Basaih priests, indicating that the family had a high status in the past. The author's grandmother shared that many members of the great matrilineal family were officials in the court and Maduen and Kadhar Guru in the

Fig. 3.4 Balamon Cham dignitaries in Ninh Thuận Province during the celebration of the Kate festival (Author, 2017)

past. Thus, the cremation rituals today reflect the status and class of the family and clan in the past.

The social structure and institutions of the Cham people used to be dominated by the four classes of Brahmanism, as described in the My Son epitaph under King Jaya Indravarman (1088). These four classes were

1. Brahmins: priests and teachers;
2. Kshatriyas: the aristocrat, kings, and martial artists;
3. Vaishyas: farmers, traders, and merchants; and
4. Sudras: laborers.

As noted by Phan Quoc Anh (2004), the Cham society still recognizes these social classes, but with different terminology. Specifically, they are referred to as:

1. Brahmin class: *Haluw Janâng*;
2. Aristocratic class: *Takai gai*;
3. Popular class: *Bal li-wa, kulit*; and
4. Slave and servant class: *Halun halak, halun klor*.

However, the class system has undergone significant changes, including changes in terms and roles within Cham society today. For example, the terms "Po Gru" and "Po Adhia" refer to folk priests and ordinary people (Bhap). In the Ahier system, there are two classes: the Basaih system and folk dignitaries. Basaih is a term used to refer to religious dignitaries of Brahmanism, who hold the highest rank in society and belong to the old aristocracy of the past Cham society.

Basaih is understood as a wise man and spiritual supporter of all classes in the Cham Ahier society, responsible for the sacred duties of religious life and possessing both intellectual and linguistic mastery of Cham culture. They maintain and preserve ancient manuscripts containing information on rituals, collective knowledge, and the Cham Sakawi calendar, which is used to keep track of dates and times for rituals and agricultural activities.

The selection of new Cham religious dignitaries is based on the principle of hereditary, as only members of the lineage of existing dignitaries are eligible to serve in this role. In addition to having a lineage connection, potential candidates must also meet certain physical and personal requirements, including being physically fit, free of any physical handicaps or deformities, capable of studying catechism and learning ancient Cham traditions, and having a wife. Once a candidate has met these requirements and been approved by the Basaih Guru teachers (the current Council of Brahman Dignitaries), they will undergo a purifying baptism ceremony. The exact timing of this ceremony is determined by the teacher of the candidate. This process reflects the influence of ancient Indian Brahmanism, which still has a significant presence in the Cham community today. The family of the candidate holds responsibility for the celebration of their Basaih position, highlighting the important role of the clan in shaping the beliefs and practices of the Cham Ahier community.

It's important to note that the Cham Ahier religion is based on the Hindu tradition and its religious dignitaries play a central role in maintaining the customs and beliefs of the community.

The Ahier dignitaries are organized in a hierarchical order, from lower to higher rank. The five levels are: Basaih Ndung Akaok, Basaih Liah, Basaih Pahuak, Basaih Tapah (On Bac), and Po Adhia, who holds the highest position and has supremacy in the Ahier religion and society.

1. *Basaih Ndung Akaok:* This is the first level of ordination, and the priest is in an apprenticeship stage.
2. *Basaih Liah:* This is the second level of ordination, and the priest has completed the apprenticeship and is officially ordained as a senior Basaih.
3. *Basaih Pahuak:* This is the third level of ordination and is given to priests who have become fully qualified and are engaged in official service.
4. *Basaih Tapah (On Bac):* This is a high-ranking dignitary who has attained the level of escapism and strictly follows the religious teachings.
5. *Po Adhia:* This is the highest level of ordination, and the priest is elected from the ranks of Basaih Tapah. They serve as the religious leader of a temple and preside over all religious rituals and ceremonies, including weddings, funerals, new homes, and other religious activities. Po Adhia is responsible for making all spiritual and cultural decisions for the Ahiér community and assigning responsibilities for implementation.

They are responsible for preserving the ancient manuscripts and traditions of the Cham people and ensuring the continuation of their religious practices. The selection and ordination of dignitaries is a complex process that is based on hereditary lineage, physical fitness, and intellectual and spiritual aptitude. The role of the Basaih in the Cham society is significant, as they play a key role in preserving the culture and traditions of the community (Fig. 3.5).

The Basaih dignitaries are subject to stringent guidelines. Ahier priests are prohibited from consuming beef, deer meat, catfish, eels, frogs, figs, and squashes. They must also refrain from eating the liver or other parts of an animal that haven't been properly prepared. Dinner must be consumed before the sun sets and, in the absence of light, they must stop eating even if they're not yet full. Before using the restroom, Ahier priests must remove their cap and recite a mantra.

The religious landscape of Ninh Thuan Province is divided into three main temple areas, including Po Klaong Girai, Po Nagar, and Po Rome. Each temple is represented by a Po Adhia, who is responsible for overseeing the spiritual activities of the Ahier community surrounding the temple, as well as maintaining the number of Ahier dignitaries. In the past, the Po Adhia of the Po Klaong Girai temple held the highest rank in the region, and was responsible for deciding the ordinations, dates, and processes of religious ceremonies. This Po Adhia stayed at home to direct any religious activities in the region, while the Po Adhia of the Po Nagar temple performed rituals under the direction of the Po Adhia of Po Klaong Girai, and the Po Adhia of the Po Rome temple conducted the Kut entrance ceremony. However, these provisions are no longer in effect (Anh, 2004). Each Po Adhia now has the autonomy to decide and manage the activities at their respective temples, performing all the duties of the three Po Adhia in the past.

Fig. 3.5 The ordination ceremony for Po Gru in Ahier religion (Courtesy of the author, 2013)

In 2017, the number of priests in charge of religious practices in the Cham community was 150, including those of the Ahier religion and the Cham folk religion. These priests were responsible for overseeing religious activities at three main temples: Po Klaong Girai, Po Rome, and Po Ina Nagar, as well as 20 shrines in Cham villages. While the Ahier priests primarily lead the religious practices, Cham folk priests such as Maduen, Ka-ing, and Kadhar continue to play a role in conducting rituals in Awal villages (Table 3.1).

In 2017, there were 150 priests of Ahier and folk religions responsible for the religious practices at three main temple areas including Po Klaong Girai, Po Rome, and Po Ina Nagar, as well as 20 shrines in all Cham villages. They primarily work with the Cham Ahier community, but Cham folk priests like Maduen, Ka-ing, and Kadhar still assist in conducting rituals at the Awal villages.

Each temple has three main scriptures that are preserved by *Po Adhia.* These scriptures consist of five large volumes, each with a number of sections that cover a wide range of topics, from the creation of the universe to customs and habits. The first volume discusses the formation of the earth, the world, and humans. The second volume focuses on religion and folk beliefs (*Ngap Yang Parang Bingu*). The third volume highlights the prohibitions, teachings on human behavior, and lifestyle in general, as well as specific rules for the Basaih priests in cultivating the Dhamma (cosmic law and order) and performing magic spells to save people. These rules are written on palm leaves in the traditional *Cham Akhar Thrah* scripts, sometimes alternating between *Akhar Rik, Akhar Tuer, Akhar Yok,* which are the old styles of Cham writing systems.

According to customary customs, the five large volumes of scriptures are used during large rituals, such as ordination ceremonies for *Ahier priests, Palao Kaxah or Pa Cakap Hlau Kraong* rituals for praying for peace at water downstream or upstream, and Kamruai Pakap ceremony for exterminating bad omens in the village. For smaller, ordinary rituals, such as the Purification rite for land and house and purification offerings for priests, small scriptures are used.

In addition to the strict codes of conduct for the Basaih dignitaries, the Cham folk beliefs also include the preservation of certain hymns and exorcism practices. Three

Table 3.1 List of Cham Ahier custodians in Ninh Thuan Province (Report of Council of Cham Brahmanism Dignitaries 2017)

Priests	Number of priests	Role
Basaih	38	Within Ahier communities
Kadhar	11	Both Ahier and Awal communities
Maduen	19	Both Ahier and Awal communities
Camânay	08	Only at the Hindu temples
Muk Pajuw	03	At Hindu temples and Ahier villages
Guru orang (Master worship man)	53	Only at Ahier villages

prominent dignitaries, *Ong Kadhar, Ong Maduen, and Ong Gru Kaleng,* each have specific responsibilities for preserving these traditions.

1. *Ong Kadhar* is in charge of preserving the hymns used in various temple and community rituals, including *Yuer Yang, Kate, Cambur, Peh Bambeng Yang, Thrua, Payak Puis, Kaya Pandiak, and Kaya Yuer.*
2. *Ong Maduen* is responsible for preserving hymns used in family and clan rituals such as Rija Dayep, Rija Praong, Rija Nagar, and Rija Harei.
3. *Ong Gru Kaleng* is responsible for preserving the chanting of evil spirits and the mantra used in family and clan rituals.

While religious practices in the Cham Ahier communities may differ from traditional Brahmanism, they are still closely tied to the community's agricultural rituals and involve offerings to the gods for good luck and a bountiful harvest. The Basaih priests also play a significant role in funeral rituals and weekly offerings to the deceased.

Ancestral worship is a cherished tradition in the Cham Ahier community, reflecting the principle of "Remembering the source of the water you drink." This tradition is honored through various rituals such as funerals, weekly offerings, and the Kut entry ceremony. The Cham Ahier's ancestral worship has been deeply influenced by religion and has undergone various changes in the community over time. Religions that are prevalent in society often attempt to infiltrate this form of worship.

The Cham have incorporated elements of Indian religion into their own beliefs, creating a distinct religion for their community. The worship of ancestors and Indigenous gods has been incorporated into the form of Indian deities (Anh, 2004; Bien et al., 1991; Dop et al., 2014). However, these Indian elements are merely the outer form that encapsulates the Indigenous beliefs, which are primarily focused on the worship of ancestors (Anh, 2004; Dop et al., 2014).

The priests in the Cham Ahier community have designated duties that vary by region. For example, in Ninh Thuan, the religious worship and ceremonies are divided into ten units, consisting of seven mosques (*Sang Magik*) and three temples (*Bimong Kalan*) referred to as *"Tijuh hahlau, klau bimong"* or *"Seven mosques, three temples."* Each village also has its own shrine (*Danaok*) or God's house (*Sang Po Yang*).

The Cham people in each region coordinate festivals, rituals, ceremonial events, and annual meetings with the common consensus of the entire community. The allocation of dates and division of responsibilities among each area is consistent, reflecting the unity among the dignitaries. Despite having different roles and positions, the dignitaries closely manage the process of carrying out ceremonies and rituals related to community beliefs to ensure unity in their roles, duties, and mission (Fig. 3.6).

The diagram summarizes the traditional social and religious structure of the Cham people in Ninh Thuan and Binh Thuan Provinces, highlighting the main roles of the two major religious systems (Ahier and Awal priests) and the folk dignitaries. Some other folk dignitaries, not shown on the diagram, are closely related to the Kadhar and Maduen religious systems. Before 1834, the Cham community was organized into four groups: the royal court, the priest systems, the communities (villages),

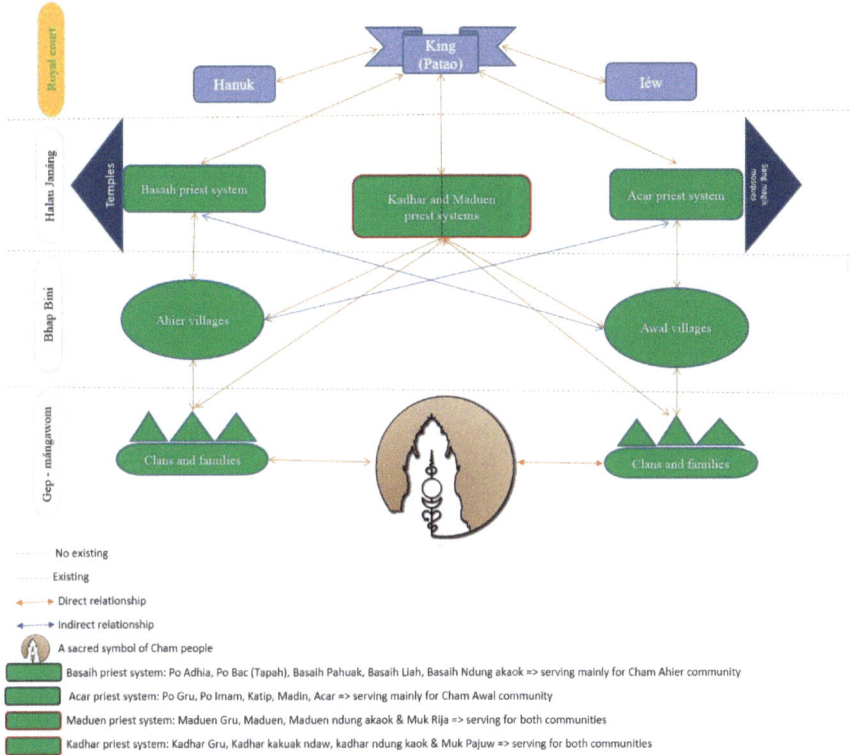

Fig. 3.6 The Management System of Cham Religious Practices and the Interconnections Among Religious Groups (Author, 2018)

and the clans and families. However, following the fall of the Champā Dynasty in 1834, the Cham social structure was reduced to three groups—the priest systems, the communities (villages), and the clans and families. The roles, positions, and functions of each group are described and explained in detail in the sections above.

The Evolving Role of Priests: Past and Present

The role of Cham priests both in the past and today has been crucial to Cham society and spirituality. During the time of the Kingdom of Champā, religious elites occupied high positions in the court and society, including the role of Po Ganuer Matri, Po Gru, and Po Adhia, and other lower religious classes (Abdul, 2013). Today, Po Ganuen Matri no longer exists, and Ahier and Awal priests have taken on these roles. Before the fall of Champā in 1834, the religious elites played a highly important role in Cham society and the kingdom (Abdul, 2013). Abdul (2013) especially highlights the role of Po Ganuer Huer as a spiritual advisor to the king, who was valued for the wise spiritual and supernatural knowledge. Abdul (2013, pp. 33–34) notes that the religious elite were seen as divine intermediaries to the gods, and the Cham political elite recognized their usefulness in legitimizing their rule and increasing their spiritual powers. The religious elite also played a key role in identifying the Cham kings who possessed the "markings" of a ruler.

The role of religious priests in the Cham society has significantly changed after the collapse of the Kingdom of Champā in 1834. The loss of the political power resulted in the wiping out of the ruling elite and *Po Ganuer Matri,* who had close connections with the rulers. In response to this, religious priests stepped in to fill the leadership gap and protect the culture and spiritual life of the Cham people. As noted by Effendy (2013, p. 118), the religious priests emerged as spiritual leaders who took over the role previously held by the political elite.

The role of religious priests has been crucial in preserving Cham traditions, culture, and identity. They play a leading role in conducting rituals and festivals, which are important for the Cham spiritual and social life. These rituals help to convey the wishes for agricultural fertility, good health, and the memory of ancestors (Dop et al., 2014; Sakaya, 2003). The priests also serve as keepers of the Cham language, religion, culture, history, and pride in their monarchs of Panduranga (2013). In addition, the religious priests serve as *"Pakreng Nagar" or "govern the Nagar"* (Abdul, 2013), and are responsible for conducting Cham rituals and arranging the ceremonial life of the Cham community. They also serve as time-keepers, resolving conflicts between Cham Ahier and Awal religious events and ensuring the accuracy of the Cham calendar.

The significance of the role of religious priests in the Cham society cannot be overstated, as they play a critical role in preserving Cham traditions and cultural heritage.

In sum, the role of priests in Cham society has a rich history that dates back to the days of the Kingdom of Champā. During that time, religious elites held a prominent position in the court and society, playing a crucial role in Cham spiritual life. They were viewed as divine intermediaries to the gods and were supported by the Cham political elite, who recognized the usefulness of religious learning in legitimizing their rule and increasing their spiritual powers. The religious elite, such as Po Ganuer Matri and Po Gru, also played an important role in identifying Cham kings who had the "markings" of a ruler (Abdul, 2013). After the collapse of the Cham principality in 1834 and the subsequent wiping out of the ruling elite, religious priests emerged to fill the leadership gap. They continued playing a leading role in Cham traditions and cultural life, serving as spiritual leaders and protectors of Cham culture and identity (Abdul, 2013; Phan, 1996). The priests, especially the dignitaries, have a broad role in conducting Cham rituals and festivals, which are central to Cham spiritual and social life. They help convey the wishes of the community for agricultural fertility, good health, and the memory of ancestors, and play a crucial role in preserving Cham language, religion, culture, and identity, as well as Cham pride in their monarchs (Abdul, 2013; Dop et al., 2014; Sakaya, 2003).

In the contemporary society, however, the role of priests has declined, leading to a lack of leadership and guidance in Cham ceremonial practices and cultural preservation. Despite the decline of their role in modern society, they still play a crucial role in preserving a significant amount of knowledge regarding Cham culture, customs, and religion. The role of dignitaries in preserving Cham culture is unparalleled. Not only do they perform rituals in temples, but they also have a broad role in Cham Ahier villages. Indigenous folk priests also participate in various Cham Ahier and Awal ceremonies. However, in contemporary society, their role has greatly diminished, leading to a lack of leadership and guidance in preserving Cham cultural practices and heritage. The decline of those who conduct the ceremonies may also negatively impact the living heritage sites of the Cham people.

Cham Brahman Dignitary Council (Hội Đồng Chức Sắc Balamon)

The traditional Cham management systems have undergone changes and evolution in the present society, often merging with or being transformed into new administrative organizations (Phan, 2010). Despite these changes, the Cham religious priests continue to manage religious activities and maintain the traditional religious systems. The new organizations, which are made up of religious dignitaries and intellectuals, are recognized by the government as a means to effectively support the management of authorities and to quickly address issues within the Cham community.

In Vietnam, the state recognizes two Cham religious beliefs, known as "Old Islamic" religion and Brahmin religion, as written in Cham texts and academic materials. However, the Cham people refer to their religious beliefs as "Awal (Bani)" and "Ahier." Although the community prefers to use these names, the government has not yet officially recognized them. In recent studies, most Cham scholars and some foreign researchers use these terms, and in this study, the author uses "Ahier" to refer to Brahmanism and "Awal" to refer to Old Islam. Nevertheless, some official terms used by the state, such as the "Balamon Dignitary Council," will also be utilized.

The Council of Interim Dignitaries of Cham Brahmanism (Hội đồng Chức sắc Lâm thời Balamon tỉnh Ninh Thuận) was officially established on October 13, 2010, and recognized by the Chairman of the Ninh Thuan Provincial People's Committee on June 18, 2012 through Decision No. 1192/QD-UBND. The first meeting of the Council, which was held in the term of 2012–2017, aimed to consolidate Cham traditions and customs, and preserve traditional cultural heritage in accordance with the policies and laws set by the Party and State.

The Council is composed of intellectuals and senior Basaih and folk dignitaries from the three Ahier communities in Ninh Thuan Province. There are 27 board members in the Council, organized into a Standing Committee, four specialized boards, and three regional custom boards. They are organized as following (Fig. 3.7):

1. *The Standing Committee* is composed of seven members, including the president, four vice presidents, and two secretaries. The secretary in charge of Cham scripts and customs is a Basaih priest, while the layperson secretary is responsible for general administrative and financial planning.
2. *Cham Sakawi Calendar Board* made up of six members, is responsible for solving problems related to the dates of Cham rituals. They often collaborate with the

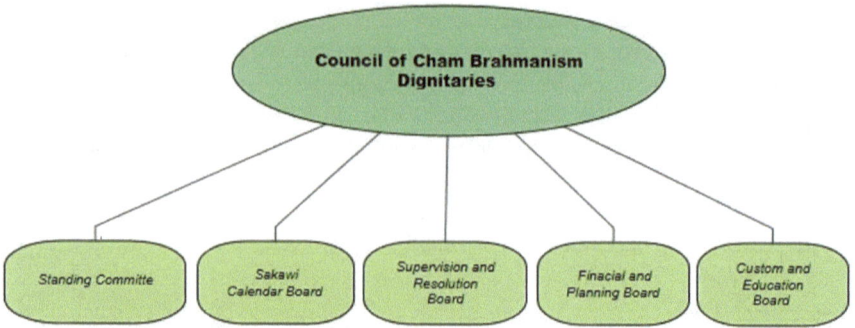

Fig. 3.7 Organizational structure diagram of the council

Cham Sakawi Calendar Board of the Awal religion to determine suitable dates for both Ahier and Awal communities.

3. *Supervision and Resolution Board* consists of 06 members.
4. *Financial and Planning Board* consists of 06 members.
5. *The Customs and Education Board* consists of 07 members.

The Council strengthened three regional custom boards for three temples in the region (Fig. 3.8):

1. Custom Board of Po Klaong Girai temple: 17 members.
2. Custom Board of Po Ina Nagar temple: 20 members.
3. Custom Board of Po Rome temple: 11 members.

Fig. 3.8 Composition of the executive members of the council of interim dignitaries of Cham Brahmanism in Ninh Thuan Province. *Source* Author, 2017

The Council of Cham Brahman Dignitaries in Ninh Thuan Province has also re-established Custom Boards in each Cham Ahier village. These boards are composed of 5 to 11 members, selected by the elders of each village and include a headperson, a deputy, a secretary, and several other members. In the past, these village-level organizations were referred to as the Elders Association, but today they are called the Custom Boards.

The role of the Custom Boards is to support the religious system and cere-monies, manage cultural and natural resources, and protect customs. They also orga-nize rituals and festivals, such as the Rija Nagar (Cham New Year), Kate festival, Ramâwan ceremonies, and other spiritual celebrations. Furthermore, the Custom Boards serve as a resolution mechanism in cases where village members violate traditions, customs, and habits. To enhance their problem-solving capabilities, the boards often collaborate with the local government and rely on their power to address issues related to faith and customs. The Council of Cham Brahman Dignitaries and its sub-organizations, including the Custom Boards, play a crucial role in preserving and promoting traditional Cham culture in Ninh Thuan Province (Phan, 2010).

In essence, the Council of Interim Dignitaries of Cham Brahmanism is a contin-uation of a long-standing tradition of Cham organizations consisting of intellectuals and senior Basaih and folk dignitaries. However, unlike the past, this organization is now directly overseen by the government's Internal Affairs Department, leading some to believe that the traditional power of the Cham Ahier priests has dimin-ished. A Cham scholar states, *"From the highest authority and the largest right in the Cham community, this system is under the direction of a provincial department of government. The Cham Ahier priests are losing their traditional power in the Cham community by being an official board under government direction"* (Orang_ Kaya006). Theoretically, this recognition by the government shows the recogni-tion of the Cham community and their traditional management systems for cultural heritage management. It also highlights the early stages of collaboration in Cham cultural heritage management. However, so far the new organization doesn't seem to be much involved in many heritage management activities. As a case in point, the Po Klaong Girai temple operates under two parallel Cham management systems. The first is managed by the Ahier dignitaries of the temple, who are responsible for temple and religious activities and is composed purely of Ahier priests. The second system is the Council of Ahier Dignitaries, which includes both intellectuals and priests, manages all three temples, and works closely with local authorities and is seen as the representative voice for the Cham Ahier community in Ninh Thuan.

The folk and religious dignitaries play a crucial role in preserving the cultural heritage and the identity of the Cham people. They are responsible for safe-guarding and preserving multiple ancient manuscripts written in Cham script, as well as maintaining their rituals, beliefs, folk songs and dances, anecdotes, legends "damnây," offering gifts, traditional musical instruments, and various types of tradi-tional clothing. These cultural elements serve as external expressions of their cultural heritage. Additionally, the dignitaries are responsible for organizing and conducting traditional ceremonies and festivals, thereby ensuring the continuity of the Cham society.

Philosophies and Traditions of the Cham Community

Significance of Ahier and Awal Dualism in Representing Cham Unity

The Champa temples hold a significant place not only in the hearts of the Cham Ahier community, but of the entire Cham population as it serves as a symbol of their veneration for intelligent and meritorious god-kings from their glorious past. However, it is important to understand the relationship between the different Cham groups, particularly the relationship between the Cham Ahier and Cham Awal.

Previous research has often divided the Cham in South Central Vietnam into two separate communities: the Cham Ahier and the Cham Awal (Duong, 2007; Khanh, 2009; Ninh, 2006) or as Cham Bani and Cham Jat (Phan, 2011). However, from the perspective of the Cham people, their communities should not be divided into two separate entities, but rather considered as united under one traditional religion with a cosmology of dualism (Nakamura, 2009; Phan, 1996, 2011; Yasuko, 2012).

The term "Ahier" refers to the Cham Balamon who adhere to an indigenized form of Brahmanism and later came to believe in the God of Islam, Allah. "Ahier" means "the latter or last" in Cham. This group venerates their gods, Po Yang and deified kings, and performs their ceremonies in temples (bimong) and at home with their families. Beef is traditionally taboo in the Cham Ahier community, and they are cremated after death with funerals led by Ahier priests (Nakamura, 2009).

On the other hand, the term "*Awal*" refers to the Cham influenced by Bani Islam. "*Awal*" means "before or first." This group primarily worships their god, Po Awluah (*Allah*), in mosques (*Sang magik*) and at home. Pork is taboo in the Cham Bani community, and they are buried after death with services led by Acar priests (Nakamura, 2009). Although both the Cham Ahier and Awal venerate Po Awluah, the Cham Awal conduct rituals and festivals for Allah, while the Cham Ahier hold ceremonies for the gods known to them prior to the introduction of Islam to Champā (Nakamura, 2009).

According to the Cham people, Awal and Ahier, though seemingly opposing each other, are always attached as a couple and cannot exist without the other, much like males and females, fathers and mothers, who are inseparable (Yasuko, 2012, p. 500). In fact, these two communities are always bonded together as a pair of Likei - Kumei (men and women) or a couple of Hadiip - Pasang (husband and wife) and are considered as the traditional cultural identity of the Cham people. The Cham Awal community symbolizes the female aspect (female/kumei, wife/hadiip), while the Ahier Cham community symbolizes the male aspect (male/likei, husband/pasang). This reflects the unique and rich culture of the Cham people who have lived in the South Central region for a long time and have a diverse and distinct cultural identity (Phan, 2011; Yasuko, 2011, 2012). Despite the fact that Cham society is matrilineal and matriarchal, this dualism is opposite to the typical Muslim view in which men are considered superior to women.

The dialectical relationship between Ahier and Awal continues to play a significant role in Cham culture, serving as a foundation for linking the two religious communities. This concept is seen as a pair of philosophical categories and is used in the performance of rituals and ceremonies in the religious beliefs of both communities. Furthermore, the Cham people use the Awal-Ahier dialectic to explain phenomena related to the universe and their overall worldview (Phan, 1996, 2011; Yasuko, 2011). The importance of the relationship between Ahier and Awal cannot be overstated and remains a central aspect of Cham identity and tradition.

The enduring dualistic relationship between the Awal and the Ahier is evident in the cultural and spiritual life, as well as the material culture, of the two Cham communities in the provinces of Ninh Thuan and Binh Thuan today. Based on this concept, the Cham people have incorporated this symbol of unity through the use of the Homkar. In fact, the Homkar symbol originated from the Hindu AUM symbol, but Cham intellectuals today have given it a unique narrative meaning. According to Nakamura (2009, pp. 89–90), the symbol's center is a circle that represents the sun, under which there is a crescent. The number 6 is placed above the sun, while the number 3 is placed below the crescent. In Cham belief, the sun and the number 3 represent the Ahier, while the crescent and the number 6 represent the Awal. The number 9 is considered the largest number in Cham script, and it is formed by the combination of the Ahier number 3 and the Awal number 6. Thus, the Homkar symbol, which is composed of both Ahier and Awal elements, represents the most complete form of existence, including unity, balance, stability, and peace. In essence, the coexistence of the Ahier and Awal creates unity in the Cham world (Fig. 3.9).

The Homkar symbol represents the unity of the Cham community, transcending religious boundaries and distinctions. The temples that reflect this symbol are not only important to the Cham Ahier but also to the entire Cham community. These temples are seen as beacons of Cham culture and heritage, preserving their history and traditions for future generations. As such, it is the responsibility of both the Cham Ahier and Awal to protect these places of worship and preserve the rich cultural legacy of their people. By coming together to protect their temples, Cham people are symbolizing the unity and harmony embodied in the Homkar symbol, which represents stability, balance, peace, and wholeness. The preservation of the Cham temples is, therefore, a crucial aspect of preserving their cultural heritage and ensuring that it is passed down to future generations (Phan, 2011; Yasuko, 2012).

Delve into the World of the Cham: Uncovering the Perception of Sacredness

The Cham people of Southeast Asia have a unique perspective on the concept of sacredness. In their culture, the term "hacih/suci" encompasses both the ideas of purity and holiness. They also use the term "Ganreh" to describe the power associated with speaking about a sacred site. Both human-made objects and natural

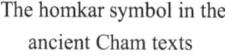

The homkar symbol in the ancient Cham texts	The homkar symbol on the stone pillar of the top of the Po Rome temple (1624-1651)

Fig. 3.9 The Homkar is a sacred symbol of Champa (Sakaya, 2013)

phenomena can be considered sacred places, as they are believed to have mysterious or supernatural powers that can protect or harm humans.

The Cham culture recognizes a close relationship between the gods, the dead, ancestors, and the living. The world of the gods and ancestors is considered separate from the profane and protected from disturbance. This relationship is maintained through spiritual and religious ceremonies, during which the spirits of the gods, dead, and ancestors are connected to descendants. The living have the obligation to ensure proper burial or cremation of their relatives, and to protect their graves (Awal graves and Ahier Kuts) from disturbance. Access to these sacred places is limited to religious ceremonies, and failure to properly uphold these traditions is believed to result in harm to both the dead and the living.

The Cham temples are among the most revered sacred sites in the Cham culture, where the king-gods and national heroes are honored and worshipped. According to Cham beliefs, the Yang gods are incredibly powerful and sacred, and they have the ability to both protect and bless human beings. However, if the sacred sites are disturbed or changed, the Yang Gods will punish those who did so.

Every Cham person is responsible for protecting the sacred sites and maintaining the religious beliefs associated with them. The Cham people hold a strong stance against any activities that could negatively affect the sacred sites. To maintain the sanctity of these places, they must remain peaceful and free from disturbance.

The Cham temples are located in various terrains, including the plains, sealed valleys, large rivers, seashores, slopes, and the tops of hills. They are isolated from residential areas to maintain their purity and are only opened for religious rituals conducted by priests. These sacred places are dedicated solely to worship, and the Cham people both fear and respect them. To this day, the Cham avoid using disrespectful language or behavior at sacred sites like the temple, as it is believed to make the site impure and lead to punishment from the gods.

In the Cham culture, the doors of the temples were traditionally only opened when the Ahier priests performed a ceremony to ask permission. The opening of the temple doors was a sacred ritual that required the participation of four important dignitaries in the Cham Ahier religion: the Po Adhia, Ong Kadhar, Ong Camnei, and Muk Pajuw.

The ritual began with the Po Adhia performing a ritual in the small courtyard of the temple. Then, the Ong Camnei and Po Adhia conducted the Shiva (Şiva) water ritual, while Ong Kadhar sang the appropriate hymn in front of the temple. The Muk Pajuw and Ong Camnei then performed the bathing and dressing rituals for the king-god inside the temple.

This elaborate ceremony demonstrated the importance and sacredness of the temples in the Cham culture. The doors of the temples remained closed most of the time, and only opened during specific religious rituals. The rituals conducted by the dignitaries emphasized the reverence and respect that the Cham people held for their temples and their gods.

The Cham culture places a great emphasis on the maintenance and preservation of sacred sites, with many still being in use today in the Ninh Thuan Province of Vietnam. The three major temples in this region, known as "bimong kalan," are each governed by a Po Adhia, the leader of the Ahier priests. Each temple serves the Cham villages in its respective area and it is the responsibility of these villages to worship at the closest temple to them. In particular,

1. *The Po Klaong Girai* temple serves the villages of Padra, Baoh Dana, Baoh Bini, Caok, Mblang Kacak, Tabeng, Bal Riya, and Baoh Hadeng.
2. *The Po Ina Nagar* temple serves the villages of Hamu Tanran and Hamu Craok.
3. *The Po Rame* temple serves Thuer, Palao, Pabhan, Aia Li-U, Bal Caong, and Caklaing.

There is a famous temple in this province called Ba Thap temple but it is forgotten by the Cham. The temple is considered as a "dead" heritage site because the Cham no longer practiced religion there.

In addition to the temples, the Cham also worship many human gods at shrines located in different villages. These shrines, known as Danaok, are revered and protected by the Cham communities. Some of the notable shrines in Ninh Thuan Province include:

1. Danaok Po Patao Bin Thuer, Po Bia Choi, Po Bia Binan, Po Ina Nagar Hamu Kut in Bal Riya village;
2. Danaok Po Gaol/ Po Gilai Baok located near Kraong Pha River;
3. Danaok Po Klaong Kachait in Cang village;
4. Danaok Po Klaong Girai in Kacak village;
5. Danaok Po Sah in Baoh Dana village;

6. Danaok Po Klaong Girai in Baoh Bini village;
7. Danaok Po Nai Riki Nai Rikit in Padra village;
8. Danaok Po Klaong Haluw in Hamu Tanran village;
9. Danaok Po Klaong Can in Hamu Caok village;
10. Danaok Po Riyak in Caklaing village;
11. Danaok Po Nai located at Cah Mbang Mountain; and
12. Danaok Po Rome in Thuer village.

These shrines play an important role in the spiritual lives of the Cham people and serve as places of worship and veneration (Fig. 3.10).

The Cham people also worship at various natural sacred sites to pray to supernatural beings and at numerous Kut and Ghur cemeteries found in every Cham village. In the past, Kut cemeteries were situated far from the villages, but with the growth of the Cham population, many have now been established within the villages. Nevertheless, like the temples and shrines, these cemeteries are only opened for rituals on specific days and times, after which the gates must be closed to provide a peaceful space for their ancestors. The Cham's cultural and religious philosophy holds that the spiritual world is made up of all members of the community and is composed of spiritual, mental, and tangible elements of life. This belief is closely tied to folk cultural activities and the integration of the divine and human world through various ceremonies, which all members of the Cham accept as a spiritual and sacred legacy. Many Cham people believe that this system of beliefs is unalterable and that no one

Fig. 3.10 A ritual being performed at the Po Nai Shrine located on Cah Mbang Mountain in Ninh Thuan Province. *Source* Author, 2014

has the right to add or modify it without the consent of the Cham community. Any changes made to the meaning or structure of a Cham ritual or rite could be perceived as an offense against their sacred beliefs.

Understanding the Cham's Views on Dates, Timing, and Rituals

In addition to the two main religious groups in the Cham community, including the Ahier influenced by Brahmanism and the Awal influenced by Islam, there are also two types of calendars used for religious purposes. The first is the Islamic calendar, which is limited to use in mosques for the Ramâwan and Ikak Waha festivals. The second is the common calendar, which is widely used by both the Cham Ahier and Awal in a variety of ceremonies such as funerals, weddings, festivals, agricultural rituals, the opening of a new house, house construction, and other rituals. Despite the two different religious beliefs, the Cham people are considered as one community due to their participation in these shared ceremonies (Dai, 2016; Sakaya, 2016).

For the Cham, time is regulated by God Luah Tala for each year, month, day, and hour for each ritual. The Cham calendar has twelve months, which are represented by twelve animals of the Cham zodiac in sequential order: rat, ox, tiger, rabbit, dragon, snake, horse, goat or ram, monkey, cock, dog, and pig. A year with thirteen months is called a leap year or bilan bhang or bilan biruw (a new month) (Sakaya, 2016).

The date is a crucial aspect of Cham customs. A Cham month can have either 30 days or 29 days. The months with 30 days are January, March, May, July, September, and November, while the months with 29 days are February, April, June, August, October, and December. The days in a Cham month are organized based on the lunar phase, with the first quarter (bingun) starting from the 1st to the 15th day and the last quarter (Klam) starting from the 16th to the end of the month. The first quarter, known as the full moon (harei porami), and the last quarter, known as the moon off (harei aia bilan abih). The Cham also recognize good days, bad days, and taboo days, as well as good times, bad times, and taboo times in a day. A Cham day is divided into 8 tuk, where each tuk equals 1.5 h (Dai, 2016; Phan, 2007; Sakaya, 2016). The significance of time is especially evident in Cham customs related to weddings, house-building, and new home ceremonies.

The Sakawi Calendar was created by Champā scholars in response to a problem faced by the Cham people after the introduction of the Hijri Calendar (Islamic religion) in Champā in the fifteenth century. The term "Sakawi" is derived from "Saka" (universal calendar) and "wi" (an abbreviation of Jawi, meaning Islam), and the calendar is a hybrid that combines the Cham calendar, based on twelve months, with the Islamic calendar. The main objectives of the Sakawi calendar are to respect the cycle of the seasons (i.e., January must bring rain and summer months must be sunny) and to avoid coincidence between the Kate festival and the Ramawan season.

The formulation of the Sakawi calendar was passed down through the Ariya Sakawi tradition and remains in use today.

The Cham people use the dates in the Sakawi Ahier calendar in conjunction with the dates in the Sakawi Awal calendar, and the calendar is used not only to determine the dates for opening the door of the temples and performing rituals of Rija, Paralao Pasah, Kate, Cambur, and Yuen Yang, but also to choose the dates for important ceremonies, such as weddings, funerals, house-building, and new house ceremonies, and various family rituals for both Cham Awal and Ahier.

The Cham people do not rely solely on the dates in the Sakawi Ahier calendar. Instead, they consistently align the dates in both the Sakawi Ahier and Sakawi Awal calendars. This ensures that the Sakawi Ahier calendar is utilized not only for determining the dates for important religious ceremonies such as the opening of temple doors, Rija rituals, Paralao Pasah, Kate, Cambur, and Yuen Yang, but also for planning significant life events such as weddings, funerals, house-building and inauguration ceremonies, and various familial rituals for both the Cham Awal and Ahier communities.

The Cham have well-defined beliefs about the auspicious and inauspicious days and times. For the purpose of this research, which focuses on the appropriate days for temple openings, only the favorable and taboo days and times will be discussed. The following are the characteristic traits associated with each day:

1. Sunday (Adit): the day of fire and the sun.
2. Monday (Som): the day of wood, symbolizing growth and new beginnings.
3. Tuesday (Angar): the day of stone, power, and strength.
4. Wednesday (But): the day of the earth, symbolizing stability and grounding.
5. Thursday (Jip): the day of human creation.
6. Friday (Suk): the day of the breath of the soul.
7. Saturday (Sanacar): the day of the moon (Phan, 2014; Sakaya, 2016).

The Cham people utilize the characteristics of the Cham Sakawi calendar to distinguish between favorable and unfavorable days in their lives. This research, however, is limited to understanding the dates and times related to communal and temple ceremonies only. The following are the months during which the Cham conduct their communal ceremonies:

8. January, February, and March are considered leisurely months for conducting Rija ceremonies, which are presided over by Maduen priests. These months are referred to as Maduen's months (Sakaya, 2016, p. 130).
9. April is the month for conducting the Yuen Yang ceremony to honor the Fire God, as well as the ploughing ceremony, which marks the start of the rice-growing season.
10. July is the month for conducting the Kate festival to worship the gods and for giving thanks for the watering of the rice fields.
11. September is the month for conducting the Cambur ceremony to worship the goddesses.

12. November is the month for conducting the Peh Mbeng Yang ceremony, which involves opening the doors of the temples (Dai, 2016).

The Cham have special significance attached to certain days and times, and they follow these beliefs in their daily activities and ceremonies.

13. *The 1st Klam and 6th Klam* are considered auspicious days as they coincide with sunrise. However, these days are reserved for the king and ordinary people are not allowed to perform ceremonies or rituals on these days as it is believed to offend the gods. These days are reserved for the opening of the temple doors and the ordination of priests (Dai, 2016; Phan, 2014; Sakaya, 2016).

14. *The 6th and 7th hours (tuk)* that coincide with the 6th Klam or 2nd Klam are considered favorable days for humans. This time is believed to represent Brah or God Yang Sri, the rice god. These days are often chosen for housewarming ceremonies and weddings. Conversely, if the 8th hour coincides with the 1st Klam or 11th Klam, these are considered unfavorable hours (Mabih) and no rituals are performed at these times (Dai, 2016; Phan, 2014; Sakaya, 2016).

According to the Cham, there are many sorts of hours, each having a specific effect. It is believed that performing activities on taboo days (Harei Juak Nathak) can result in a day of great disaster (Harei Main Taming) and bring tragedy and catastrophic events to individuals or families. As a result, the Cham are cautious when choosing the time for their daily activities and ceremonies (Dai, 2016; Phan, 2014; Sakaya, 2016) (Fig. 3.11).

As previously mentioned, religion plays a significant role in the social life of the Cham people. It greatly influences their socio-economic and cultural activities. With the aid of the Cham Sakawi calendar, the Cham select appropriate days to worship Yang gods and conduct rituals and festivals (Sakaya, 2003).

According to Sakaya, the Cham currently have at least 75 Yang gods and perform over 115 different ceremonies and festivals, which are held on a yearly, biennial, quinquennial, or longer cycle basis (Sakaya, 2003). These events are connected to the life cycles, such as weddings, funeral ceremonies, and temple-based thanksgiving festivals to specific deities. In addition to these, the Cham have several Indigenous beliefs-based ceremonies and rituals, including those related to agriculture (Sakaya, 2003). Throughout the year, the Cham conduct a diverse range of public and family ceremonies at the village or clan level.

The Cham people hold four main public ceremonies and festivals in Ninh Thuan, including Yuer Yang in April, Kate in July, Cambur in September, and Peh Pabah Mbeng Yang in November. These ceremonies and festivals aim to bring good weather, abundant crops, and growth of life, and are conducted in a specific order based on the Cham Sakawi calendar (Dai, 2016; Phan, 2014). The Kate Festival is the largest traditional festival of the Cham people in Vietnam and was recognized by the Vietnam Ministry of Culture, Sports, and Tourism as a national intangible cultural heritage in 2017 (Dop et al., 2014; Bien et al., 1991; Sakaya, 2003). The festival takes place on July 1st according to the Cham calendar and commemorates Cham kings, national heroes, and ancestors, while praying to the gods for favorable weather, bountiful

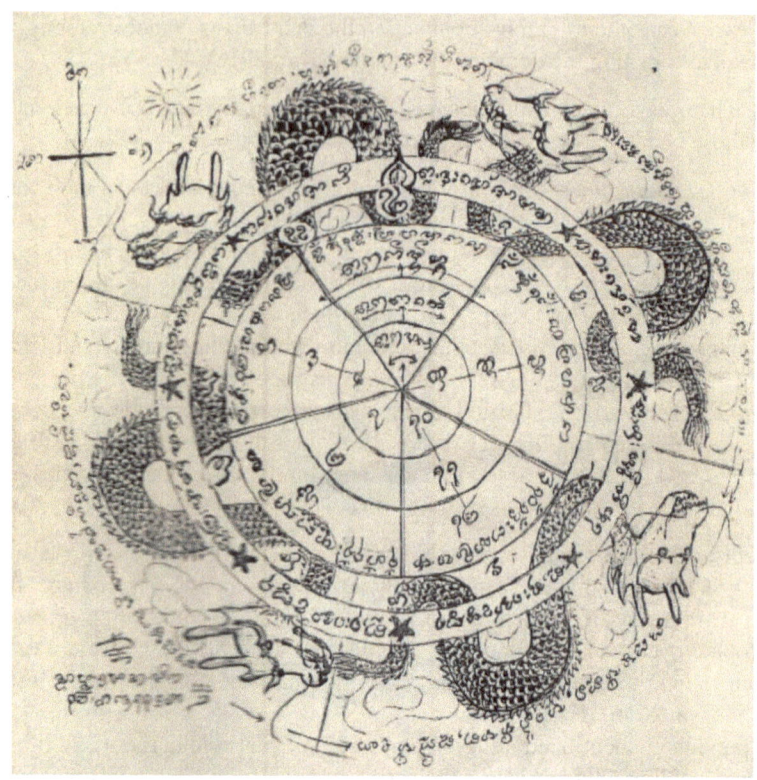

ປິເທິລ ຄໍ

ແລລ ຕາາຖ i – *Canh Tý* - 2020

ອາງຄົຕ Chủ nhật	ລຄໍ Thứ Hai	ອາງືລ Thứ Ba	ແລຕ Thứ Tư	ກຄໍລ Thứ Năm	ລະຄ Thứ Sáu	ລາແາາລ Thứ Bảy
			ຄໍ 22.4.2020	໔❀ ຕາລ 23	໔❀☾ 24	໔ 25
ຄໍ 26	໔ 27	໔ 28	໔ 29	໔ 30	໑໔ 1.5.20	໑໑ 2
໑໔ 3	໑໔ 4	໑໔ 5	໑໔ 6	໑ 7	໔ 8	໔ 9
໔ 10	໑ 11	໔ 12	໔ 13	໔ 14	໔ 15	໑໔ 16
໑໑ 17	໑໔ 18	໑໔ 19	໑໔ 20	໑໑ 21		

◫ ປິເທິລ ລາາງຄົຕ ເລ. – ແລລ ຄໍ – ອາງຕ

❀ ໔ລຄໍ ລຕລາ : 23 - 24/4/2020

☾ ຕາຖ ໔ລນຄໍຍ ຄໍ ແລລ ລຄໍ : 25/4/2020

Fig. 3.11 A *Sakawi* Ahier calendar in January, 2020

harvests, and prosperity, peace, and happiness (Dop et al., 2014; Bien et al., 1991; Sakaya, 2003).

Given the advanced paddy rice culture of the Cham people, they have a deep understanding of weather and crops (Thu et al., 2010). They have a long-standing reputation for their knowledge of astronomy, which they use to predict the weather by observing the sun, moon, stars, and the behavior of animals and plants (Thu et al., 2010). The activities related to Cham ceremonies take place throughout the year, not only in agricultural production and social activities but also in religious beliefs (Dai, 2016; Dop et al., 2014; Bien et al., 1991). The precise schedule in the Cham Sakawi calendar helps the Cham people to understand good days, good months, non-leap years, leap years, and taboo days, making it an indispensable part of the Cham people's lives (Dai, 2016; Phan, 2014; Sakaya, 2016).

Significance and Evolution of the Kate Festival

The Katé festival is a significant cultural event for the Cham community, where they come together to commemorate the memory of gods like Po Klaong Girai, Po Rome, and their ancestors who have protected and maintained the community over the past year. They also offer prayers for bumper harvests and the well-being of all beings (Bien et al., 1991; Dop et al., 2014; Sakaya, 2003).

The festival takes place at various locations, from the temples to villages, and even within families (Sakaya, 2003). The official venues for the festival are the temples of Po Klaong Girai, Po Inâ Nâgar, and Po Rome, where ceremonies are conducted simultaneously with similar rituals and procedures (Sakaya, 2003). The festival starts with a procession of the royal clothing of three deities, which are kept by the Raglai ethnic minority, from three Cham Ahier communities in Ninh Thuan to the temples. The procession is a formal event attended by dignitaries, Cham and Raglai dancers, and members of the Cham community (Sakaya, 2003).

The Kate festival is a significant cultural event among the Champā people in Panduranga and is marked by several ceremonial events, including the opening door ceremony, the statue bathing ceremony, the wearing clothes of the statues ceremony, and the great ceremony (Sakaya, 2003). The festival begins at the temple and continues in villages and within families (Sakaya, 2003). The process of the ritual parts of the Kate festival involves various ceremonies such as welcoming new costumes for the gods, opening the temple gates, bathing the statues of the gods, changing their costumes, and offering goat meat, chicken, rice, wine, fruits, and other offerings. The order of these rituals is based on the Cham's belief in good or bad times and requires early preparation by participants (Sakaya, 2003).

One notable aspect of the Kate festival is the presence of the Raglai people who organize and perform dances and music. Furthermore, the festival extends beyond the temple and encompasses the villages and families in their homes (Sakaya, 2003, p. 258). According to Sakaya (2003), the Kate festival symbolizes the shared cultural heritage of the Champā people, including the Cham Ahiér, Cham Awal, and the Raglai group in the Central Highlands of Vietnam. In conclusion, the Kate festival is owned by the entire Champā community.

In terms of its form, the Kate festival has undergone significant changes over time, growing in size and number of participants. Despite these changes, the Cham people have maintained its spiritual essence (Dop et al., 2014; Noseworthy, 2013). Prior to 1965, the Kate festival was merely one of the four main temple rituals performed in the presence of Cham Ahiér elders and was not a compulsory event for participants to bring offerings for the gods. As a result, the Kate festival was not widely attended, particularly among younger generations (Dop et al., 2014).

However, in 1965, Mr. Duong Tan So, the district head of An Phuoc, recommended to the Ahiér religious leaders that cultural performances be included during the Kate festival to welcome visiting Vietnamese delegations (Noseworthy, 2013). This suggestion, considered an "invented tradition" by Hobsbawm (1983), was embraced by the Cham community and since then, the Kate ceremony has incorporated more festive activities. Consequently, the Kate festival has become increasingly rich and inclusive, involving participation from all generations (Dop et al., 2014).

The Cham people have a saying, "Katé patok dah ka Yang Amâ - Cambuer patok dah ka Yang Ina," which translates to "Katé is a ritual for the Gods and Cambuer is a ritual for the Goddesses" (Shaklikei, 2016). During the Kate festival, the Cham people worship and honor their ancestors and gods, and pray for the health and wealth of their families and communities (Noseworthy, 2015).

The roots of the Kate festival can be traced back to at least the seventeenth century and the cultural traditions of the Cham people. After the fall of Vijaya-Champā, which was associated with Hindu civilization, the Champā king of Panduranga renounced Hindu worship and instead promoted the practice of Po Yang, a form of polytheistic worship (Sakaya, 2013). As a result, many Cham people today do not remember the names of Hindu gods and are more familiar with Po Inâ Nâgar, Po Klaong Girai, and Po Rome, gods who were once local kings (Noseworthy, 2015).

Since then, the Cham community has transformed Hindu-style temples and gods into spiritual heritage sites of Indigenous significance. For instance, Bhagavati, a Hindu goddess believed to be the wife of Shiva and once worshipped at a temple in Nha Trang, was transformed into Po Inâ Nâgar, the Cham people's god of creation who is said to have given birth to the country (Noseworthy, 2015). The purpose and meaning of the Kate festival have thus become a celebration of Indigenous symbolism and the majority of the gods worshipped have origins in the Indigenous Cham region, derived from local tales and historical figures (Sakaya, 2013). In conclusion, these festivals illustrate the long-term transformations in the "tradition" of the Cham people.

Similarly, Cham people transformed the temple in Phan Rang, which was originally dedicated to Shiva and named Singhavarmalingesvara, built by King Jaya Singhavarman III at the end of the thirteenth century (Aymonier, 1891), into the altar of Po Klaong Garai, the legendary king and Indigenous deity of Panduranga. This transformation is evidenced by the transformation of the Hindu linga-yoni symbol, a manifestation of Shiva worship, into a statue of Po Klaong Girai (Lafont, 2014). Researchers often suggest that Po Klaong Girai (the legendary king of the Panduranga principality) is just a symbol of Jaya Simhavarman III (King of the Champā Federation) based on this transformation (Dharma, 1999; Lafont, 2014). This transformation also demonstrates the cultural identity of the Cham and their ability to adapt to changes in their traditional culture (Noseworthy, 2014).

A few remnants of Hinduism are still maintained through the Sanskrit mantras recited by Basaih, such as "Om nāmasibayong" or OM in the name of Shiva. However, the significant parts of the Katé ritual originate in Cham culture and include the contents of hymns of Kadhar that appear during Katé rituals, such as the door opening, bathing, and dressing for the god's ceremonies, and hymns praising the gods, although these processes are similar to Hinduism. All of these rituals are conducted entirely in the Cham language and recorded in Akhar Thrah (Dharma, 2012).

In short, Katé is a ritual festival among the Cham Balamon (Ahier) to make offerings to Indigenous spirits (Noseworthy, 2014). Throughout history, the Cham have incorporated architectural styles from Hindu temples, religious practices of worshipping Shiva, and local innovations in worshipping local spirits. The Hindu elements of Katé are remnants of the long "Indianized" period of Champā. However, Katé remains a custom associated with Indigenous beliefs, localized and attached to a language that dates from the 16th and the seventeenth centuries.

The Katé festival is a celebration that reflects the rich and diverse culture of the Cham community. As noted by Dop et al. (2014) and Noseworthy (2014), the festival is associated with ancient Cham temples and showcases the technical and artistic traditions that reached their peak in Cham history. In addition to offerings, cuisine, and clothing, the festival features unique music, hymns, and praise for the kings, people, and nation, as well as public performances of folk dance and music.

According to Biên et al. (1991), Lafont (2014), and Sakaya (2003), the Cham culture is a fusion of Indigenous cultural elements and foreign influences, such as early Han Chinese, Indian cultures, and religions like Buddhism and Islam. Mus (1934) argues that the Cham culture transformed exogenous religions into beliefs familiar to the Cham people, resulting in specific adaptations of religious practices. This fusion of Indigenous and foreign elements in Cham culture is the result of the interaction of ecological, social, and historical conditions.

Today, the Katé festival is not only a means of preserving the intangible cultural value for the Cham community but is also intended to introduce the unique features of the Cham community and Ninh Thuan Province to local and international tourists, as noted by Dop et al. (2014) and Noseworthy (2013).

Distinguishing Between Living and Dead Heritage Sites

The majority of Cham temples in Vietnam today are located in or near the Cham and Kinh communities due to population growth. Despite this proximity, the current Cham community mostly resides in the Ninh Thuan and Binh Thuan Provinces of South Central Vietnam and does not use these temples for religious practices.

The Cham people have various heritage sites, including shrines (danaok), tower-temples or temples (Bimong Kalan), and ancestral mausoleums (ghur and kut). Most of these sites are considered "living" sacred sites because the Cham maintain and use them for spiritual worship. However, this research focuses on the temples, known as bimon in the Cham language, that have been categorized into two types: bimon bhaw and bimon hadiep. A "dead site" or "bimon bhaw" in Cham language means "no one knows or cares" and has been abandoned without any cultural or spiritual connections due to historical changes, mainly related to the departure of Cham populations from the northern regions of Central Vietnam. In contrast, "living sites" or "bimon *hadiep*" are considered "*living*" heritage sites, with both tangible and intangible elements, and close connections with the contemporary Cham community. The Cham community maintains its rich culture in the region and conducts its religious practices through various spiritual activities at these sites.

Regardless of whether the Cham temples are "living" or "dead," they must still be traditionally located far from Cham settlements to prevent disturbance by the profane actions of the living. This distance is crucial for maintaining the sacredness of the heritage sites. Table 3.2 shows the distribution of the two different types of Cham temples in Vietnam today.

This table highlights the significance of Cham temple names in reflecting the status of the temple as either a "dead" or "living" heritage site. Temples that retain their Cham names and are still maintained and used by the Cham community are considered "living" heritage sites, such as the Po Inâ Nagar, Po Dam, Po Xah Inâ, Po Rome, and Po Klaong Girai temples. On the other hand, regions without Cham residents have resulted in the temples becoming "dead" heritage sites, as they are no longer connected with the Cham community from a spiritual perspective.

It is worth noting that despite the growth of population and the presence of people living near the temples, the Cham still maintain a certain distance from their sacred sites to allow the gods to rest.

Despite the crucial role that the Cham temples play in maintaining the cultural and spiritual heritage of the Cham community, the Vietnamese government authorities and heritage managers have not yet adequately acknowledged and protected the different features of these temples. The absence of clear definitions and distinctions between living and dead heritage sites has resulted in a one-size-fits-all approach to heritage conservation, which has negatively impacted the Cham community's close association with their living heritage.

One of the most prominent and complex aspects of Cham's living heritage is the spiritual practices that the Cham communities undertake at the temples. The Cham have many different ceremonies, rituals, and festivals that usually take place at regular intervals, such as every year, every two years, and every five years (Nose-worthy, 2013). Several of these ceremonies and rituals derive from Indigenous beliefs, including those related to agriculture, and most commemorate the gods, kings, and ancestors. These ceremonies are powerful ethnic symbols for the Cham community.

Today, more and more Cham youth are gaining a growing awareness of their cultural identity and are reviving their culture. The Cham temples and festivals provide spaces where they can gain a deeper understanding of their culture and

Table 3.2 The classification between the living heritage sites and the "deserted" heritage sites of the Cham people

No	Locations (Provinces)	Temples	Classifications		Heritage status
			"Dead" heritage sites from the Cham community	Living heritage sites	
1	Huế	Mỹ Khánh	*Bimon bhaw*		
2	Quảng Nam	Mỹ Sơn	*Bimon bhaw*		*World Heritage Site*
3		Chiên Đàn	*Bimon bhaw*		
4		B`ăng An	*Bimon bhaw*		
5		Khương Mỹ	*Bimon bhaw*		
6	Bình Định	Phú Lốc	*Bimon bhaw*		
7		Bình Lâm	*Bimon bhaw*		
8		Dương Long	*Bimon bhaw*		
9		Bánh Ít	*Bimon bhaw*		
10		Cánh Tiên	*Bimon bhaw*		
11		Đôi	*Bimon bhaw*		
12	Phú Yên	Nhạn	*Bimon bhaw*		
13	Đak Lak	Yang Praong	*Bimon bhaw*		
14	Khánh Hòa	Po Ina Nagar	*Bimon hadiep (co-worshipped by the Cham and Kinh communities)*		
15	Ninh Thuận	Po Rome		*Bimon hadiep*	*National Cultural Heritage*
16		Hòa Lai	*Bimon bhaw*		
17		Po Klaong Girai		*Bimon hadiep*	
18	Bình Thuận	Po Dam		*Bimon hadiep*	
19		Po Xah Ina		*Bimon hadiep*	

history, and reinforce their personal and collective identities (Noseworthy, 2013). As a result, the Cham temples are becoming increasingly significant and inspirational for the Cham community and are closely connected to the everyday life of Cham villages and the memory of their ancestors.

Because of the significance of the temples, the Cham have continuously maintained their traditional management systems at these living heritage sites through many historical periods from the era of Champā kingdoms, through French colonialism, to before and after the American War ended in 1975. The traditional custodians are human repositories of religious and ritual knowledge from the upper classes of Cham society (Abdul, 2013) and are held in high repute in Cham communities

(Sakaya, 2003). Although the last kingdom of Champā collapsed in 1834, the religious elite has continued to play a crucial role in maintaining the culture, religion, and society of the Cham until the present day. In his recent research, Effendy states that "the religious elite contributed to the development of a strong sense of Cham identity rooted in their lands" (Abdul, 2013). For example, the Ahier religion is a localized form of Brahmanism in the Cham community. Ahier dignitaries have the highest status in Cham society. They maintain and preserve the ancient manuscripts concerning rituals, collective knowledge, and the Cham Sakawi calendar. They also conduct religious rituals. Regarding their social status, they once were the aristocracy and the religious elite and on that basis now maintain Cham "hereditary" customs (Phan Xuan Bien, et al., 1991; Sakaya, 2003; Phan, 2010). They play the highest role in guiding the Cham community to conduct ceremonies and also have an important role in protecting and maintaining the temples.

One example to see how they work in living heritage sites is in Ninh Thuan Province, which is divided into three Ahier community areas encompassing the Po Klaong Girai, Po Nagar, and Po Rome temples. Each temple has its own Ahier religious system led by Po Adhia priests who look after spiritual activities and the Ahier community surrounding the temple and maintain the number of Ahier dignitaries.

The preceding discussion highlights the significance of the Cham temples, which embody a continuity of use, care, connection, and cultural expression and truly embody the idea of a "living heritage" site. This study asserts that the Cham temples encompass more than just the towers and stone/brick structures in their vicinity, but also include surrounding structures, supporting villages, and lands. Over the years, numerous Champā relics and remains have been lost due to wars and natural disasters. Some sculptures have been preserved in museums such as those in Da Nang, Ho Chi Minh City, Hanoi, and other central provinces, while others have been kept by individual collectors. However, much of the Cham heritage is no longer in its original location and has been forgotten by the community due to geographical distance and historical events. Only a few temples in the former principality of Panduranga (present-day Ninh Thuan and Binh Thuan Provinces) are still maintained by the Cham community.

References

Abdul, M. E. (2013). *Nager Cam and the Priests of Prowess: A history of resilience*. University of Hawaii at Manoa.

Anh, P. Q. (2004). The religious system of the Bramanism of the Cham people in Ninh Thuan Provvince [Hệ thống chủ lễ của ngưởi Chăm Balamon ở Ninh Thuận]. *Nghiên Cứu Đông Nam A, 3*(66). http://vanhoahoc.vn/nghien-cuu/van-hoa-viet-nam/van-hoa-cac-dan-toc-thieu-so/525-phan-quoc-anh-he-thong-chu-le-cua-nguoi-cham-balamon-o-ninh-thuan.html

Aymonier, É. (1891). Première étude sur les inscriptions tchames. *Journal Asiatique, 8*(17), 5–86.

Bien, P. X., An, P., & Dop, P. Van. (1991). *The Cham culture* [*Văn hoá Chăm*]. KHXH.

Dai, Q. Van. (2016). *Cẩm nang nghi lễ truyền thống Chăm Ninh Thuận* [*A gude of Cham traditional rituals in Ninh Thuan province, Vietnam*]. Tri Thuc Press.

Dharma, P. (1999). The Contribution to Understanding the History of Champa [Góp phần tìm hiểu lịch sử Champa]. *Nghiên Cứu Lịch Sử Văn Minh Champa (Champaka)*, 1.

Dharma, P. (2012). *Vương quốc Champa: lịch sử 33 năm cuối cùng*. (I. – Champa, Ed.). San Jose.

Dop, P. Van, Anh, P. Q., & Thu, N. T. (2014). Văn hóa phi vật thể người Chăm Ninh Thuận [Intangible cultural heritage of the Cham people in Ninh Thuan]. NXB Nông Nghiệp TP.HCM. http://chamstudies.net/2016/02/18/van-hoa-phi-vat-the-cua-nguoi-cham-ninh-thuan/

Duong, N. H. (2007). *Một số vấn đề cơ bản về tôn giáo, tín ngưỡng của đồng bào Chăm ở hai tỉnh Bình Thuận, Ninh Thuận hiện nay*. KHXH Publishing House.

Hobsbawm. (1983). The invention of tradition. In E. J. Hobsbawm & T. O. Ranger (Eds.), *The invention of tradition* (pp. 1–14). Cambridge University Press.

Khanh, V. (2009). *Người Chăm*. Thong Tan Press.

Lafont, P. B. (2014). *The kingdom of Champa: Geography, population, history*. International Office of the Champa.

Manguin, P.-Y. (2001). The introduction of Islam into Champa. In Alijah Gordon (Ed.), *The Propagation of Islam in the Indonesian-Malaysian Archipelago* (pp. 287–328). Malaysian Socialogical Research Institute.

Mus, P. (1934). *India Seen from the East: Indian and Indigenous Cults in Champa*. Monash Asia Institute.

Nakamura, R. (2009). Awar-Ahier: Two keys to understanding the cosmology and ethnicity of the Cham people (Ninh Thuan province, Vietnam). In A. Hardy, M. Cucarzi, & P. Zolese (Eds.), *Champa and the Archaeology of Mỹ Sơn (Vietnam)* (pp. 78–106). NUS Press Pte Ltd.

Ninh, L. (2006). *Vương quốc Champa [The kingdom of Champa]*. DH Quoc Gia Ha Noi.

Noseworthy, W. (2013). Reviving traditions and creating futures | International Institute for Asian Studies. The Newsletter (pp. 12–13). https://iias.asia/the-newsletter/article/reviving-traditions-and-creating-futures

Noseworthy, W. (2014). Mối Quan Hệ Giữa Lễ Katé và Lễ Ramâwan: Một Sự Bản Địa Hóa Trong Lễ Hội Truyền Thống của Dân Tộc Chăm. In *Lễ Hội Cộng Đồng – Truyền Thống và Biến Đổi* (pp. 338–349). NXB DH Quốc Gia Tp. HCM.

Noseworthy, W. (2015). The Mother Goddess of Champa: Po Inâ Nâgar. *SUVANNABHUMI, 7*(1), 107–137. http://suvannabhumi.iseas.kr/pdf/suvannabhumi0701_05.pdf

Phan, T. (1996). Religious organizations and traditional soceity of the Cham people in Phan Rang region [Tổ chức tôn giáo và xã hội truyền thống của người Chăm ở vùng Phan Rang]. *Tap San Khoa Hoc [Đại Học Tổng Hợp Tp. HCM], 1*(1), 165–172.

Phan, T. (2007). *Danh mục thư tịch Chăm ở Việt Nam [The Catalogue of Cham manuscripts in Vietnam - Tapul Akhar Cam di Biénam]*. Tri Thuc Press.

Phan, T. (2010). Some Research Issues related to Traditional Beliefs and Religions of the Cham people in Vietnam today [Một số vấn đề nghiên cứu liên quan đến tín ngưỡng - tôn giáo truyền thống của người Chăm hiện nay ở Việt Nam]. In P. T. Y. T. Lương Văn Hy, Ngô Văn Lệ, Nguyễn Văn Tiệp (Ed.), *Hiện đại và động thái của Truyền thống ở Việt Nam: Những cách tiếp cận Nhân học* (tập 2) (pp. 215–227). HCM National University.

Phan, T. (2011). Một số vấn đề nghiên cứu liên quan đến tín ngưỡng – tôn giáo truyền thống của người Chăm hiện nay ở Việt Nam. In N. V. L. . . Luong Van Hy (Ed.), *Hiện đại và động thái của truyền thống ở Việt Nam: những cách tiếp cận nhân học* (pp. 215–227). DH Quoc Gia.

Phan, T. (2014). Bảo tồn và phát huy nét đẹp văn hóa truyền thống qua lễ tục Ew muk kei, Lễ hội Katé – Ramâwan và Lễ hội Rija Nâgar. In T. Phan (Ed.), *Những vấn đề văn hoá – xã hội người Chăm ngày nay* (pp. 5–31). TP. NXB Trẻ.

Phu, B. T. (2005). The community of islamist Chams in Vietnam with social life the present time [Cộng đồng người Chàm Islam giáo ở Việt Nam với đời sống xã hội]. *Nghiên Cứu Tôn Giáo, 2*, 39–41.

Phu, B. T. (2008). Bani Islam Cham in Vietnam. In O. FAROUK & H. YAMAMOTO (Eds.), *Islam at the margins: The Muslims of Indochina*. CIAS Discussion Paper No. 3 (pp. 24–34). Center for Integrated Area Studies, Kyoto University. https://www.cias.kyoto-u.ac.jp/files/pdf/publish/ciasdp03.pdf

Sakaya. (2003). *The festivals of the Cham people [Lễ hội của ngư`ời Chăm]*. NXB Van Hoa Dan Toc.

Sakaya. (2013). *Tiếp cận một số vấn đề văn hóa Champa [Approaching some problems of Cham Culture]*. Tri Thuc Press.

Sakaya. (2016). *lịch pháp của ngư`ời chăm [cham calendar]*. Tri Thức Press.

Shaklikei. (2016). *Đặt lại vấn đề lịch sử vua Po Klaong Garai [Reconsidering history of King Po Klaong Girai]*. Retrieved June 11, 2018, from http://www.champaka.info/index.php/quandiem/quandiemlichsu/1342-dat

Sharma, J. (1992). *Temples of Champa in Vietnam*. Khoa Hoc Xa Hoi.

Thu, N. T., Truong, T. L., & Thanh, P. Van. (2010). *Lễ nghi nông nghiệp truyền thống tộc ngư`ời Chăm - Raglai Ninh Thuận [Agricultural rituals of the Cham An Raglai groups in Ninh Thuan]*. NXB Nong Nghiep.

Xuyen, H. T. (1999). *Mư`ời tôn giáo l´ờn trên thế gi´ời*. NXB Chính Trị Quốc Gia.

Yasuko, Y. (2011). A study of the almanac of the Cham in south-central Vietnam. In *The Cham of Vietnam: History, society and art* (pp. 323–336). https://www.scopus.com/inward/record.uri?eid=2-s2.0-84895182374&partnerID=40&md5=f8b3dfc502294c1d8f7fd217d35d87c5

Yasuko, Y. (2012). A study of the Hồi giáo religion in Vietnam: With a reference to islamic religious practices of Cham Bani. *Southeast Asian Studies, 1*(3), 487–505. http://repository.kulib.kyoto-u.ac.jp/dspace/bitstream/2433/167310/1/sas_1_3_487.pdf

Open Access This chapter is licensed under the terms of the Creative Commons Attribution 4.0 International License (http://creativecommons.org/licenses/by/4.0/), which permits use, sharing, adaptation, distribution and reproduction in any medium or format, as long as you give appropriate credit to the original author(s) and the source, provide a link to the Creative Commons license and indicate if changes were made.

The images or other third party material in this chapter are included in the chapter's Creative Commons license, unless indicated otherwise in a credit line to the material. If material is not included in the chapter's Creative Commons license and your intended use is not permitted by statutory regulation or exceeds the permitted use, you will need to obtain permission directly from the copyright holder.

Chapter 4
The Conservation of Cham Cultural Heritage in Vietnam

Introduction

This chapter provides an overview of the conservation of Cham cultural heritage in Vietnam and its significance to the country's rich cultural history. It specifically focuses on the heritage sites and artifacts in Ninh Thuan Province, which is home to a significant number of Cham communities. The chapter highlights the importance of preserving Cham cultural heritage for future generations and for understanding the cultural diversity of Vietnam. The aim of this chapter is to give readers an understanding of the history and current state of Cham cultural heritage conservation in Vietnam, and provide a foundation for further exploration and analysis.

Tracing the History of Heritage Conservation in Vietnam

In Vietnam, the protection of cultural heritage is seen as a crucial aspect of preserving national independence (Binh, 2001). Throughout its history, Vietnam has been enriched by the cultural contributions of various ethnic communities, resulting in a unique and diverse cultural heritage. The Vietnamese embrace and incorporate various customs and traditions, regardless of their origin, into their cultural identity (Thien, 2017). The conservation of cultural heritage in Vietnam has been shaped by different approaches, from the French colonial period to the present day.

The preservation of Cham cultural heritage has not only been carried out by Vietnamese authorities, but also by foreigners, especially the French. Upon their arrival in Southeast Asia, the French paid special attention to the remaining relics and cultural heritage of the kingdom of Champā, a Hindu-influenced civilization. Consequently, the conservation of cultural heritage in Vietnam has evolved unevenly throughout its history.

© The Author(s) 2023
Q. D. Tuyen, *Heritage Conservation and Tourism Development at Cham Sacred Sites in Vietnam*, Global Vietnam: Across Time, Space and Community, https://doi.org/10.1007/978-981-99-3350-1_4

Initially, the French researchers who arrived in Vietnam during the late nineteenth century showed great enthusiasm for preserving cultural heritage. However, a hundred years later, after the defeat and withdrawal of the French colonial government from Southeast Asia, heritage conservation came to a halt. The country's subsequent civil war between the North and the South, in which available resources were directed towards the battlefields, further hindered the preservation of cultural heritage.

Finally, with the reunification of Vietnam on April 30, 1975, the conservation of cultural heritage reappeared and has continued until the present day.

In the French colonial period (1887–1945), the French had a significant impact on heritage conservation in Vietnam (Chapman, 2018; Phuong, 2006; Stubbs et al., 2016). In 1898, the École française d'Extrême-Orient (EFEO) was established in Saigon and later moved to Hanoi, which was the French capital of Indochina. The EFEO's mission was to conduct scholarly research and carry out architectural restoration and conservation of key historical monuments in Vietnam and its surrounding areas (Chapman, 2018; Stubbs et al., 2016). In addition to preserving architectural ruins, the EFEO was also interested in Vietnamese history, language, and prehistoric archaeology, such as the Sa Huynh, Oc Eo, Bac Son, and Dong Son cultures. However, the Champā civilization was the main focus of their attention, and several projects were launched to document, study, and conserve Cham cultural heritage (Chapman, 2018; Stubbs et al., 2016). These efforts greatly improved the Western world's understanding of Vietnamese languages, history, and cultural expression (Stubbs et al., 2016). Today, these documentation and conservation methodologies are still employed in Vietnam (Chapman, 2013; Kinh, 2012; Stubbs et al., 2016).

In pre-unified Vietnam, various policies and laws were enacted for the preservation of the country's cultural heritage (Phuong, 2005; Saltiel, 2014). In November 1945, President Ho Chi Minh signed Decree No 65, which prohibited the destruction of temples, historical sites, and documents of historical significance (Phuong, 2005; Thuc, 2015). However, these directives were largely ignored during the land reform from 1953 to 1955, as the state aimed to establish control over religious affairs in local communities (Roszko, 2011). As a result, many sacred objects from temples, shrines, and pagodas were destroyed and deemed to be "powerless effigies" by the state (Roszko, 2011, p. 156). Some structures that were not destroyed were repurposed for secular use. Although religious sites were referred to as "historical monuments," "heritage of feudalism," or "monuments of resistance to foreign aggression," they were officially recognized as having national heritage significance, but not religious significance (Roszko, 2011).

Years later, several institutions were established in Vietnam to manage and protect cultural heritage more effectively (Saltiel, 2014). One such institution is the Vietnam Oriental Institute, which was founded for the protection of the country's antiquities. In 1955, the Ministry of Culture and Information was established to supervise and manage culture and museums in Vietnam. In 1957, Ho Chi Minh passed the Decree on the Management, Classification, and Methods of Organizing the Protection and Restoration of Historical and Cultural Monuments [Di tích lịch sử văn hóa] in Vietnam (Thinh, 2012, pp. 212–213). This decree, which strengthened the provisions of the 1945 decree, was aimed at protecting and restoring tangible cultural heritage, including historic and cultural relics and revolution monuments (Roszko, 2011).

It is said that the conservation of cultural heritage in Vietnam from the 1940s to 1950s mainly focused on immovable heritage due to the economic difficulties brought about by years of war. Many intangible cultural heritages were overlooked during this time (Phuong, 2005). However, since the 1960s, the state has paid more attention to preserving intangible cultural heritage and has carried out research and training in this field. For example, the Vietnam Commission of Social Sciences, which is now known as the Vietnam Institute of Social Sciences, was founded and has collaborated with the Ministry of Culture (currently known as the Ministry of Culture, Sports and Tourism) to collect, study, and promote the cultural values of Vietnam to build a modern cultural life (Phuong, 2005). The cultural heritage of ethnic minorities has also become a focus of national attention, leading to a range of research on the ethnology, folklore, and folk art performance of these groups (Binh, 2001; Phuong, 2005).

In the 1980s and 1990s, during the economic and governmental reforms of Đổi Mới, Vietnam ratified the World Heritage Convention and issued the Ordinance on the Protection of Historical Cultural Relics and Scenic Sites (Stubbs et al., 2016). The government then signed the World Heritage Convention in order to develop its cultural heritage management systems (Stubbs et al., 2016). During this period, several important heritage sites in Vietnam received international support, including the royal tombs of Minh Mang and Ta Tung Tu (Hue), Hội An Old Town and My Son Sanctuary (Quang Nam province), and the Old Town and Temple of Literature (Hanoi city) (Chapman, 2013; Logan, 2001, 2009; Stubbs et al., 2016).

To further protect and promote the cultural values of Vietnam, the government launched and implemented the "National Programme for Safeguarding of the Cultural Heritage" in 1994 (Stubbs et al., 2016). This period marked the government's efforts to issue laws and policies for the preservation and promotion of cultural heritage in the country. In 1998, the 5th Plenum of the Party Central Committee, 8th Tenure, adopted "Resolution No. 5 on Building a Progressive Culture, Imbued with National Identity" which emphasized the importance of the nation's culture in modern life during industrialization, modernization, and international integration (Salemink, 2012; Thien, 2017; Thinh, 2012). These efforts demonstrate the government's commitment to protecting and promoting cultural heritage in Vietnam, both through domestic initiatives and international collaboration.

Cultural heritage plays a crucial role in the socio-economic development of the nation and is recognized by the government as a valuable resource. It acts as a link between the ethnic communities and forms the foundation of national identity, facilitating the creation of new values and cultural exchange. To maximize the benefits of cultural heritage, the government places a high value on the conservation, preservation, and promotion of traditional cultural values, including scholar and folk culture, as well as revolutionary culture, both tangible and intangible. This includes studying and educating on the national ethics passed down from previous generations.

Cultural heritage plays a crucial role in connecting the ethnic community and forms the foundation of national identity. It is imperative to safeguard and enhance traditional cultural values, including both scholar and folk cultures, as well as revolutionary culture, whether tangible or intangible. The education and study of the national ethic passed down from our ancestors is also crucial. In order to protect and promote the values of heritage, we must value, preserve and promote traditional values, cultivate new values in the culture, literature and arts of ethnic minorities, and protect and develop the languages and scripts of different ethnic groups. (Thien, 2017)

In recent years, the significance of cultural heritage has become increasingly important in the national development and preservation of Vietnam. To address this, the National Assembly of the Socialist Republic of Vietnam established a modern legal framework for the preservation of cultural heritage in 2001 through the passage of the Law on Cultural Heritage (National Assembly Vietnam, 2001). This law encompasses seven chapters and 74 articles that cover both natural and cultural heritage, with a full chapter dedicated to intangible cultural heritage, highlighting the state's importance placed on it.

According to the law, cultural heritage encompasses both tangible and intangible cultural heritage, which are spiritual and material products embracing cultural, historical, or scientific values and passed down through generations in Vietnam. They are closely related but can also be comparatively separate. In particular, tangible cultural heritage encompasses material forms of historical, cultural, or scientific value, such as historical-cultural relics, famous landscapes and beauty spots, vestiges, antiques, and national precious objects. Meanwhile, intangible cultural heritage encompasses spiritual products of historical, cultural, or scientific value, such as speech, scripts, literary and artistic works, oral philology, folk oratorios, life style, way of life, rites, traditional craft know-how, knowledge about traditional medicine and pharmacy, gastronomic culture, traditional costumes, and other folk knowledge, which are saved in memory or scripts, handed down orally and through professional teaching and performance (National Assembly Vietnam, 2001).

The law requires all policies related to cultural heritage preservation to have both economic and social benefits for the nation's development (Lask & Herold, 2004). However, this law does not cover cultural tourism policies and strategies, which could potentially lead to issues related to mass tourism and its impact on cultural heritage sites. A solution for a sustainable use of heritage for future generations is yet to be pursued (Council of Europe, Committee of Ministers, 1996 cited from Lask & Herold, 2004).

Since the passing of the 2001 law, numerous National Target Program projects have been initiated to study, document, and collect Vietnamese cultural heritage (Binh, 2001; Van, 2001). The law has also been amended to enhance the management of intangible cultural heritage and to adapt to the 2003 UNESCO Convention for the Safeguarding of Intangible Cultural Heritage. The preservation and protection of cultural heritage should prioritize the cultural carriers who embody these intangible cultural practices (Salemink, 2012).

Leveraging International Partnerships for Cultural Heritage Preservation

Heritage conservation in Vietnam has been greatly influenced by international policies and approaches since the French colonial era, independence, and the Doi Moi reform process. During these periods, collaborations between Vietnam and international organizations have been established (Chapman, 2013; Hoi, 2001; Kinh, 2009; Kazimierz, 1995; Stubbs et al., 2016). The collaboration became particularly significant when Vietnam joined UNESCO and the protection and promotion of the country's cultural heritage became a major focus of collaboration between Vietnam and international organizations (Saltiel, 2014). The first technical and financial support was provided by UNESCO to protect the cultural heritage of Hue in the 1990s, followed by the protection of Hanoi cultural heritage.

Vietnam has been actively participating in international institutions in cultural heritage preservation and has collaborated on a range of projects with numerous countries and institutions (Binh, 2001; Phuong, 2005). For example, the Vietnamese government and the Polish Ateliers for Conservation of Cultural Properties signed an agreement for support in conservation work on Cham heritage sites between 1981 and 1991 (Kinh, 2009; Kazimierz & Kinh, 1995). Polish conservationists and Vietnamese archaeologists worked together to document, examine, restore, and preserve various Cham temples, such as My Son, Chien Dan, Duong Long, Hung Thanh, Po Klaong Girai, and others (Chapman, 2013; Stubbs et al., 2016).

In 1992, the Moon Gate of Hue received support from the UNESCO Japanese Trust for Preserving World Heritage. The An Dinh Palace was also conserved in 2008 through a collaboration between the Hue Monuments Conservation Centre and the German Conservation, Restoration, and Education Project (GCREP). Many other projects were also undertaken in the 1990s, and in 1993, Hue became the first Vietnamese heritage site to be recognized as a World Heritage Site. Later, My Son Sanctuary and Hoi An Ancient Town were both listed as World Heritage Sites in 1999. In the same year, Vietnam and UNESCO signed an agreement in Paris to continue the effective implementation of cultural heritage projects in the country. For the My Son World Heritage Site, UNESCO organized a project team with the collaboration of the Italian government, the Italian Lerici Foundation of Milan's Polytechnic University, and Vietnamese authorities to establish a master plan and conduct extensive restoration work. In 1994, the American Express Corporation, through the World Monuments Fund, preserved the commemorative stele at the Temple of Literature, a Confucian Temple of the Imperial Academy.

Vietnamese heritage sites have received international technical assistance for heritage conservation from countries such as Australia, Belgium, Canada, France, Germany, Japan, and the United States (Stubbs et al., 2016).

As a member of the Association of Southeast Asian Nations (ASEAN), the Vietnamese government has made significant efforts to protect and promote cultural heritage in the region. Vietnam's commitment to cultural heritage is demonstrated by its signing of the "ASEAN Declaration on Cultural Heritage" in 2000, which aimed to carry out projects to protect and promote cultural heritage in Southeast Asia (Hoi, 2001).

To further its efforts, Vietnam has established international collaborations with organizations such as UNESCO, ICOMOS, ICCROM, ASEANCOCI, and SPAFA (Binh, 2001). These organizations have established various bilateral and multilateral diplomatic relationships with Vietnam to protect cultural heritage. These international collaborations have provided Vietnamese conservationists with the opportunity to learn advanced technology and conservation methodologies for heritage protection and enhancement in Vietnam (Binh, 2001, p. 64).

The Ministry of Culture, Sports and Tourism is the major federal institution responsible for heritage management in Vietnam. It works in consultation with other smaller agencies such as the Conservation of Monuments and the Department of Cultural Heritage, which oversee architectural heritage and the conservation of heritage architecture (Binh, 2001; Dung, n.d.). In 2003, the Museum Conservation Department was renamed to the Department of Cultural Heritage, forming the management board of world cultural heritage. The National Council of Cultural Heritage was established in 2004 to advise the government on the preservation and promotion of cultural heritage values (Thuc, 2015). In the same year, the Vietnam Cultural Heritage Association, a non-governmental organization, was established to bring together members in the country. The Prime Minister of Vietnam issued a decision on November 23, 2005, declaring it Vietnam Cultural Heritage Day (President Ho Chi Minh signed Decree No. 65) (Thuc, 2015).

These efforts show that the Vietnamese government takes the preservation and promotion of cultural heritage seriously and is committed to ensuring that this important aspect of its culture is protected for future generations to appreciate and learn from.

To be recognized as a local, national, or specific national cultural heritage, a cultural heritage must be documented in a technical file. The Provincial People's Committees are provided with guidelines for establishing the technical file, and the Ministry of Culture, Sports and Tourism decides on the procedures for evaluating the technical file. The National Council of Cultural Heritage, which examines the scientific value of intangible cultural heritage, provides comprehensive advice to the Ministry to determine which cultural heritage should be considered as national cultural heritage (Dung, n.d.).

Vietnam has made great strides in recent years, with several of its cultural heritage sites being listed by UNESCO as globally significant sites. This recognition highlights the diversity and richness of Vietnamese cultural heritage and shows that Vietnam is actively contributing to the global inventory of heritage and diversifying humanity's spiritual life (Stubbs et al., 2016). Furthermore, these cultural heritage sites have become a significant economic resource and attract international tourists to Vietnam. Despite this progress, Vietnamese cultural heritage, like in many other countries, is facing the challenges of modernization and conservation failures, though the country continues to be a regional leader in conservation efforts (Stubbs et al., 2016).

Principles of Conservation and Promotion of Cultural Heritage in Vietnam

The principles of conservation and promotion of cultural heritage in Vietnam aim to protect and preserve the unique elements and qualities of these sites. As recognized by Thinh (2012), the essence of conservation activities lies in maintaining the original features of cultural heritage sites. To do so, it is important to understand the cultural heritage within its specific historical, economic, and cultural context, as Bai (2013) emphasized. This requires clarifying the relationship between the cultural heritage and the historical period in which it was created to gain insight into its history, experience, and even lessons, particularly in regard to its integrity and authenticity.

Integrity, as defined by Bai (2013) and Kinh (2012), refers to the constituent physical parts of a historical monument as it was originally created. Authenticity, also defined by Bai (2013) and Kinh (2012), pertains to the creative style of the monument. These two factors contribute to the value of cultural heritage sites and distinguish them from copies or imitations. The root element, as stated by Thinh (2012), refers to the heritage's original source and creativity, while authenticity differentiates it from a counterfeit. These elements are based on factual evidence rather than conjecture or misinformation (Bai, 2013).

The preservation and transfer of cultural heritage to future generations is crucial, and the renovation and restoration of monuments in conjunction with sustainable tourism development has become a widely adopted modern trend (Bai, 2013; Thinh, 2012). Cultural heritage conservation should be seen as a scientific effort to achieve its fundamental goals, including removing elements from the heritage that do not contain historical, cultural, or scientific value, and establishing the material and technical conditions to showcase the valuable elements of the monument with the greatest efficiency for visitors (Bai, 2013).

Moreover, the acceptance of the principle of adaptation and necessary changes in protected areas, including relic protection zones, is crucial to the success of conservation efforts. This view is supported by provisions in the Cultural Heritage Law (Bai, 2013). The preservation of cultural heritage not only requires its protection, but also its ability to continue to meet the diverse needs and enjoyment of human use, making it a dialectical way to connect the past with the present and prepare it for future generations (Bai, 2013).

In terms of intangible cultural heritage, each type of intangible cultural heritage is a product of a certain environment and its preservation requires the protection of the whole cultural system as a principle. This includes the protection of the traditional ecological culture in which the cultural heritage is embedded (Thinh, 2012). Changes to the human environment and displacement of the local population can negatively impact the traditional practitioners who act as keepers of cultural heritage (Salemink, 2016; Thinh, 2012, pp. 94–95).

The conservation of cultural heritage should be approached flexibly, taking into account the historical and natural conditions, as well as the characteristics and values of each specific site (Thien, 2017). However, some heritage authorities prioritize development, especially sustainable tourism development, over the preservation of cultural heritage (Thinh, 2012). This can lead to development goals taking precedence over preserving cultural heritage, which is a problem currently observed in the conservation of cultural heritage in Vietnam.

The history of cultural heritage conservation in Vietnam has been shaped by various periods of influence, including French colonialism, a long period of war (1946–1975), national reunification, Soviet influence, and the market economy. The conservation of cultural heritage in Vietnam has been influenced by French conservation practices in the past, and by international conservation efforts in recent times, through collaborations with various countries and organizations (Thinh, 2012).

Cultural Heritages of Ethnic Minorities in Vietnam

Vietnam is home to 54 different ethnic groups, each with its own unique cultural heritage that makes up the rich and diverse Vietnamese culture, referred to as a "garden of many colorful flowers" (Van, 2001, p. 37). The preservation and promotion of the cultural heritage of these ethnic groups is not only the responsibility of the cultural sector but also of the entire Party and community, as it serves the goals of national pride, unity, and economic development (Thinh, 2012; Van, 2001).

The Vietnamese government is committed to building unity in diversity, and recognizes the importance of respecting and celebrating the cultural similarities and differences of each ethnic group in Vietnam (Hong, 2015; Van, 2001). To this end, the state has implemented plans to preserve and promote the cultural heritage of these groups, in order to protect cultural diversity and prevent threats to national cultural identity in the face of globalization and acculturation (Lask & Herold, 2004; Thinh, 2012).

Furthermore, the state affirms the equality of all cultures in Vietnam and does not accept the concept of "high" or "low" culture (Van, 2001). Each of the 54 ethnic groups contributes greatly to the cultural heritage of the Vietnamese people, regardless of their population size or economic status. The government is dedicated to implementing the National Targeted Programme on Culture policy to care for and promote the cultural features of these groups and enrich their cultural heritage legacies (Salemink, 2013; Van, 2001).

The culture of ethnic minorities plays a crucial role in the rich and diverse fabric of Vietnamese culture, and as such, the Vietnamese government places great importance on preserving, protecting, and promoting the cultural heritage of these communities (Thien, 2017). The Cultural Heritage Laws of 2001 and 2009 establish a comprehensive framework for the preservation of cultural heritage in Vietnam, without differentiating between the cultural heritage of various ethnic groups (Thinh, 2012).

In order to specifically address the preservation of ethnic cultures, the government has implemented the "General Inventory of the Cultural Heritage of Vietnamese Ethnicities" (Salemink, 2013). Central and local institutions such as the Association of Vietnamese Folklorists, the Society of Minority Peoples' Culture, and the Department of Culture and Information have established policies and programs aimed at collecting and preserving the cultural heritage of these communities (Hong, 2015). In addition, national and regional museums such as the Museum of the Cultures of Ethnic Groups of Vietnam and the Museum of Minority Peoples' Culture in Thai Nguyen have been established to showcase the rich cultural heritage of Vietnam's ethnic minorities (Lask & Herold, 2004).

In order to preserve and promote cultural heritage, the Vietnamese government also recognizes the role of tourism, particularly cultural tourism, as a key economic and diplomatic tool. The Strategy on Cultural Development of Vietnam to 2020, with a vision to 2030, links cultural development with national economic and social development, highlighting the economic value of cultural heritage, and promoting creative diversity among individuals, groups, and communities (Binh, 2001; Thien, 2017). All provinces of Vietnam are encouraged to follow this strategy and promote the cultural heritage of their localities as an important economic resource (Thien, 2017; Thinh, 2012). Today, the cultural heritage of ethnic groups is a significant source of income for Vietnam, contributing to the country's social and economic development and providing funds for the preservation of cultural heritage for future generations (Logan, 2009).

Issues of Heritage Law in Vietnam

In recent years, the Vietnamese government and people have placed great emphasis on the protection and promotion of cultural heritage. The new awareness about the crucial role of cultural heritage in Vietnam is reflected in the Resolution of the 5th Plenum of the Central Committee, 8th Tenure (Roszko, 2011), the Resolution of the 9th Plenum, 11th Tenure, and the basic contents of the Law on Cultural Heritage (Giang, 2015). At the same time, many policies have been implemented to exploit the potential of heritage for socio-economic development. However, the implementation of the Law on Cultural Heritage has resulted in the transformation of all types of cultural and religious heritage into only one type of cultural heritage (Roszko, 2011). This has led to the secularization of many spiritual sites and the governmentalization of many folk festivals, which are a part of intangible cultural heritage (Cham, 2017). For example, the Cham Po Klaong Girai temple and the Cham practices of ceremonies and festivals have become increasingly secularized and have lost their inherent values in their conservation practices (Cham, 2017).

The protection and preservation of heritage in Vietnam has been a concern since the establishment of the state in 1945. The first mention of the protection of heritage in Vietnam was in the Constitution of 1980, when article 45 was added to prepare for Vietnam's accession to the World Heritage Convention in 1987 (Giang, 2015). The recognition of the Complex of Hue Monuments as a World Cultural Heritage Site in 1993 with the support of UNESCO marked a turning point in the heritage conservation of Vietnam, leading to greater consideration and interest in participating in international conventions related to heritage (Giang, 2015). To date, Vietnam has participated in 9 Conventions and Protocols related to the protection of world cultural and natural heritage (Giang, 2015).

According to the United Nations Educational, Scientific and Cultural Organization (UNESCO), Vietnam has participated in several international conventions and protocols related to the protection and preservation of cultural and natural heritage. These include:

1. The World Heritage Convention 1972
2. The Convention on the Means of Prohibiting and Preventing the Illicit Import, Export and Transfer of Ownership of Cultural Property 1970
3. The Convention for the Safeguarding of the Intangible Cultural Heritage 2003
4. The Ramsar Convention on Wetlands 1971
5. The Convention on International Trade in Endangered Species of Wild Fauna and Flora 1973
6. The Convention on Biological Diversity 1992
7. The Cartagena Protocol on Biosafety to the Convention on Biological Diversity 2000
8. The Nagoya—Kuala Lumpur Supplementary Protocol on Liability and Redress to the Cartagena Protocol on Biosafety 2010

These international agreements demonstrate Vietnam's commitment to the protection and preservation of its cultural and natural heritage for future generations.

Furthermore, based on the UNESCO World Heritage Convention, the National Assembly of the Socialist Republic of Vietnam adopted the Law on Cultural Heritage in 2001 and revised and supplemented it in 2009 with provisions related to the management of different types of heritage. Although this law primarily focuses on the management of tangible and intangible cultural heritage, it is also applicable to natural heritage management as Vietnam currently does not have a specific law for this area. The management of natural heritage is also governed by other laws such as the Law on Environmental Protection, the Biodiversity Law, the Law on Forest Protection and Development, the Land Law, and various implementing guidelines for these laws (National Assembly of the Socialist Republic of Vietnam, 2001, 2009).

In the law of cultural heritage, intangible cultural heritage (ICH) is considered importantly and receives significant attention. As a State Party to the 2003 Convention on the Safeguarding of the Intangible Cultural Heritage, Vietnam revised its legislation in 2009 to improve its compliance with the Convention and address practical considerations (Park, 2013, p. 130). The 2009 Cultural Heritage Law was supplemented with several articles, including the requirement for an ICH inventory and the establishment of an ICH database as legal professional activities (Park, 2013, p. 130). However, the law still lacks provisions that would make it more effective in many cases in Vietnam.

According to Nguyen Linh Giang (2015), the Cultural Heritage Law, in general, provides protection for human rights related to cultural heritage such as property rights, cultural rights, and other rights. However, the author also points out several limitations in the provisions, such as the absence of the right to participation of individuals or communities in decision-making processes related to their own cultural heritage. The law also does not include provisions regarding the traditional use of cultural heritage by communities. Additionally, the law does not mention traditional and religious ceremonies of host communities that are connected to cultural heritage in protected areas. Issues related to religion and belief are governed by the 2004 Ordinance on Belief and Religion, which lacks specific regulations regarding the practice of religion and belief in heritage areas. Finally, the law fails to provide provisions regarding the obligations of the state and organizations to ensure the rights of people living in heritage areas (Giang, 2015, p. 7).

As discussed previously, the Cultural Heritage Law of Vietnam incorporates strong influence from UNESCO's conventions and adjusts to address current issues at the national and international levels. However, it appears that sacred places are not specifically mentioned in the law. These sacred places are associated with various issues such as religious and cultural practices, land ownership, and other factors that can negatively impact communities if only the current cultural heritage law is applied.

In Vietnam, there is a need for special provisions to accommodate Indigenous cultures within its territory. Sacred places play a significant role in Indigenous groups in Vietnam, but they are not acknowledged in the cultural heritage law. However, there is a need for a clear definition of sacred places as they are not just related to spirituality, but also to land use rights, economic benefits, and cultural rights.

A research team from Quang Binh University presented the issues faced by the Rem Indigenous people after the Phong Nha—Ke Bang National Park was inscribed on the World Heritage List in 2003 and designated as a protected area. This area is the living space of many Indigenous groups, including the Arem people, who rely on the forest for their livelihoods and conduct many spiritual ceremonies there. However, after the area was protected, the Arem people were prohibited from using forest resources for their daily needs and were also banned from entering their ancestral lands for spiritual ceremonies (Luong et al., 2015). This demonstration shows that applying the law within a national framework may not be appropriate in the local context where Indigenous people are closely connected to their environment. This can result in the loss of cultural rights, livelihoods, and habitats.

The Cham culture highlights the crucial role of spirituality in its connection to ancestors and nature. The sacred in the Cham culture, referred to as "ganreh," encompasses objects, both human-made and natural, that possess mysterious powers that can either protect or harm human beings. The Cham people believe that by respecting these sacred places, they will be protected, and by neglecting them, they will be punished. In Cham culture, there is a close relationship between gods, ancestors, and descendants, with the spirits of the gods, ancestors, and the dead connected to the living through spiritual and religious ceremonies. Temples and graves, such as Awal graves and Ahier Kuts, serve as the resting place of these spirits and are protected from disturbance. The living have a duty to ensure that their relatives are buried or cremated in the proper place and manner, and to protect them from desecration. The failure to perform these duties not only harms the dead, but also the living. These traditions exhibit a strong continuity in Cham culture.

Despite the importance of sacred places in Cham culture, they are not specifically mentioned in the Cultural Heritage Law of Vietnam. While the Ordinance on Belief and Religion in 2004 recognizes the right to the spiritual practices of any group, it has no specific regulations regarding the practice of religion and belief in heritage areas. It is important to supplement the spiritual aspect into the Cultural Heritage Law and to have specific regulations for the Cham people to ensure the protection of their cultural heritage.

Conservation of Cham Cultural Heritage in Vietnam and Ninh Thuan Province

History of the Conservation of Cham Cultural Heritage

The French Colonial Period: 1902–1954

French archaeologists Henri Parmentier and Charles Carpeaux, working with the École française d'Extrême-Orient (EFEO), made significant contributions to the inventory and preservation of Cham cultural heritage in Vietnam (Baptiste, 2009). Through clearing debris, preparing annotated descriptions, taking photographs, conducting excavations, documenting, and evaluating the conditions of Cham temples, Parmentier and Carpeaux helped to establish an important body of information for the study and conservation of Cham heritage (Baptiste, 2009).

The EFEO also played an important role in the management and restoration of Cham monuments in the twentieth century. During the period of 1931–1942, several Cham temples, including My Son, Bang An, and Po Inâ Nâgar, were preserved and reconstructed (Phuong, 2006, 2011). In 1931, Jean-Yves Claeys consolidated and restored the main temple of Po Inâ Nâgar in Khanh Hoa Province, building upon Parmentier's restoration of the southern temple in 1902 and 1907 (Phuong, 2006, 2011). Claeys also collaborated with irrigation engineer Crocquet in 1933 to restore the vestibule of Bang An temple in Quang Nam Province (Phuong, 2006, 2011).

In 1937, Louis Bezacier and Nguyen Xuan Dong began the restoration work at My Son, which involved the use of cement, gravel, and iron to shore up the foundations and walls of the structures (Hy, 2012). To address the damage caused by the course of the Khe Thể river, the conservators built a dam in 1939 (Patrizia, 2009; Phuong, 2011). Despite the use of brute force in the restoration, the aim was to preserve the original surfaces of the structures as effectively as possible, with broken structural elements being repaired accordingly (Phuong, 2008).

The Polish-Vietnamese Conservation Period: 1975–1998

During this time, the conservation of Cham cultural heritage was a collaborative effort between Polish architects and Vietnamese preservationists. In the 1980s, Professor Tadeusz Polak, General Director of the Polish Federation of Historical Heritage Restoration Workshop, initiated the Federation's efforts to preserve Champā's cultural heritage. He proposed a bilateral cooperative effort and established the Poland Joint Sub-Committee for the conservation of Champā's architectural heritage, based in Vietnam (Kinh, 2009). From 1980 to 1986, conservators conducted an inventory and evaluated the condition of Champā's heritage in Central Vietnam, including the Po Klaong Girai temple, after the American War (Tieu et al., 2000). Polish conservation workers followed the principles and techniques of archaeological restoration, using the conservative anastylosis method (Kinh, 2009, p. 27), which involves the use of original materials as much as possible. They used both fallen bricks and modern cement to restore damaged walls and temples and applied methods of consolidation, anastylosis, and fragmentary restoration to preserve the authenticity of the temples (Phuong, 2002). Decorative reliefs on walls were restored at Po Klaong Girai and other temples. However, the use of sanding to restore original brick walls sometimes resulted in indentations in the reinforced walls that were 5 cm deeper/wider than the original walls. This was due to the extensive bombing raids of the American War that reduced many temples to ruins, leading to large numbers of broken bricks being moved and rearranged in many Central Vietnamese temples (Hy, 2012, p. 3).

The Contemporary Period: From 1999 to Today

The My Son temple, a Cham heritage site in Central Vietnam, was recognized as a UNESCO World Heritage Site in 1999 and has been preserved through the efforts of conservation specialists. However, the preservation of other Cham heritage sites, such as Po Klaong Girai, is carried out by individual Vietnamese archaeologists and architects who have used their own methods, some of which have been untested and improvised. For example, the Center for Design and Conservation Vestiges, as noted by Kien (2000) and Kien and Tuyen (2012), used a brick-making technique that contradicts the original Cham design and has resulted in modifications that have damaged the surfaces and diminished the aesthetic value of the decorative motifs. Despite these efforts, as Phuong (2006) notes, there have been instances of adverse impacts on the Cham temples, particularly during the later period when Vietnamese conservators applied their own techniques. Nevertheless, the combined efforts of these conservators, as Phuong (2002, 2006) points out, have created a valuable resource for future research and conservation. Additionally, they have acted as advocates, protecting the Cham temples through international legislation and diplomacy.

The conservation and restoration efforts of Cham's architectural heritage have undergone three distinct periods. In the first period, French archaeologists Henri Parmentier and Charles Carpeaux, working with the EFEO, greatly contributed to the inventory of Champā's remains through excavation, documentation, photography, and preparation of annotated descriptions (Baptiste, 2009). During this period, the EFEO also investigated the management of the restoration of Cham monuments, resulting in the preservation and reconstruction of many temples such as My Son, Bang An, and Po Inâ Nâgar (Phuong, 2006, 2011). In the second period, Polish architects and Vietnamese preservationists conducted conservation work through a bilateral cooperative effort, using a conservative anastylosis method that empha- sized the use of original materials (Kinh, 2009; Phuong, 2002). During the 1980s, the Poland Joint Sub-Committee for the conservation of Champā's architectural heritage was established and conducted an inventory of Champā's heritage in Central Vietnam (Tieu et al., 2000). Finally, in the third period, individual Vietnamese archaeologists and architects have used untested and improvised methods to preserve and protect Cham heritage sites, including Po Klaong Girai (Phuong, 2002, 2006). However, some of these methods have resulted in adverse impacts on the temples, such as the modification of original decorative designs (Kien & Tuyen, 2012). Despite these instances, the collective efforts of these conservators have provided a valuable resource for future research and conservation efforts, and have acted as advocates in providing protection and security for the Cham temples through international legislative and diplomatic efforts.

In short, the conservation and restoration efforts of Cham's architectural heritage have undergone three distinct periods. In the first period, French archaeologists Henri Parmentier and Charles Carpeaux, working with the EFEO, greatly contributed to the inventory of Champā's remains through excavation, documentation, photography, and preparation of annotated descriptions (Baptiste, 2009). During this period, the EFEO also investigated the management of the restoration of Cham monuments, resulting in the preservation and reconstruction of many temples such as My Son, Bang An, and Po Inâ Nâgar (Phuong, 2006, 2011). In the second period, Polish architects and Vietnamese preservationists conducted conservation work through a bilateral cooperative effort, using a conservative anastylosis method that empha- sized the use of original materials (Kinh, 2009; Phuong, 2002). During the 1980s, the Poland Joint Sub-Committee for the conservation of Champā's architectural heritage was established and conducted an inventory of Champā's heritage in Central Vietnam (Tieu et al., 2000). Finally, in the third period, individual Vietnamese archaeologists and architects have used untested and improvised methods to preserve and protect Cham heritage sites, including Po Klaong Girai (Phuong, 2002, 2006). However, some of these methods have resulted in adverse impacts on the temples, such as the modification of original decorative designs (Kien & Tuyen, 2012). Despite these instances, the collective efforts of these conservators have provided a valuable resource for future research and conservation efforts, and have acted as advocates in providing protection and security for the Cham temples through international legislative and diplomatic efforts.

Conservation of Cham Cultural Heritage in Ninh Thuan Province

Vietnamese government's Policies for the Preservation of Cham Cultural Heritage

Indigenous Cham heritage plays a prominent role in the larger project of Vietnam's development, specifically in the tourism sector. Since reunification in 1975, the Vietnam Communist Party and State have issued many policies and guidelines for the socio-cultural and social development of ethnic minorities in general and Cham people in particular. On October 26, 1981, the Prime Minister issued Directive No.121/CT stipulating the protection and preservation of typical historical relics and culture:

> *The cultural sector should continue to collect the cultural heritage of the Cham. For precious cultural heritages scattered among Cham families, it should be active in collecting them for effective preservation and maintenance as well as building a museum of ethnic Cham culture. At the places where Cham are living, the establishment of professional art needs to be at the core of the development of the popular Cham cultural movement.*

The legal basis for policy construction in the Provinces of Thuan Hai, Ninh Thuan, and Binh Thuan is Directive No. 121/CT issued by the Prime Minister on October 26, 1981, as described by Dop et al. (2014). This directive tasked the Culture and Sports and Tourism Department with protecting and preserving the cultural heritage of the Cham people, including collecting valuable cultural objects and establishing a museum of ethnic Cham culture. However, evidence suggests that the collection of cultural objects for preservation has resulted in the removal of many objects from the daily life and religious practices of the Cham people, rendering them "dead" cultural objects within the museum.

After a decade of implementation, a conference was held by the Secretariat in 1991 to review the progress of the Circular No.03/TT-TW dated October 17, 1991 on the work of Cham people. This conference led to plans for restoring Cham temple-towers and re-establishing the Cham Cultural Center in Phan Rang city, as well as continued investment in teaching the Cham language, rewriting textbooks, and consolidating the establishment of a Cham Folk Art Troupe.

Finally, Directive No. 06/2004/CT-TTg, issued by the Prime Minister on February 28, 2004, emphasized the importance of continuing socio-economic and cultural development, ensuring security in the regions of the Cham people. This directive specifically highlighted the task of developing cultural forms to preserve and promote the traditional culture and identity of the Cham people.

The Ninh Thuan Province's Ministry of Culture and Information (now the Ministry of Culture, Sports and Tourism) has made significant efforts to preserve and promote Cham culture. The provincial Party committee and People's committee have worked to enhance the capability of the Cham Cultural Research Center and established the Cham Folk Art Troupe to carry out cultural exchanges. The Ministry organized the "Cham Cultural Days" which comprised of events to publish, disseminate, and compile cultural studies, literary, and artistic works. The aim of these activities was to increase the understanding of Cham culture and promote tourism in the province.

Tourism is considered a crucial industry for the province's economic development, second only to the energy sector. In line with this, the Ninh Thuan Province issued Resolution No. 07-NQ/TW (Ninh Thuan Tourism Development from 2012 to 2020 with a vision towards 2030) on April 10, 2012. The purpose of this plan was to establish sustainable and effective guidelines for the province's economic, social, and tourism development and create a unified basis for managing and utilizing the potential of the tourism market.

Ninh Thuan Tourism specifically emphasizes the comprehensive development of marine tourism, ecotourism, and cultural tourism. Cham culture is prioritized for preservation to support the development of tourism, which will contribute to the socio-economic development of the province and the Cham community.

The Provincial Department of Culture, Sports, and Tourism has initiated a project to develop ecological and cultural tours, with a specific focus on Cham tourist destinations (Anh, 2012). Additionally, local authorities have restored Cham temples and improved the infrastructure at these sites, such as the newly built downhill path at the Po Klaong Girai temple and the exhibition area of the Cham Cultural Research Center (Anh, 2012).

Phan Quoc Anh, former director of the Department of Culture, Sports, and Tourism, emphasized the crucial role of stakeholders in contributing to the development of the provincial tourism. These stakeholders include travel agents, central and local tourism associations, hotels, and facilities (Anh, 2012). However, the roles and responsibilities of cooperation between the Cham people and government authorities have not yet been clearly defined, and most notably, the role of the Cham community in the tourism development of Ninh Thuan Province seems to have been overlooked.

Safeguarding Intangible Cultural Heritage

Since the re-establishment of Ninh Thuan Province in 1993, local authorities have made significant efforts to preserve and promote the intangible cultural heritage of the Cham people. These efforts include renovating and embellishing cultural monuments, promoting the recognition of these monuments, and establishing cultural institutions like the Cham Cultural Research Center, the Provincial Museum, the Committee for Drafting School Textbooks in the Cham Language, and the Cham Folk Art Group.

The Cham Cultural Research Center, in particular, has been tasked with the research, collection, conservation, and development of Cham culture, not just in Ninh Thuan Province but throughout the country. Despite facing challenges such as limited human resources, funding, and equipment, the center has conducted numerous surveys, fieldwork investigations, and research projects in recent years. However, these research projects tend to be small, scattered, and unsystematic, with limited dissemination of the findings beyond the provincial level. Given the rich cultural heritage of the Cham people, it is important to conduct a comprehensive survey of the Cham culture in Ninh Thuan Province to identify what has been lost, what remains, and what may be at risk in the future. This will provide a basis for more informed and effective preservation and promotion efforts in the future.

The preservation and promotion of Cham manuscripts has been an important focus for local authorities and scholars in Ninh Thuan Province. Written in the Akhar Thrah script, these manuscripts hold significant value for the Cham community as they contain valuable information on literature, history, astronomy, medicine, religious beliefs, ceremonial practices, and daily activities of the Cham people (Hao, 2015; Phan, 2012). Despite being maintained primarily by Cham families, many manuscripts have been deteriorating and disappearing due to the humid and hot conditions in the Cham regions (Hao, 2015). To address this, numerous initiatives have been undertaken in recent years. For instance, the Center for Vietnamese and Southeast Asia Studies has digitized manuscripts in collaboration with Dr. Phan Hao of Northern Illinois University, and has trained Cham people to preserve them. These documents are now easily accessible through the British Library. Additionally, a joint project between the Cham Cultural Research Center and the State Records Management and Archives Department of Vietnam is underway to renovate, restore, and digitize all Cham manuscript collections at the Center. Furthermore, scholars such as Thanh Phan, Inrasara, and Sakaya have individually collected, preserved, and studied many Cham manuscripts. These documents remain a significant part of the living heritage of the Cham community and are still used for religious practices and daily life, such as the popularly kept stories of King Po Klaong Girai in Cham families.

The transmission of traditional Cham culture to future generations is a crucial aspect of preserving and revitalizing the intangible cultural heritage of the Cham community. To achieve this goal, the Ninh Thuan Province has implemented various projects focused on promoting handicraft skills, festival activities, and other cultural traditions.

The Cham Cultural Research Center took the lead in this effort by conducting a project from 1994 to 1996 entitled "Festivals of Cham people in Ninh Thuan Province." In 2003, the project results were published in a book by author Sakaya, providing a comprehensive investigation of the Cham festival system, including an in-depth analysis of the natural and social factors that have shaped and sustained these festivals.

With over 75 festivals and rituals, the Cham have effectively passed down their cultural heritage through generations, making Ninh Thuan Province a thriving center of Cham cultural heritage. This is a testament to the Cham community's commitment to preserving their cultural traditions, and the efforts of the Ninh Thuan Province to support and enhance these efforts.

Temple Reconstruction as a Method of Preserving Tangible Culture

In Ninh Thuan Province, there are three clusters of Cham temples, namely Po Klaong Girai (13th–fourteenth centuries), Hoa Lai (eighth century), and Po Rome

(17th–eighteenth centuries), that symbolize the construction techniques and architectural styles of the Cham people throughout history. These temples are significant in preserving the tangible cultural heritage of the Cham people.

The Po Rome temple, located about two kilometers west of the Cham village in Ninh Phuoc district, is a group of towers built during the final period of Cham architecture in the 17th and the eighteenth centuries (Doanh, 2002). The temple consists of a Kalan erected in honor of King Po Rame, a temple dedicated to his wife, and his relative's tomb. At the beginning of the last century, it also included a repository for offerings, but only traces remain today due to severe damage. It is considered the last tower showcasing the art, history, architecture, and sculpture of the Cham people.

Hoa Lai or Ba Thap temple (Yang Bakran in the Cham language) is dedicated to Adidiveshavara, a form of Shiva (Schweyer, 2011). The temple, which was once comprised of three Kalans, saw the destruction of the middle tower during the American war. At the beginning of the twentieth century, French scholars documented the remains of a wall surrounding the three kalans and other sites such as a main tower (Mandapa) and a Gorupa (gateway tower) (T. K. Phuong, 2008, p. 103). The Hoa Lai complex is constructed in traditional Cham style, but the decorative patterns on the temple are unique. This temple is believed to be a style typical of the end of the 8th and the beginning of the ninth centuries (T. K. Phuong, 2008, p. 106). It is considered one of the most valuable art forms among the existing temples in Ninh Thuan Province (Doanh, 2002; Parmentier, 1909; Tieu et al., 2000). According to Parmentier, it is a masterpiece of ancient Cham architecture that features a multi-tower complex with unique design patterns reflecting cross-cultural influences. The "Hoa Lai style," which marked the end of the first phase of Cham art, is characterized by square shapes, themes of symmetry, and the absence of small decorative towers on the floor of the complex, with motifs such as cylindrical flower motifs and naturalistic foliage (Parmentier, 1909, pp. 118–120).

Conservation works have been undertaken at the Hoa Lai temple and at Po Rome temple. As well as these restoration projects, heritage authorities have undertaken conservation works at a range of heritage places to build facilities to promote the purpose of tourism development (Binh, 2001). However, the conservation of Cham heritage sites and objects is faced with numerous challenges, including a lack of funding (Dharma, 2001), inappropriate policies, and the inadequate abilities of heritage practitioners (Binh, 2001; Dharma, 2001) (Fig. 4.1).

A Case Study of Po Klaong Girai Temple: Preserving Cham Heritage in Vietnam

The Po Klaong Girai temple complex is located on the Hala hill in Phan Rang—Thap Cham city and is considered one of the most iconic and visually distinctive Cham temples. The complex was constructed during the late thirteenth century to the early fourteenth centuries (Doanh, 2006). According to local Cham beliefs, the temple was dedicated to King Po Klaong Girai in the late fourteenth century by the

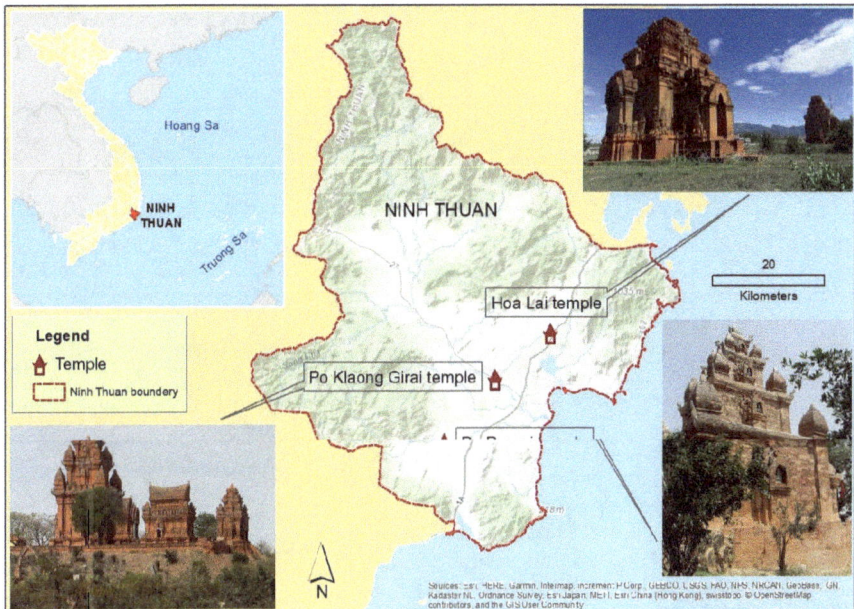

Fig. 4.1 Locations of Cham temples in Ninh Thuan Province

Champā monarch Jaya Simhavarman III. This king played a significant role in the development of the Champā kingdom in the late thirteenth century, having helped the Cham people in the Panduranga principality with infrastructure improvements and irrigation projects (Doanh, 2006).

King Po Klaong Girai is credited with the construction of many dams and canals (ditches) that helped regulate the supply of water to rice fields. Many of these irrigation systems, such as the Nha Trinh and Lâm Cấm networks, are still in use today and serve as a testament to the king's contributions (Dharma & Weber, 2005). Further details on these irrigation systems can be found in Appendix 1 and 2 and Dharma and Weber's (2005) publication.

Po Klaong Girai temple is a prime example of the intricate and sophisticated construction techniques utilized by the Cham people (Viet, 2007). Despite being in ruins today, the temple was once a unique testament to the Cham architectural style, with its abundance of intricate details, according to Parmentier (1919, p. 96). Currently, only a few structures of the temple complex remain, including vestiges of the central tower, the entrance tower, and the southeast building (Fig. 4.2).

Schweyer (2011, p. 88) has written extensively about the architecture of the remaining structures at Po Klaong Girai temple, pointing out that the structure is open from east to west to allow passage and features false doors on the south and the north. The central tower, which stands at 20.50 m high and is 13.80 m long and 10.71 m wide, is an impressive example of Cham architecture. The tower features five flat pilasters on each side, with capital decorations of delicate lotus petals and a

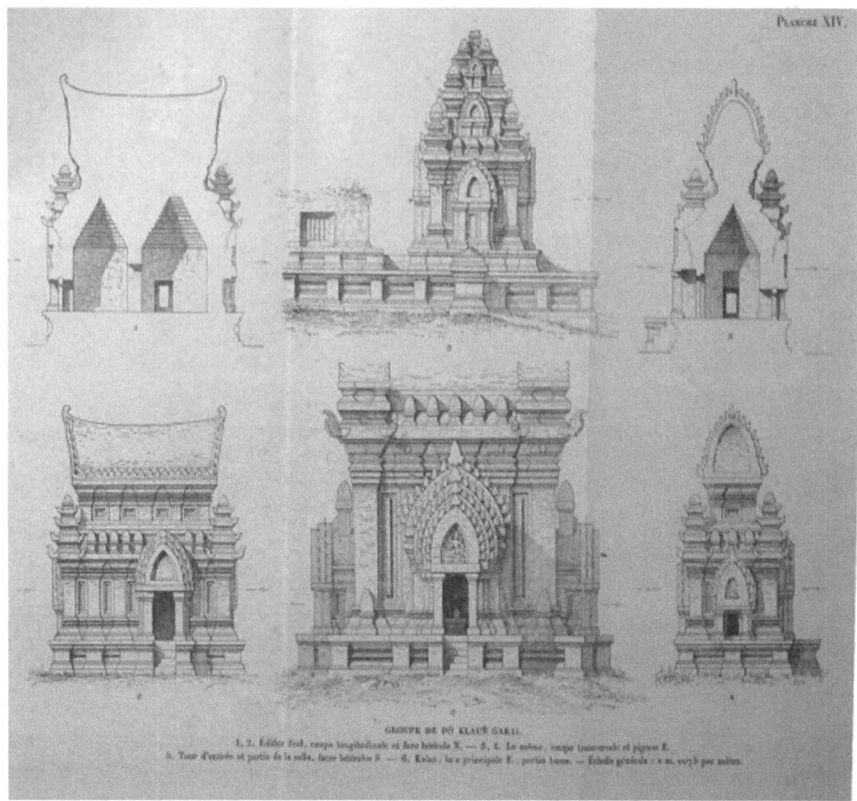

Fig. 4.2 Plans of Po Klaong Girai temple (Parmentier, 1909)

three-tiered roof, as described by Schweyer (2011, p. 89). The corners of the tower feature small towers in the shape of a lotus bud and the summit is decorated with accentuating details in stone, including spirals and figures in prayer. The entrance and false doors are surmounted by four superimposed arches, decorated with flame-like leaves, and the carved pediment above the door depicts a dancing Shiva (Schweyer, 2011, p. 89) (Fig. 4.3).

Inside the temple's vestibule, a statue of the bull Nandin can be found. The main tower houses a Mukha-linga, a unique type of linga featuring a painted image of King Po Klaong Girai's face (Fig. 4.4). A wooden pyramid has been erected above the Mukha-linga. On the opposite side of the entrance to the sanctuary, wooden columns demonstrate the sophisticated building techniques employed by the Cham people, supporting the lightweight roof. According to Doanh (2006), the structure adjacent to the Mukha-linga served as the original key entrance to the temple. A nearby hill bears a rock inscription from the year 1050 that commemorates the erection of a linga by a Cham prince.

Fig. 4.3 Some architectural features of the Po Klaong Girai temple (Courtesy of the author, 2012)

The Po Klaong Girai temple is an important center of the traditional Cham belief system, hosting many festivals and ceremonies annually, such as the Katé festival, Cambun festival, Peh Bambeng Yang, and Yuen Yang. As a result of its significance, the temple has undergone several preservation and restoration efforts over the years, particularly between 1982 and 1987 under the direction of Polish experts.

Fig. 4.4. King Po Klaong Girai, painted on the Mukha-Linga (Courtesy of the author, 2012)

The conservation efforts began with reinforcing damaged elements with steel bars and consolidating materials in 1982. The following year, the fundamental parts of the temple were restored and consolidated, with one-third of these parts being listed as severely damaged. In 1983, the main tower was restored by removing damaged bricks and restoring stone statues inside the tower. In 1985, restoration work was conducted on the three towers in the Po Klaong Girai group, with almost 500 sculptural details or designs on arches being restored and replicated to their original designs. In 1987, the conservators repaired falling walls, bringing the conservation efforts to a close.

As a result of these efforts, the Po Klaong Girai temple is considered to be the best conservation project in the Ninh Thuan Province in comparison to other central Vietnamese provinces (Phuong, 2006, 2011; Tieu et al., 2000). Although the temple is still in good condition today, the use of cement during the restoration work has led to the rapid erosion of the original brickwork and the spread of conditions to surrounding bricks. Furthermore, the intervention has created a black patina of surface lichens on the new bricks. While the conservation work at Po Klaong Girai temple has helped to restore some damaged decorative elements and has placed original features back into place as harmoniously as possible, the use of cement has ultimately done more harm than good.

The recognition of all Cham temples in Vietnam as national historical sites by the Ministry of Culture, Sports and Tourism highlights the cultural significance of these sacred sites. The Hoa Lai and Po Klaong Girai temples in Ninh Thuan, in particular, have been designated as special national architectural relic sites and the Katé festival of the Cham people has been recognized as the national intangible cultural heritage. This dual recognition acknowledges the rich cultural heritage of the Cham community and helps to preserve and promote its heritage values for local economic development. In 2005, the local government invested 15 billion VND (approximately USD $643,000) to construct a tourism area at the Po Klaong Girai temple, covering 7.8 hectares. This area includes an exhibition hall, art performance space, a traditional game area, and a traditional Cham house located behind the temple. The project has had both positive and negative impacts on the temple and the Cham people. The positive impacts include the cultural presentation of Cham culture to tourists and the economic benefits of preserving the temple. On the other hand, the project has also had negative impacts on the temple and the Cham community, which are the focus of the research for this book.

The author aims to conduct an assessment and analyze the implications of this project on the Cham cultural heritage, highlighting the importance of preserving cultural heritage while also considering the impact of tourism and development on these sacred sites.

References

Anh, P. Q. (2012). Văn hóa Chăm v´ới phát triển du lịch ở Ninh Thuận [Cham culture with the development of tourism in Ninh Thuan]. In Bảo tồn, phát triển văn hóa dân tộc Chăm trong bối cảnh công nghiệp hóa, hiện đại hóa và hội nhập quốc tế (pp. 11–20). Phan Rang- Thap Cham: Bộ VHTTDL.

Bai, D. Van. (2013). Quan điểm bảo tồn di sản văn hóa trong chiến lược phát triển văn hóa đến 2020 [Cultural heritage conservation perspectives in the cultural development strategy toward 2020]. Culture and Arts, 346. Retrieved from http://vhnt.org.vn/tin-tuc/y-kien-trao-doi/27707/quan-diem-bao-ton-di-san-van-hoa-trong-chien-luoc-phat-trien-van-hoa-den-nam-2020

Baptiste, P. (2009). The Archaeology of ancient Champa: The French excavations. In P. Z. Andrew Hardy, Mauro Curcazi (Ed.), Champa and the archaeology of Mỹ Sơn (Vietnam) (pp. 14–25). NUS Press.

Binh, T. Q. (2001). The protection and enhancement of cultural property in Vietnam. In A. Galla (Ed.), Protection of cultural heritage in Southeast Asia (pp. 63–65). Ha Noi: Asia Pacific Organisation of the International Council of Museums in partnership with the Vietnam Ministry of Culture and Information.

Cham, N. T. P. (2017). A number of trends in folk festival celebration today. Vietnam Social Sciences, 2(178), 72–84.

Chapman, W. (2013). A heritage of ruins: The ancient sites of Southeast Asia and their conservation. A heritage of ruins: The ancient sites of Southeast Asia and their conservation. University of Hawaii Press. https://doi.org/859157590

Chapman, W. (2018). Adjuncts to empire: The EFEO and the conservation of Champa antiquities. Bulletin of the History of Archaeology, 28(1), 1. http://doi.org/10.5334/bha-584

Dharma, P. (2001). The intangible cultural heritage of two provinces of central Viet Nam – Ninh Thuan and Binh Thuan. In O. Salemink (Ed.), Viet Nam's cultural diversity: Approaches to preservation (pp. 265–270). UNESCO.

Dharma, P., & Weber, N. (2005). Numérisation des Manuscrits Cam Fonds de l'EFEO. Kuala Lumpur: Ministry of Culture, Arts and Heritage Malaysia Centre EFEO.

Doanh, N. Van. (2002). Champa Ancient Towers: Reality and Legend. Thế gi´ới.

Doanh, N. Van. (2006). Champa: Ancient towers, reality & legend (2nd ed.). The Gioi.

Dop, P. Van, Anh, P. Q., & Thu, N. T. (2014). Văn hóa phi vật thể ngư`ời Chăm Ninh Thuận [Intangible cultural heritage of the Cham people in Ninh Thuan]. Ho Chi Minh: NXB Nông

Nghiệp TP.HCM. Retrieved from http://chamstudies.net/2016/02/18/van-hoa-phi-vat-the-cua-nguoi-cham-ninh-thuan/

Giang, N. L. (2015). Legal analysis: Current framework, challenges and opportunities. In *Understanding rights practices in the world heritage system: Lessons from the Asia Pacific* (p. 16). The Viet Nam Academy of Social Sciences & Ha Noi UNNESCO Office.

Hao, P. (2015). Cham manuscripts, the endangered cultural heritage from a lost Kingdom. *Restaurator, 36*(2), 101–120. https://doi.org/10.1515/res-2014-0019

Hoi, N. (2001). Heritage management and international legal instruments in Vietnam. In A. Galla (Ed.), *Protection of cultural heritage in Southeast Asia*. Asia Pacific Organisation of the International Council of Museums in partnership with the Vietnam Ministry of Culture and Information.

Hong, N. V. (2015). Conservation of cultural heritage from cultural stakeholders. In Universidad Complutense de Madrid (Ed.), *Proceedings of the II Internacional Conference on Best Practices in World Heritage: People and Communities* (pp. 614–625). Servicio. https://doi.org/978-84-606-9264-5

Hy, N. T. (2012). Thinking about Conservation and Aesthetic Issues of Conservation of the Cham temples [Suy nghĩ về việc tu bổ tháp Chăm và vấn đề thẩm mỹ]. In Cham civilizational linkages between India and Vietnam. Da Nang, Vietnam: Da Nang city.

Kien, N. H. (2000). The temples of Champa [Đền tháp Champa]. *Kiến Trúc, 4*(84), 49–52.

Kien, N. H., & Tuyen, Q. D. (2012). Problems in studying, preserving, and educating of Cham cultural vestiges. In *Workshop on Champa Art Research*. Institute of Art.

Kinh, H. D. (2009). Champa: The Vietnam-Poland Conservation. In M. C. and P. Z. (eds.. A. Hardy (Ed.), *Champa and the Archaeology of Mỹ Sơn.* (pp. 26–32). NUS Press.

Kinh, H. D. (2012). Selected Conservaton of Architectural Art of the Cham people [Lựa chọn giải pháp bảo tồn nghệ thuật kiến trúc của dân tộc Chăm]. In *Cham cilivizational linkages between India and Vietnam*. Da Nang city.

Kwiatkowski Kazimierz & Hoang Dao Kinh. (1995). Cooperation profile between Vietnam and Poland: Remodeling and restoration of cham architectural monuments: The Po Klaong Girai complex, Phan Rang [Hồ sơ hợp tác Việt Nam - Ba Lan: Tu sửa và phục hồi các di tích kiến trúc Chàm: Nhóm tháp Pô Klaong Girai, Ha Noi.

Kwiatkowski Kazimierz. H. D. K. et al. (1995). Hồ sơ hợp tác Việt Nam - Ba Lan: Tu sửa và phục hồi các di tích kiến trúc Chàm: Nhóm tháp Pô Klaong Girai, Phan Rang [Cooperation profile between Vietnam and Poland: repair and restoration of the Cham architectural monuments: The Po Klaong Girai complex,. Hà Nội: Viện Bảo Tồn Di Tích.

Lask, T., & Herold, S. (2004). An observation station for culture and tourism in Vietnam: A forum for World Heritage and public participation. *Current Issues in Tourism, 7*(4–5), 399–411.

Logan, W. (2001). Heritage significance and the intangible in Hanoi. *Vietnam. Historic Environment, 15*(3), 46–55.

Logan, W. (2009). Hanoi, Vietnam: Representing power in and of the nation. *City, 13*(1), 87–94. https://doi.org/10.1080/13604810902726251

National Assembly Vietnam. Law on Cultural Heritage, Pub. L. No. Law#28/2001/QH10, 23 (2001). Vietnam. http://www.unesco.org/culture/natlaws/media/pdf/vietnam/vn_law_cltal_heritage_engtof.pdf

The National Assembly of Vietnam. (2009). Law Amending and Supplementing A Number of Articles of the Law on Cultural Heritages, Pub. L. No. #32/2009/QH12 (2009). Vietnam. http://www.moj.gov.vn/vbpq/en/lists/vn%20bn%20php%20lut/view_detail.aspx?itemid=10463

Nguyen Duy Luong, & research team. (2015). Mapping cultural landscape in Phong Nha - Ke Bang region: several results. In *Understanding rights practices in the world heritage system: Lessons from the Asia Pacific* (p. 11). The Viet Nam Academy of Social Sciences & Ha Noi UNNESCO Office.

Park, S.-Y. (2013). *On intangible heritage safeguarding governance: An Asia-Pacific context.* Cambridge Scholars Publishing. https://books.google.com/books?id=WlkxBwAAQBAJ&pgis=1

Parmentier, H. (1909). Inventaire descriptif des monuments Cams de l'Annam: vol.I. Description des monuments. de l'Ecole francaise d'Extreme-Orient V 11. Leroux, Paris: de l'Ecole Francaise d'Extrême- Orient.

Parmentier, H. (1919). Surveys and Descriptions the Cham ruins in Central Vietnam in the early 20th century - Vol 2 (Vietnamese version). Paris: Leroux [Publications de l'Ecole Francaise d'Extrême- Orient 11].

Patrizia, Z. (2009). Results of the Archaeological Investigations at My Son G Group (1997–2007). In P. Z. Andrew Hardy, Mauro Curcazi (Ed.), *Champa and the archaeology of my son* (pp. 177–237). Singapore: NUS Press.

Phan, T. (2012). Language and hand writing documents of the Cham indigenous people in Vietnam in the study of cultural anthropology [Tiếng nói và văn bản viết tay của dân tộc bản địa ở Việt Nam trong Nghiên cứu Nhân học văn hóa]. In The Annual Conference of the Association for Asian Studies (AAS). Toronto, Canada. http://www.asian-studies.org/Conferences/AAS

Phuong, D. L. (2005). Preservation and promotion of the intangible cultural heritage in Vietnam (Some results and practical experiences). In *Sub-Regional experts meeting in Asia on intangible cultural heritage: Safeguarding and Inventory-Making Methodologies* (p. 6). Asia-Pacific Database on Intangible Cultural Heritage (ICH) by Asia-Pacific Cultural Centre for UNESCO (ACCU).

Phuong, T. K. (2002). Champa ruins: Essays on the temple-tower architectural form [Phế tích Champa: Khảo luận về kiến trúc đền-tháp]. *Nghiên Cứu Và Phát Triển, 1*(35), 75–78.

Phuong, T. K. (2006). Cultural resource and heritage issues of historic Champa states: Champa origins, reconfirmed nomenclatures and preservation of sites. SSRN Electronic Journal. https://doi.org/10.2139/ssrn.1317157

Phuong, T. K. (2008). *Vestiges of Champa Civilisation*. Thế Giới Publishers.

Phuong, T. K. (2011). The preservation and management of the monuments of Champa in central Vietnam: The example of my son ssanctuary, a world cultural heritage site. In G. Y. G. and S. O. John N. Miksic (Ed.), *Rethinking cultural resource management in Southeast Asia preservation, development, and neglect* (pp. 218–235). Anthem Press.

Roszko, E. (2011). *Spirited dialogues: Contestations over the religious landscape in central Vietnam's littoral society*. Martin-Luther-Universität Halle-Wittenberg. https://d-nb.info/102535 2424/34

Salemink, O. (2012). "Di sản hóa" văn hóa Việt Nam: Di sản văn hóa phi vật thể giữa các cộng đồng, Nhà nước và thị trường [The 'heritagization' of culture in Vietnam : Intangible cultural heritage between communities, state and market]. In The 4th International Conference on Vietnamese Studies: Vietnam on the Road to Integration and Sustainable Development (pp. 243–291). Hanoi: Vietnam Academy of Social Sciences.

Salemink, O. (2013). Appropriating culture: The politics of intangible cultural heritage in Vietnam. In H.-T. H. T. M. Sidel (Ed.), *State, society and the market in contemporary Vietnam: property, power and values* (pp. 158–180). https://doi.org/10.4324/9780203098318

Salemink, O. (2016). Described, Inscribed, Written Off: Heritagisation as (Dis)connection. In P. Taylor (Ed.), *Connected and disconnected in Vietnam: Remarking social relations in a post-socialist Nation* (pp. 311–345). ANU Press.

Saltiel, L. (2014). Cultural governance and development in Vietnam. *University of Pennsylvania Journal of International Law, 35*(3), 893–915. Retrieved from https://scholarship.law.upenn.edu/jil/vol35/iss3/6

Schweyer, A.-V. (2011). *Ancient Vietnam: History, art and archaeology*. River Books.

Stubbs, J. H., Thomson, R. G., & Menon, A. G. K. (2016). Architectural conservation in Asia: National experiences and practice. *Architectural Conservation in Asia: National Experiences and Practice*. London UK: Rougtledge. https://doi.org/10.4324/9781315683447

Tang, D. G. K., & L. H. (1994). *Lễ hội truyền thống trong đời sống xã hội hiện đại [Traditional Festivals in Modern Life]*. Social Sciences Publishing House.

Thien, N. N. (2017). Linking preservation of intangible cultural heritage with socio-economic development in Vietnam today. *Communist Review*, (892). http://english.tapchicongsan.org.vn/Home/Culture-Society/2017/1032/Linking-preservation-of-intangible-cultural-heritage-with-socioeconomic-development-in-Vietnam-today.aspx

Thinh, N. (2012). Di sản văn hóa Việt Nam: Bản sắc và những vấn đề về quản lý và bảo tồn [Vietnam's Cultural Heritage: Identity and Issues in Management and Conservation]. Xây Dựng.

Thuc, N. H. (2015). Nhận thức về di sản văn hóa Việt Nam qua một số văn bản của Đảng và Nhà nước [Awareness of Vietnamese cultural heritage through some legal documents of the Party and State]. *Vietnamese Cultural Heritage, 52*(3), 6–9.

Tieu, L. T., Doanh, N. Van, & Hung, N. Q. (2000). Giữ gìn những kiệt tác kiến trúc trong nền văn hóa Chăm [Preservation of the architectural masterpiece of the Cham culture]. Hanoi: Nxb Văn hóa Dân tộc.

Van, D. N. (2001). Preservation and development of the cultural heritage. In O. Salemink (Ed.), *Viet Nam's cultural diversity: Approaches to preservation* (pp. 33–62). UNESCO.

Viet, T. B. (2007). Champa temple-towers: Mysterious construction [Đền tháp Champa: Bí ẩn xây dựng]. Ha Noi: Construction.

Open Access This chapter is licensed under the terms of the Creative Commons Attribution 4.0 International License (http://creativecommons.org/licenses/by/4.0/), which permits use, sharing, adaptation, distribution and reproduction in any medium or format, as long as you give appropriate credit to the original author(s) and the source, provide a link to the Creative Commons license and indicate if changes were made.

The images or other third party material in this chapter are included in the chapter's Creative Commons license, unless indicated otherwise in a credit line to the material. If material is not included in the chapter's Creative Commons license and your intended use is not permitted by statutory regulation or exceeds the permitted use, you will need to obtain permission directly from the copyright holder.

Chapter 5
Living Heritage in the Everyday: Roles of Po Klaong Girai Temple in the Cham Community

Introduction

Pak ngaok hu Yang, pak ala hu Bimong
[In heaven are Gods, on the earth are temples]

This Cham idiom illustrates the vital position of temples as the most sacred places on earth for the Cham. If the gods hold the highest position in heaven, then on earth, temples secure the highest respect as they are the soul and the sacred symbols of the Cham community. Temples are the Yang's home on the earth, from where they reign and protect human beings.

Po Klaong Girai temple was named after the famous Cham King Po Klaong Girai. This temple holds a prominent position in the Cham community because of its unique architectural characteristics and its place in the historiography of South Central Vietnam. It is also one of the best-known Cham temples in Vietnam today since it is still closely connected to the Cham people through religious activities and cultural practices. The temple is a *"living sacred site"* because Cham people frequently visit the place and perform sacred rituals there. In this chapter, I explore the role of the Po Klaong Girai temple in the life of Cham people today. I investigate contemporary Cham views about the Po Klaong Girai temple, specifically concerning how it is used as a symbol for many cultural activities and everyday life events by the Cham community. A significant part of this chapter is devoted to the examination of how the Katé festival, as a living heritage performance, has become the most significant moment for many members of Cham communities to demonstrate their cultural identity and pride in their cultural heritage. I argue that inappropriate conservation and development that conflicts with Cham cultural values are likely to be rejected by the Cham community because this sacred living site is where the Cham maintain their spirituality, culture, and identity.

© The Author(s) 2023
Q. D. Tuyen, *Heritage Conservation and Tourism Development at Cham Sacred Sites in Vietnam*, Global Vietnam: Across Time, Space and Community,
https://doi.org/10.1007/978-981-99-3350-1_5

Contemporary Cham Views About the Po Klaong Girai Temple

King Po Klaong Girai holds a central place in the heart of the Cham people. He is considered a great king whose merits and contributions to Cham history and culture are worthy of recognition. The king has been worshipped in the Po Klaong Girai temple for generations, although no one knows precisely when this practice started. To shed light on the place of the Po Klaong Girai in Cham heritage, I explore contemporary Cham thoughts about the Po Klaong Girai temple through a review of informal dialogues and conversations I held with Cham religious leaders, elders, intellectuals, women, and youth. Those most closely connected with the Po Klaong Girai temple are the Ahier religious priests such as *Basaih, Kadhar, Muk Pajuw,* and *Ong Camânay.* They are not only in charge of preparing and performing the religious ceremonies but also help to ensure the temple is upkept and protected. The temple is closely associated with their lives, especially from the first days after which they inherit the position of religious dignitaries:

> When I was young, I often followed my Dad to the temple to worship. At that time, I did not know anything; I just knew that after rituals, there would be much food. Later, when I succeeded in my father's religious position, I would often go to the temple and act as the religious leader there. Who would have thought I would become the head of religion and administration at this temple! Po Klaong Girai temple has been attached to me since childhood and will continue to be even when I die. (Orang-Gu005)

Other religious dignitaries have also witnessed numerous changes at the temple over the decades:

> My life from childhood has been firmly attached to the temple. The temple is a part of my heart. I am a Basaih priest, so I often go up there so that I can easily recognise the transformation of the temple. I can see which bricks fall or which new bricks are inserted in the body of the temple. The temple is very sacred and has status because it is the place for the Gods - Yang and the Kings of the Cham. For religious dignitaries, the temple is even more sacred. In the past, nobody was allowed to come here. Only priests were allowed here. The rituals must have four *bangsa* (dignitaries) including Basaih, On Camânay, On Kadhar and Muk Pajuw. Without one of them, the door of the temple would not be allowed to open. For me, my life is too attached to the temple and I cannot separate myself from it. The temple is something so sacred that I cannot describe it. I feel proud and love it very much. I do not want to leave my temple. (Orang-Gu001)

It is not only priests who hold such sentiments about the Po Klaong Girai temple. Many other Cham people share these feelings. In numerous cases, temples are considered the most critical inheritance in the legacy of Champā people. Furthermore, according to a significant sector of the Cham population, the most important of all the temples is Po Klaong Girai, because of its association with King Po Klaong Girai:

> I think Po Klaong Girai temple is both Cham heritage and a place for the Cham community to serve in their spiritual life. Cham people are proud of the former king and honour him because he built the most significant agricultural works that are still in use by people today. For myself, the Cham temples are essential, but most especially Po Klaong Girai temple. Although the researchers have not clearly defined him yet, the Cham community still recognises Po Klaong Girai as one of the greatest kings of the Cham. (Orang-Ta002)

Ong Camânay is the Cham temple keeper, or in other words, the person directly tasked with taking care of and protecting the temple. He is proud of his role as a cultural steward, as well as a community coordinator connecting the temple to the community. *Ong Camânay's* son told me:

> Spiritually speaking, my old father did his duty here. Later he fell ill and handed all this over to me in the form of a contract as a security guard from 1995 to now. Currently, the temple is under the management of the State. However, I still have a responsibility, with my ancestors, to protect the temple. We must preserve the temple for the following generations. For me, as a Cham, Po Klaong Girai temple is a sacred place that should be guarded. I am proud of being a security guard to protect the temple because I continue my ancestor's work. There is nothing to compare to this joy. (Orang_Ta003)

Temples (*Bimong*) incorporate Cham history, architecture, art, and culture. They are physical manifestations of all of the symbolic elements of the Cham communities. The Cham people view Po Klaong Girai as a fulcrum around which the community can be centered and a point from which the history of Champā can be leveraged to promote solidarity in the Cham community, especially in the wake of traumatic historical events, such as the genocidal policies inflicted upon Cham communities during the reign of Minh Mang of Vietnam kingdom. Because of the fear of losing their cultural inheritance, many generations of Cham have been promoting the Katé festival to raise consciousness about preserving Cham culture in younger generations. I was fortunate to discuss this matter with one Katé organizer, Mr. Thanh Phu Ba, who in the 1950s began promoting the Katé festival to raise Cham awareness. As he explained, his generation tried to promote the Katé festival at Po Klaong Girai temple to preserve Cham culture, where temple is the host to the four most significant ceremonies among the Cham community. Today, whenever Mr. Thanh sees the image of people coming to the temple to celebrate the Katé festival, he explained how he feels a sense of happiness because he knows he and his friends have significantly contributed to helping Cham people become aware of, and feel proud about, their culture.

For Cham people, the temple awakens the spirit of their communities and the Katé festival is the activity during which Cham people express that spirit. For many local scholars, a sense of pride is furthermore found in how this temple contributes to the treasure of Vietnamese cultural heritage. One Cham scholar explained to me:

> I have seen Po Klaong Girai temple since I was a kid. My grandparents told me that the gods had made the temple because it is grandiose. I mean at that time, I did not understand how the temple appeared; when I grew up, I understood that the Cham temple was built by humans, by our Cham ancestors. I am very proud of Cham heritage today and feel that Cham temples have many significant cultural and historical values for the Cham people, as well as for the Vietnamese people. (Orang_Ka004)

For the younger Cham generation, the modernization of contemporary society has had a substantial impact on them. Although many young Cham people are now swept into the vortex of urban society, the majority of people in the younger generation view the temple as a sacred symbol of pride for the nation. The temple is, first and foremost, a place where Cham people practice religion and is also where they can maintain the value of Cham culture.

In the memory of many young Cham people, the temple was, during their child-hood, considered a quotidian part of Cham cultural heritage that demanded little attention. However, as adults, many people that I have grown up with expressed to me how they have begun to understand the significance of Po Klaong Girai. Today, more and more Cham people want to visit this sacred space to respect the glory of the ancient Champā kingdom and to connect with other Cham people. The temple has also become a space for Cham people to display their culture for tourists so that they can contribute to the development of tourism. Among these sacred and performative motivations for visiting this site, many people are increasingly proud of being Cham as their caretakers and elders have raised them with the knowledge about the role of the temple in the history of the Champā kingdom. One of my younger informants explained:

> When I was a child, my grandfather told the story about King Po Klaong Girai, the Champā kingdom and building temples. I dreamed that I would follow him to the temples. When I was 13 years old, he brought me to Po Klaong Girai temple. I was overwhelmed by the beauty of the temple and loved it. Since then, I often read books about the history of Cham to learn about the story of our Cham kings. I feel nostalgic when I think about how Champā disappeared, but I am very proud of the ancestors that left this beautiful temple. (Orang-De006)

Through my informal conversations, I have recognized that among teenagers the majority do not know much about the temple and do not see it as sacred in the same way as the older generations. In their eyes, Po Klaong Girai temple is a heritage site like any other part of Cham cultural heritage. However, one significant finding is that, for many, the temple awakens a sense of cultural pride and historical awareness. In particular, this growing metacultural awareness often develops in experiences taking their non-Cham friends to visit the temple. As some younger friends reflected:

> When I took my Kinh friends to the temple, they asked me why I saw Cham people often wear traditional Cham dresses to the temple, but you do not wear it. I felt ashamed at that time, but after that, I bought a new Cham traditional dress for the Katé festival. (Orang_Ra002)

> Sometimes, when we come here, my non-Cham friends ask us about Cham culture and the temple but we do not know how to explain it. This made us feel ashamed, but it led us to find out more about Cham culture on the internet. I found much information about Cham temples and the history of my Cham people. I was so surprised because Champā was an advanced civilization and had its kingdom, which I have never known before that. It was sad about the history of Champā but thanks to taking friends here [Po Klaong Girai temple], I discovered much more about the origins of Cham. (Orang Ra001)

In this way, Po Klaong Girai temple has become a connecting point to help younger generations develop a newfound sense of identity and spirituality when visiting the temple, or by seeking Cham cultural and historical information on the internet. Through these practices, the younger Cham generation can develop their understanding of the history and culture of their people, and further deepen their awareness of, and the desire for, preserving their ethnic culture.

Traditionally, each Cham family prepares offerings for worship at their temples during the Katé festival. Many visitors to Po Klaong Girai temple during this occa-sion are often impressed with the images of women who carry offerings to conduct religious ceremonies at the temple. Indeed, Cham women play a critical role in the ritual worship because they prepare offerings for the gods while men act only as supporters. Thus, women's views about the temple also help to underscore the role of Po Klaong Girai in their spiritual lives. With many women, the temple and the gods are sacred, and women have to know the taboos associated with them. Elders often pass down lessons on taboos to their daughters to ensure they do not inadvertently (or deliberately) defile the temple, for example by entering the temple while menstruating and thereby being punished by the Yang (gods). Although this may appear to be a minimal and seemingly insignificant issue, it can adversely affect perceptions of such a sacred place in Cham culture. With the current trend for tourism, many visitors do not pay attention to this problem; in fact, they are mostly completely unaware of the prohibitions and thereby unwittingly contribute impurity to the holy temple. Two women who participated in the Katé festival in 2017 elaborated:

> I remember when I was a teenager, my mother always advised me to stay at home if I was having my period. Other members of the family can go to worship. She said to me that Yang [Gods] and the temple are very sacred, and the place must be cleaned; hence, one cannot go to the temple during menstruation because the temple will be unclean, and Yang will punish members of the family. Therefore, I always advise my daughters and her friends to pay attention to this taboo because Po Klaong Girai temple is a holy place, so we all need to respect it and avoid making this place impure. (Orang-Ku001)

> The temple is very sacred to me. Every year, we must go there for our traditional ceremonies to pray for health and prosperity for our family members. That is our belief, but if there are days of taboos within the family, they will not go to worship. I believe in holy Yang for the Cham. All Cham also think like that. (Orang-Ku002)

Over the course of the twentieth and early twenty-first centuries, the temple has become a space for cultivating shared heritage and collective pride of the Cham community beyond the boundaries of religion. For example, there are ceremonies at the temple that incorporate the participation of Bani (Cham Awal) practitioners. According to folkloric tales, the kings or the generals who are worshipped in Cham temples, especially in Po Klaong Girai temple, are those who made great contributions for the entire Cham population. Thus, the legacy of the temples is for all Cham people without religious discrimination. In the Panduranga region, the last realm of the Cham people before 1834, the kings and generals of the Cham who are worshipped in the temples are the ancestors of the present-day people of the region. Although Hinduism strongly influences the Cham temples in this area, the gods are local, from the kings and contributors of the Cham people in history. As a *Cham Awal* priest told me:

> Po Klaong Girai temple is the legacy of all Cham, not just the Cham following Ahier (localised Hinduism). I followed Awal, but the king worshiped in the temple is our king and the common god of [all] Cham. Who can deny the history of our ancestors? The Cham following Ahier or Awal is of Cham blood. (Orang-Gu008)

For ordinary Cham Awal people, visiting the temples for worshiping or other activities is very common, but it is rarer with Awal religious dignitaries because of their traditional norm of not being allowed to go to Ahier temples. However, for some progressive Awal priests, the temples should not be distinguished as a product of religion only. According to them, Cham ancestors were also Hindu, and therefore, this temple is not only made by, and for, Cham Ahier, but rather the Cham population as a whole:

> There are very few Awal priests visiting the temple [now], but for me, I want to visit here. There is no taboo against Awal priests visiting the legacy of Cham people. When you conduct ceremonies, you do it at home. That is a part of your belief. Po Klaong Girai temple here is like ancestral heritage passed down to us. I come here to admire the miracle of our ancestors who created it. I also learn more about how Ahier Cham people celebrate the Katé festival. I do not distinguish whom the temples belong to because all are the descendants of Po Klaong Girai, the blood of Cham. (Orang-De008)

The many members of the Cham community who follow Islam are also proud of the Cham temples because they argue the temples are their ancestral cultural heritage too. However, at present, Cham Muslims do have a different view of the meaning of Cham temples. Because Islam is based on the religious belief in Allah as the single most important tenet of their religion, the kings/gods worshipped at temples are generally totally ignored, even though Cham Muslims are also their descendants. One young Cham Muslim recounted the following episode:

> Once, an Imâm called on me to talk. He asked why I wore Cham clothes to go to the Katé festival. He said "Our God is only Po Auluah, not some of those at the temple. We have our religious clothes". You know what? I was shocked about that perspective. I responded to him right away. I said "the kings are our Cham ancestors, not outsiders. Why did you say I did wrong?" I also wear traditional Cham clothes. I visit the temple for the pride of my national history. Nothing affects my Islam religion. I still practice Islam, but I am visiting Po Klaong Girai temple to participate in the ceremonies of the Cham people to know our Cham culture. You should not confuse the kings/the gods of the Cham with the religion of Islam. (Orang-De008)

The majority of Cham who are of the Sunni Islam faith are less associated with the temples than the Awal and Ahier communities. Meanwhile, both Awal and Ahier religious communities also worship Allah (Po Auloah in Cham), while the Awal continue to venerate certain supernatural beings and the kings/gods of the Cham. Currently, there is increasing recognition among Cham Muslims in the distinctions between their ancestral kings and their religion. As a result, a small part of the Cham Muslims in Chau Doc community (An Giang Province) do not deny their ancestral Champā history and their kings (Taylor, 2007). This demonstrates the secure place of Cham temples as a common heritage of all Cham people.

Po Klaong Girai temple plays a crucial role in the spiritual life of the Cham people, and it became one of the most important topics discussed at a 2017 conference held in remembrance of the 185 years since the loss of the Champā kingdom (1832–2017). At this conference, many activists and researchers discussed issues relating to the conservation and management of Cham temples. Following the conference, the Cham Council submitted a petition to the Vietnamese government with many clauses. The issues outlined in this document include the current major problems in the management of Cham temples in Vietnam in general and in Ninh Thuan Province in particular, which is mainly focused on the Po Klaong Girai temple.

In sum, the Po Klaong Girai temple holds immense significance for the Cham community, being considered as a sacred and vital part of their cultural identity and spirituality. The temple serves as a space to pay homage to King Po Klaong Girai and to raise awareness about the Indigenous heritage of the Cham people. For community leaders, it is a place to continue the legacy of their ancestors in preserving and promoting Cham culture and serving Cham spiritual life. Despite religious differences, the temple serves as a common ground for all members of the Cham community to connect and preserve their cultural heritage.

As a living heritage site, the members of the Cham community take their responsibilities to protect the temple and its cultural values seriously. The elders pass on their knowledge and teachings about the associated taboos to the younger generations, to maintain the purity and spirituality of the temple. Despite the decline of the Champā civilization, the Po Klaong Girai temple remains a symbol of spiritual and cultural identity for the contemporary Cham community. They celebrate their heritage through events such as the Katé Festival, which not only gives a deeper sense of identity to the modern and future generations of Cham people, but also presents their culture to the outside world. This makes the festival a colorful and meaningful celebration of Cham heritage.

Celebrating Living Heritage at Po Klaong Girai Temple: An Insight into the Katé Festival

The Po Klaong Girai temple plays a crucial role in the four main public ceremonies of the Cham people—Peh Bambeng Yang, Yuer Yang, Katé, and Cambur. Of these, the Katé festival is the most well known and well attended. In this section, I examine the role of the Katé festival in illuminating the evolution of Cham community traditions surrounding temple rituals. The Katé festival serves as a testament to the ongoing adaptation of Cham traditions to changing circumstances. Despite its evolution over time, the festival remains an important expression of Cham cultural heritage and identity.

Connections Between Cham and Raglai Cultures in Relation to Cham Temples

A unique aspect of the Katé festival is the involvement of the Raglai community, who are regarded as having a close relationship with the Cham compared to other ethnic minorities in Vietnam. According to Cham beliefs, the Cham and Raglai are considered siblings from the same family, with the Cham being the elder and the Raglai being the younger. Under the Cham matriarchal system, the youngest sibling is entitled to inherit property, keep family heirlooms, and serve the ancestors. As a result, in ancient times, the Raglai were tasked by Cham kings with the responsibility of safeguarding the king's belongings. Today, the Raglai still preserve traditional Cham clothing in their villages, and during the day of worship, they bring these traditional garments to the temple for the rituals. In return, the Cham prepare a special ceremony to welcome the Raglai participants.

Raglai people are warmly welcomed and considered as family members when they visit Cham villages. Before the main ceremonies at the temple, the Raglai people spend a day with the Cham community and participate in gatherings. This is the only official religious event where the Cham and Raglai communities come together throughout the year. The two communities then carry costumes to the temple, accompanied by musical performances and dances. During this procession, Raglai people, represented by village chiefs, elders, and dancers, take part in the ceremonial procession of King Po Klaong Girai along with dignitaries, Cham dancers, and the surrounding crowds—creating a sense of unity (see Fig. 5.1). Once at the temple, Cham women, musicians, and Raglai musicians perform their traditional music and dances. This event highlights the strong bond between the Cham and Raglai communities and adds to the vibrant atmosphere of the Katé festival.

The presence of Raglai people at the Katé festival reflects the former Champā administrative system. In the past, Raglai were responsible for safeguarding some of the king's possessions, while the Ong Camânei, the temple keepers, held onto the rest. The presence of Raglai at the Katé festival today perpetuates the historical relationship between the Cham and Raglai peoples and underscores the multi-ethnic character of the Champā kingdom (Dharma, 2012). The Katé festival thereby showcases the close connection between the Cham and Raglai while celebrating the unique

Fig. 5.1 Traditional clothing procession: Raglai men accompany the Cham community with musical instruments as they bring the King's attire to the Po Klaong Girai Temple *Source* Author, 2016

values of Cham cultural heritage. The Po Klaong Girai temple, as the venue for the festival, serves as a sacred space for the Cham people to express their spiritual and cultural values. Despite financial challenges that sometimes prevent many Raglai from attending other sites, the tradition of Raglai visiting Po Klaong Girai persists, thanks to the significance of the living cultural connection between the two groups.

The Role of Cham Religious Dignitaries in the Temple

The temple is a central place of worship for the Cham community and serves as a venue for various community rituals. It is here where they come to pay homage to their kings and gods. The activities of the Katé festival at the temple are managed by the Ahier priests, who play important roles in the ceremony. The head of the temple, the Po Adhia, acts as the master of ceremonies. The On Kadhar sing hymns, the Muk Pajuw offer holy offerings, and the Ong Camânei preside over the statue bath. The Basaih priests also support the ceremony. Each priest has a distinct role that has been passed down through generations.

The ceremony cannot commence without the participation of the four dignitaries who perform the opening of the temple. This technical procedure has been in place for hundreds of years and is a principle and tradition that the Cham community still holds dear to protect the sacred space for their gods. However, due to government initiatives to develop tourism, the temple has been open every day for tourists since the 1990s, breaking the accepted procedures of Cham cultural and religious views regarding sacred sites.

Today, when the Cham need to perform rituals, they must first inform the Relic Management Board in advance to close the temple before the priests come to open it again, as the management of the temple is now officially undertaken by the state authorities and not by the Cham community. This shift in traditional patterns of management and use demonstrates the crucial role of the state in the management of Cham temples and highlights the need for the Cham community to seek permission from the state to conduct traditional activities.

The religious ceremonies at the Po Klaong Garai temple reflect elements of Hindu religion that have been localized and transformed into a specific form of Hinduism known as the Ahier. This localized form of Hinduism includes a cosmologically dualistic relationship with the Awal (Dharma, 1987). Although Hindu priests have influenced the ceremonies, they have been adapted to include non-Hindu religious dignitaries such as the Kadhar, Camânei, and Muk Pajaw who only started partic-ipating in temple worship in the fifteenth century (Lafont, 2014). Additionally, the musical instrument, rabap/kanyi, played by the Kadhar in the Katé rituals, is closely related to the Malaysian rabap and became more popular in Cham areas after the fifteenth century (Sakaya, 2003).

This demonstrates the adaptability of the Cham community to external cultural influences and changes, as long as they align with their agricultural lifestyle and cultural foundation. The image of the current Cham priests and the instruments they use highlight the Hindu influence, but also show that the Cham are open to accepting other cultures and changes that they see as appropriate for their life and needs, not just for preservation of tradition (Nakamura, 2008).

Cultural Performance

The Katé was once just a religious ceremony performed by Cham priests and a few elderly worshippers. However, after 1967, more cultural activities such as traditional music and dance were added to the festival, making it the largest Cham celebration. Traditional dance and music have since become an integral component of the annual Katé festival, showcasing Cham's rich cultural heritage. This new tradition was invented by the Cham community for religious purposes and has been widely accepted as it does not conflict with existing Cham traditions. Today, the performance of dances and music is not only an important aspect of the Katé festival, but also an integral part of Cham temple rituals.

Cham people have a rich musical tradition that has greatly influenced Vietnamese music throughout the country (Addiss, 1971, p. 34). They possess a diverse array of musical instruments, including those in the percussion family such as ginang, baranâng, and ceng, brass family instruments like saranai and seng, and string family instruments like kanyi and rabap. The rabap is particularly used in the main ritual at the central tower, kalan, while other types of instruments and dances are performed in front of the temple.

Cham folk dances are a particularly important aspect of the Katé festival, with many different styles and forms, each with its own unique content. These dances are also used for religious services in other rituals such as Rija Nâgar, Rija Praong, as well as for social gatherings and cultural performances on stage. Some of the most popular styles include fan dances, water carrying dances, and many others. While most of these dances are performed during on-stage performances at the Katé festival, some ritual dances also take place during different rituals.

At the Katé festival, there is a group of performers who bring to life the traditional Cham music and dance during the procession of the clothing of the gods to the temple. These dances are performed alongside the traditional Cham instruments and serve as a prelude to the great ritual at the temple. While many traditional Cham ceremonies, such as Rija Praong, Rija Dayap, Rija Harei, or Chwa, showcase different types of dances and music within families, the Katé festival provides a platform for the public display of these cultural performances. Thus, the Katé festival at the temple and in the villages is a unique opportunity for the Cham community to showcase their rich cultural heritage not only to other Cham communities but also to visitors from around the world.

Contributions to the Local Community

The Katé festival is a significant gathering for the Cham people, who gather annually to express their devotion and offer gifts to the gods. It is also a time for the Cham community to contribute their support to maintain the rituals and festivals of their temple. The Council for Cham Brahman Dignitaries, who are responsible for organizing the event, calls upon the community for financial support. As a Cham priest stated, "They are delighted to support the council because they see the meaningful work that dignitaries are carrying out."

Through my fieldwork at Po Klaong Girai temple during the Katé ceremony, I observed that the Cham people are eager to contribute their support, with many donating what they can, regardless of the amount. As one member of the community noted, "Every year, I always donate a little money for dignitaries. I will give as much support as I can as long as I have a heart. 'Many a little makes a mickle'; that helps the dignitaries have money to prepare for the next rituals for the Cham community."

These donations from the community are essential as they serve as the primary source of funding for the dignitaries to maintain and promote the festival in the long term. The funds collected from tourism, while they may provide additional support, are not the sole source of funding for the event.

The Katé festival is also a chance for the Cham people to preserve and promote their unique cultural heritage. Through the performance of traditional dances and music, as well as the transmission of myths, legends, hymns, and folk stories, the festival provides a space for the preservation and promotion of Cham culture. The Po Klaong Girai temple, as the site of the Katé festival, serves as a sacred and cultural symbol for the Cham people, representing their pride and cultural identity.

In conclusion, the Katé festival is not only an opportunity for the expression of Cham spiritual culture, but it is also a site for the preservation and promotion of Cham cultural heritage. Each year, the festival and temple provide a space for the spiritual and cultural reproduction of the Cham community, serving as a vital symbol of their identity and pride.

Preserving and Celebrating Cultural Identity: Revitalizing Cultural Pride Through Iconic Representation

> I could not choose to be a child of the President of France
> or a grandchild in direct line of the King of Brunei
> I could not choose my birthplace in Thailand or America
> I am a Cham since the first cry in life
> Either when I am rooted here
> Or when I wander to the last horizon
> I am still a Cham, even when I burn up with the pyre at the end of life.
> Be joyful when we are forgotten by history

Be joyful when we survive
Be joyful when we still could shake hands, kiss, and drink in the evening.
It's fortunate that we have our heads, bodies, and four limbs intact
More fortunate that we still have parents, siblings, and friends
If by mishap something is lacking, we are still happier than the dead.
(Inrasara, 2002)

In his poem "The Riddle of Pauh Catwai" (2022), the Cham poet Inrasara captures the essence of Cham identity and the pride that the Cham community holds for their heritage and culture. Through his words, he highlights the idea that being a Cham is not a matter of choice, but an inherent part of who they are. Regardless of where they are born or live, the Cham identity is deeply ingrained and unshakable. The poet speaks to the resilience of the Cham people, who have endured adversity and suffering but have not lost their sense of pride and belonging. The preservation of their spiritual practices at the temple is a testament to the importance of their cultural heritage. Inrasara acknowledges the Cham's strong sense of community and their appreciation for the family and friends they still have. In the end, the poet declares that the Cham are happier than the dead, as they still have their heads, bodies, and limbs, as well as the relationships that they hold dear. The poem is a celebration of Cham identity, resilience, and pride. Through his words, Inrasara reminds the Cham people of their rich cultural heritage and the importance of preserving it for future generations.

Cham Temples: A Symbol of Cultural Identity and Spirituality

Cham temples are revered symbols of Cham cultural identity and spirituality. One of the most notable among them is the Po Klaong Girai temple, which is renowned for its architectural beauty and cultural significance. The Cham people use the image of the Po Klaong Girai temple in logos of organizations and associations as a symbol of their cultural identity and spirit, such as:

1. The Champā Cultural Preservation Association of United States
2. The International Office of Champā (IOC-Champā)
3. The Champā Culture and Tradition of the United States
4. The Council for the Social—Cultural Development of Champā
5. The Council of Indigenous Peoples in Today's Vietnam (CIP-TVN).
6. Cham Culture Research Center
7. Cham Studies
8. Cham Association in Saigon (Ho Chi Minh City).

The Po Klaong Girai temple serves as an iconic representation of Cham culture, history, and identity. It is a symbol of the Cham people's cultural authenticity and is a source of pride for the community. Even among young Cham people today, the

Po Klaong Girai temple continues to be used as a symbol of their cultural heritage (Fig. 5.2).

The use of the Po Klaong Girai temple image is also prevalent in Cham weddings. The temple serves as a symbol of both cultural identity and unity for young Cham couples. Through my experiences attending Cham weddings throughout Vietnam, I have observed that families often incorporate the image of the Po Klaong Girai temple in their wedding photos and decorations. This not only displays their pride in Cham culture but also adds a sense of joy and familiarity to their special day.

For many Cham couples, taking pictures at the Po Klaong Girai temple is a way to commemorate their love and make a wish for its longevity. Some even choose to wear traditional clothing at the temple to keep the traditions alive for future generations.

The Council for the Social-Cultural Development of Champa	Cham Culture Research Center	Cham Association in Ho Chi Minh City
The Council of Indigenous Peoples in Today's Vietnam	Cham Studies	Young Cham Road Trip group in Ninh Thuan
MblangKacak village	Khik Num Krung Preserving Tradition Group	Caklaing Brodace village

Fig. 5.2 Po Klaong Girai temple is frequently featured as a logo by various Cham organizations and associations

These photos serve as a historical document and a testament to the importance of preserving Cham culture.

During my fieldwork, I had the opportunity to speak with a couple taking their wedding photos at the Po Klaong Girai temple (as shown in Fig. 5.3). They shared with me their thoughts on the significance of this cultural and spiritual symbol in their lives and the lives of their community. According to the couple, they take pictures to put in their album for future generations to look back on with pride. The beauty of the Po Klaong Girai temple and traditional Cham clothing is an important symbol of their cultural identity. They believe that these photos, taken in traditional Cham clothing, will help their children and descendants understand and appreciate their cultural heritage. As Cham culture is likely to change significantly in the future, preserving these memories and symbols today will be of great value to future generations. As Orang_De006 said, *"What you keep today will undoubtedly be very valuable for your children later."*

The use of traditional clothing and the Po Klaong Girai temple as a backdrop in wedding photos is not only a display of cultural appreciation, but also a representation of Cham identity and pride. This increased visibility of Cham culture through visual media has made the Po Klaong Girai temple and Cham culture more meaningful and alive among the younger generation of Cham people. Social media has also played

Fig. 5.3 Wedding invitation from a young Cham couple (Designed by Jaya Thiên in 2016)

Fig. 5.4 Image of Po Klaong Girai is used as the banner each year for the biggest cultural performance by the Cham Association in Ho Chi Minh City (as captured in a photo by Inrajaya in 2014)

a role in this, with couples often sharing their photos as a symbol of their pride and to preserve their traditional culture.

As a founding member of the Cham Association in Ho Chi Minh City, I have witnessed the deep significance the Po Klaong Girai temple holds for young Cham people. They use the image of the temple to connect with their cultural roots and to represent the Cham community among those living in urban areas, particularly students studying in the city (Fig. 5.4). One prominent administrator of the Cham Association told me:

> The Cham Association in Saigon[1] is set up to connect the Cham members who live, study and work in Saigon to have the opportunity to sit together. The Po Klaong Girai temple is not only a logo of the association but also a crucial part of art and cultural performances of Cham people in Saigon that we aim to introduce to friends and guests of state authorities. Through this symbol, and the activity of the Cham association, we would like to introduce Cham culture here and want to raise awareness of the Cham culture in young Cham people who might be more influenced by modernity. (Orang-Gu007)

The use of the Po Klaong Girai temple image serves as a recognizable symbol for the Cham community in Ho Chi Minh City and helps to establish a sense of belonging

---

[1] Members of the Cham community often call the biggest city: "Saigon City," not Ho Chi Minh City, as "Saigon" is close to the Cham word "Baigour," and the Cham have been calling the city this name for ages.

outside of their homeland of Panduranga. A student who is a leader of a Cham youth group in the city expressed:

> We see this as a Cham national emblem so when making the logo on the soccer T-shirt, we are very proud of that. When using this logo for the group, we also want to affirm that, even when we go to study in universities far away from home, Cham culture and Cham temples will be important symbols and souls for us to strive to study, work and live here. (Orang-De007)

The image is also used as a banner in cultural performances by Cham communities in Vietnam and the United States, serving as a symbol of community affiliation, ethnic identity, and cultural authenticity. These activities help to introduce Cham culture to those outside of the community, raising awareness and encouraging preservation of Cham culture. A member of the Cham community living in the United States stated:

> Po Klaong Girai temple is used as a banner to introduce the image of Cham culture and encourage Cham people to preserve their cultural identity overseas. In parallel, through this representative image and cultural demonstration, it introduces, and calls to action different organizations and individuals from the homeland to overseas for protecting the essence of Cham culture, not only for the multiculturalism in Vietnam but also the preservation of human culture. (Orang-Ta005)

Therefore, the image of the Po Klaong Girai temple not only represents pride in Cham culture but also serves as a form of social action, through art and community programs, to preserve Cham culture and introduce it to others.

Celebrating Cultural Identity, Revitalizing Traditions, and Fostering Community Ties

The Katé festival holds a special place in the hearts of members of the Cham community as it is a time to connect with their rich cultural history. During the festival, the Kadhar priest performs a ceremony to invite the gods and former kings to attend the festival with the Cham community. Through the hymns performed by the Kadhar, Cham people learn about the history of their former kings and generals and are able to connect with their ancestry. The songs are filled with stories of the gods and legends of the Cham people. During the festival, the Ong Kadhar plays the rabap instrument and recites hymns related to each god, and the Cham people give offerings to the gods throughout the procession of the ritual.

According to one member of the Cham community, "*My grandparents told stories about the Cham former kings, but I was not interested because I was still a kid. However, today I hear the Kadhar sing the hymns and each hymn is a story of each god. When the name of each god is invited, we pray to that god for our health and peace. I learn a lot about Cham history and feel love for much of what our ancestors passed down [to us] for today*" (Orang-De005).

Another member of the Cham community said, "*I feel that this space is very sacred. Every time the name of the god is called it is like you relive the historical moments of each king and general of our Cham people. I feel that our previous generations have built and protected our kingdom and culture. That effort must be appreciated. I think that young people like us need to be responsible for preserving the legacy that our ancestors left behind. I feel proud and consider everything here as sacred*" (Orang-Ra002).

These sentiments reflect the cultural pride and connection to history that the Katé festival brings to the Cham community, and underscores the importance of preserving their cultural heritage for future generations.

These statements reveal that the Cham community has gained a deeper understanding of their history through the stories of their former kings and generals. These tales, often shared through hymns performed during the Katé festival and other Cham events, evoke a sense of pride and ethnic consciousness among Cham people and connect them to their former polities and civilizations. The combination of these hymns with the art of singing and the rabap instrument during the Katé festival creates a ritual rich in sacred cultural performance. As a result, the Katé festival serves not only as a means of preserving and promoting the tangible cultural heritage, literary values, and artistic performances of Cham culture, but also as a source of national pride for the Cham people.

In recent years, movements promoting Cham cultural pride have flourished, especially since the establishment of the Cham Association in Saigon in 2005. Before this time, attendance at the Katé ceremony was limited, with few young Cham participating and wearing traditional Cham dress to the temples. Modern and Western clothing was more prevalent, only being worn by the older generation. Many young people reported feeling uncomfortable wearing traditional Cham clothing at that time.

Nevertheless, today, traditional Cham clothing accounts for the majority of garments that people wear during the Katé (Fig. 5.5). "*I am extremely proud of our Cham attire*," says Orang-De005. "*Every year, I take the time to prepare beautiful traditional clothing for our community to wear during the Katé festival at Po Klaong Girai Temple. My friends and I take great pride in our preparations, and I feel proud seeing the stunning Cham attire worn by many of our people.*" This statement highlights the growing sense of pride in Cham culture and tradition, as evidenced by the increased popularity of traditional Cham clothing at the Katé festival.

Fig. 5.5 Cham and non-Cham friends dressed in traditional Cham attire during the Katé festival. *Source* Author, 2016

A young Cham man, aged 38, shared his thoughts on the significance of wearing traditional clothing during the Katé festival in an informal conversation with the author. He acknowledged that the resurgence of pride in traditional clothing among the younger generation has revitalized the festival and made it more appealing to the youth. As he stated, "*In the past, not many of my peers wore traditional clothes to the temple during the Katé festival. We were intimidated by it. I also didn't dare to wear traditional clothing there. But now, I can see that the younger generation is proud to don traditional attire and participate in the festival at the temple. It's even made our generation feel ashamed for not doing the same*" (Orang-Dem009).

Another young Cham expressed his feelings about the trend of wearing traditional clothing at the festival. He said, "*I have been wearing modern clothes for many years, but seeing everyone dressed in traditional Cham clothes at the festival made me feel out of place and embarrassed. Next year, I'll have to prepare some new Cham clothes for myself to blend in with the festival atmosphere, otherwise, everyone will make fun of me*" (Orang-Dem005).

This call was met with a positive response and sparked a renewed interest in the wearing of traditional Cham clothing during the festival. The increased awareness of the importance of preserving cultural heritage, as well as the desire to connect with one's roots, led to a resurgence of traditional Cham clothing at the Katé festival. As a result, the number of young people wearing traditional Cham clothes has increased significantly in recent years (see Table 5.1). The use of social media has been instrumental in spreading information about the traditional clothing and the importance of wearing it during the festival. This has helped to revitalize the festival, promote cultural heritage, and foster a sense of pride among the Cham people.

The photo challenge "Are You Ready?" during the 2017 Katé festival was a call to action for members of the Cham community to embrace their cultural heritage and participate in the festival in full traditional attire. The challenge was initiated on Facebook and encouraged members to post a photo of their traditional Cham dress, tag three or more friends to do the same, and include the hashtag "#AwChamPostChallengeKate2017." This social media campaign helped to create a festive atmosphere and increase the visibility of the Cham community's cultural heritage, as well as promote a sense of pride and unity among members.

This social media challenge quickly gained momentum, with a large number of participants from all over the world sharing their photos in traditional Cham attire. The use of Facebook as a platform allowed the message to reach a wide audience and encouraged more people to join in on the challenge. The photos that were shared as part of the challenge showed people of all ages and backgrounds proudly wearing traditional Cham clothing. The hashtag #AwChamPostChallengeKate2017 became a trending topic, showing the level of engagement and interest from the Cham community.

The success of this social media movement is a testament to the power of technology in promoting cultural pride and reviving traditions. By using Facebook, the organizers of the challenge were able to reach a large audience and create a sense of community among Cham people. This, in turn, has helped to keep the cultural traditions of the Cham people alive and flourishing (Figs. 5.6 and 5.7). Examples of photos shared as part of the "Are You Ready?" challenge during the 2017 Katé festival (*Source* Facebook, 2017).

Table 5.1 An example of calling for social movement

The response of Katé festival: "**Are you ready**?" is the name of the photo challenge for Facebook called AW CHAM POST CHALLENGE KATÉ 2017, which means wearing Cham clothing post-challenge during the 2017 Katé festival. The Katé is coming, so to make the festive atmosphere more bustling, we call to challenge all members of the Cham community. The challenge is as follows:

First, post a photo of a traditional Cham dress on your Facebook status or as an avatar

Next, challenge three friends or more to do the same by tagging them

Finally, write or copy this hashtag: #AwChamPostChallengeKate2017

We did it. What about you?

Nang Kim Uyen đã thêm 2 ảnh mới.
8 giờ · 🌐

Theo phong trào...
Chuy iêm nhà mình chuẩn bị áo mới hết rồi đợi ngày lên thôi......

hastag:#AwChamPostChallengeKate2017

Thoảng Đặng Kim Tagalau Mai Ka Vien Đang Ni Han Thi sao nè????? 😊
)))

P/s: Hoàng Vinh Bao Ngoc Hương Giang Duyen Thanh Nại Lưu Kala Lâm
Vấn năm này bọn mình đi như năm ngoái nữa hok?

Fig. 5.6 Young Cham individual posting online in response to a challenge to wear traditional Cham clothing in celebration of the Katé

Translated.

Following the movement…
Our families prepared new traditional clothes already, now just waiting to go up to the temple.
#AwChamPostChallengeKaté2017
Challenge: Thoang Đang, Kim Tagalau, Mai Ka, Hang Ni… are you ready?

p/s: Hoang Vinh, Bao Ngoc, Huong Giang, Duyen Thanh, NaiLuu Kalu, Lam Van
…

This year, will we go together like last year?

This challenge aimed to instill pride in the cultural heritage that has been preserved by many ancestors among young people. The Katé festival provided the perfect opportunity for members of the Cham community to express their pride and showcase their cultural identity. The response to the challenge was widespread, with not only Cham youth participating but also members of the Cham community, including those in Vietnam and the United States.

In the overseas Cham community, the movement served as a reminder of their cultural identity and encouraged them to maintain their cultural heritage despite

Fig. 5.7 Cultural movement in traditional dress being posted on social media

being far from their homeland. It also helped younger generations of Cham born in the United States to learn more about their cultural identity.

A Cham American, aged 54, expressed their delight at the enthusiastic response from young people and their participation in spreading the movement on social networks. The individual, who has children born in the United States who have never been to Vietnam, sees this as an excellent way for them to learn more about their national spirit and not forget their roots. They also mention that they order Cham clothes from Vietnam every year for their daughters to help keep their cultural heritage alive (Orang-Ta005).

The #AwCham challenge highlights the significance of material heritage in daily life and the influence of visual media on the preservation and dissemination of Cham cultural heritage. The challenge provides an opportunity for members of the Cham community worldwide, from Panduranga to the United States, to come together and celebrate their cultural identity, regardless of national borders, time zones, climates, political situations, and economic conditions.

The event that creates a collective sense of unity is deeply ingrained in the Cham cultural identity, which is exemplified in their traditional clothing. The Cham consider their attire to be an icon of their cultural identity, and the event reinforces this belief. Moreover, the Cham people's use of digital media and social networking to interact transnationally is an innovative practice that fosters a sense of community among them. By sharing their passion and appreciation for all things of Cham, such as their traditional clothing, food, music, and art, this practice strengthens the sense of togetherness and belonging among the Cham people, regardless of their geographical location. The practice serves as a means of connecting with others who share similar values and interests and reinforces the importance of preserving and promoting their cultural heritage. ("By sharing their love for all things Cham" refers to the Cham people using digital media and social networking to express their admiration and appreciation for their cultural heritage, such as their traditional clothing, food, music, art, and other aspects of their cultural identity. The practice helps to strengthen the sense of community among the Cham people who share a passion for their heritage and serves as a means of connecting with others who share similar values and interests.)

Today, there are several cultural movements that support a revival of ethnic self-awareness in the Cham community through the use of social media. Before each festival, many social media groups create events to inform people of the time of the festival and to encourage young people to participate in cultural movements. These efforts help address the need for preserving traditional cultural values that are at risk of being lost in contemporary society. The revival of ethnic and cultural pride of their ancestors helps maintain the traditional culture of the Cham and preserve it for future generations.

The Katé festival provides an opportunity for Cham people to connect not only through online social networks but also in person, as it is the most significant occasion for the Cham community to come together. Young Cham living in Ho Chi Minh City eagerly look forward to returning home for the festival, where they can reunite with their families and friends and participate in the cultural events. They also bring their non-Cham friends to the festival to introduce them to the Cham culture and festival, further promoting cultural awareness and understanding (Orang-Ra003).

The Katé festival serves as a platform for the promotion and preservation of Cham cultural heritage by introducing it to non-Cham friends. The presence of friends from different countries such as the United States, Malaysia, Philippines, and Cambodia adds to the significance of the event as it showcases the appeal of Cham culture beyond national borders. This year, a Cham student studying abroad brought a group of friends to the festival, including Cham descendants from Cambodia who were elated to be back in their ancestral land. As one friend said:

> Being at the Katé festival is an emotional experience for me. Growing up, I only heard stories about the Cham motherland from my grandparents and saw images of the culture on the internet. I never thought I would have the opportunity to visit. Thanks to my friend, I was able to attend the festival, meet the Cham community, and immerse myself in the rich cultural traditions. The sight of everyone dressed in gorgeous Cham clothing, making their way to the temple, was breathtaking. I hope to welcome you to Cambodia soon. (Orang_De010)

This celebration is not only a way to connect the Cham community but also to invite others to appreciate and respect the Cham cultural heritage.

Although the Katé festival is primarily known as a significant religious activity of the Cham Ahier community, members of the Awal Cham community also participate in the worship at the temple. During the festival, gods from both the Cham Ahier and Awal histories are worshipped, including Po Tang Ahaok, Po Riyak, Po Haniim Par, and Po Nai Mâh Ghang who appeared during the period of King Po Rome (Sakaya, 2013, p. 256). At the Po Rome temple, Awal community members from Pamblap villages participate in the festival because they are descendants of King Po Rome, while at the Po Klaong Girai temple, Awal families from Ram village attend (Noseworthy, 2013). One woman from the Awal community who worships at Po Klaong Girai temple explained: *"My family has been worshiping at the Po Klaong Girai temple for many years, so whenever Katé season comes, my family will bring offerings there for worship. I do not know why my family worships here, but my ancestors did that, so I have to follow. I do not think the temple belongs only to Ahier Cham; it is for all Cham. Everyone thinks like that. I am also a Cham, so I come here to worship my ancestors and my Cham gods. That is normal. My daughters will keep this tradition like me"* (Orang-Ku003).

Therefore, the Katé festival is not only a place for the Cham Ahier community to come together, but it also serves as an opportunity for other members of the community to meet friends and perform spiritual practices. The Po Klaong Girai temple, as a Cham heritage site, is a sacred space that is still very much alive and relevant to the local community. The activities and rituals performed at the temple during the Katé festival imbue the community with a deeper sense of their Cham cultural history.

The Intersection of Community, Cultural Identity, and Social Media in Shaping Self-Perception

> Identity is mostly in the process of change; it is never frozen. Being able to recreate one's identity requires bravery. It takes bravery to conquer something but knowing how to destroy it is more courageous hundred times over. If we keep embracing an [old] identity, we will isolate ourselves from the world around us. Moreover, then we will disappear! (Inrasara, 2018—my translation)

In this piece, Inrasara offers his artistic perspectives on the themes of identity, tradition, and creativity. He argues that identity is a constantly changing and evolving process, and that the ability to recreate one's identity takes bravery. He encourages the Cham people to embrace change and not to become trapped within the confines of tradition. Through this exploration, Inrasara highlights the importance of being open to new experiences and perspectives in shaping our understanding of self.

In this section, the author delves into the relationship between tradition and new cultural practices in the Cham community. It is argued that new cultural practices can complement or supplement traditional culture and meet the needs of the community in the present, rather than destroying tradition. However, challenges such as authenticity and commodification often arise from outside sources and are met with resistance from the Cham community. The author discusses the ways in which members of the Cham community perceive and respond to these threats to their cultural heritage.

Identity continues to be an important topic of discussion among Cham intellectuals, as evidenced by the numerous conversations taking place on social media platforms like Facebook and Blogger. In October 2018, several debates emerged around the topic of identity and its relation to Cham culture and traditions. The poet Inrasara sparked a debate about the balance between destruction and creation in shaping identity, while political activist Thanh Dai called for a shared sense of identity among the global Cham diaspora. The writer TraViya warned of the dangers of changing traditions too quickly and carelessly, while Ba Van Trinh explored the challenges posed by social change to traditional Cham women's costumes. These debates reinforce the idea that traditional Cham identity is under threat from contemporary society and tourism development.

Inrasara, TraViya, and Ba Van Trinh believed that Cham identity is not a fixed entity, but is constantly being negotiated and redefined within the community. They argued that tradition must be adapted and updated over time, but that this process must be carried out with caution, taking into account both positive and negative consequences. Thanh Dai, on the other hand, emphasized the importance of identity for protecting Cham traditions and securing the rights of the Indigenous community.

TraViya also shared his perspective on Cham traditions in the context of change. He argued that while some traditional practices may need to be revised or eliminated to suit modern times and lifestyles, care must be taken to ensure that the essence of Cham culture is not lost in the process. Young people must be cautious when considering changes to tradition and must thoroughly understand the consequences of their actions. He emphasized that preserving the tradition of a people requires a deep understanding of its meaning and value, and a love and hope for the tradition itself (TraViya, 12/2018).

In addition to the thoughts shared by TraViya, other members of the Cham community hold similar views about the need for caution when it comes to adopting changes to traditions. I had several discussions with village elders, intellectuals, and younger members of the community, and they all agreed that it is important to consider the impact of changes on Cham traditions.

While changes imposed from outside the community are often met with resistance and negativity, local innovations and initiatives that complement traditional practices are perceived positively. For example, the use of traditional Cham script and images of Cham temples on T-shirts was seen as a new form of expression that respects and pays homage to the history of the Champā civilization. This innovation has helped to bring elements of Cham heritage into the mainstream and has increased cultural pride among young people. However, some older members of the community expressed concern that younger generations are becoming disconnected from their ancestral roots and the rich history of the Cham people. They believe that it is important for young people to understand the significance of tradition and the importance of preserving it for future generations. In short, Cham identity is a dynamic category that is constantly being negotiated and redefined. While it is important for the community to embrace change and innovation, it is equally important to be mindful of the impact that these changes may have on the preservation of traditional Cham heritage.

The Champā civilization, which existed from the second century to the nineteenth century AD, has left a lasting impact on the Cham community in Vietnam. Today, only a small fraction of the Cham people still exist, but they have managed to maintain their cultural heritage and identity as one of the 54 ethnic groups in the country. To preserve their heritage, Cham people draw upon their spiritual beliefs and affirm their ethnic identity, as seen in places like Ninh Thuan and Binh Thuan provinces.

However, development and tourism can pose a threat to the integrity of Cham identity. The community is concerned about the risk of cultural encroachment and the need to maintain their cultural traditions and independence. To this end, Cham people have embraced some changes within the community, such as the production of Cham-themed t-shirts, to express their cultural pride and adapt to new social and historical conditions. According to Thanh Le (2015), Cham identity can be considered both "integrated" with the national culture and "becoming," as Cham people continue to preserve their cultural heritage while also embracing new elements. Thus, to preserve the culture of minority groups like the Cham, state authorities and heritage managers need to promote their relative historical and ethnic independence.

Social media has emerged as a crucial tool for expressing cultural identity and pride among Cham people in Vietnam. As observed by numerous social scientists (Baron, 2013; Postill & Pink, 2012; Sage, 2013; Sedlacik, 2015), social media has become a platform for individuals to voice their opinions on social issues and shape their impact on the world. Cham people are utilizing these online platforms to showcase their cultural heritage, particularly through the use of symbols such as the Po Klaong Girai temple as their profile backgrounds or avatars.

Not only does social media help in spreading information about Cham culture, but it also offers a space for the Cham community to reflect on the challenges and issues surrounding conservation and tourism development. As Postill and Pink (2012) argue, social media provides a multivocal representation of these issues and amplifies the voices of young Cham people who use these platforms to critique contemporary management practices.

Moreover, social media has played a significant role in preserving and promoting Cham cultural values. It has made it easier to disseminate images and information about Cham heritage and cultural events, which has helped to raise awareness and stimulate a sense of pride in Cham cultural identity among young people. This aligns with Baron's (2013) findings that social media, especially Facebook, serves as a platform for youth expression and socio-political participation, and contributes to the legitimization of information and voice building in social movements. In sum, social media has proven to be an effective means of conveying Cham cultural heritage and promoting cultural pride among young people. By providing a space for multivocal representations of cultural and social issues, social media has helped the Cham community to preserve and promote their cultural values, and has enabled the dissemination of information about Cham culture beyond national and international boundaries.

Social media platforms have emerged as a crucial tool for marginalized communities to voice their concerns and participate in preservation efforts on a local and national level (Sedlacik, 2015). In the case of the Cham people, Po Klaong Girai temple symbolizes their cultural heritage and serves as a source of inspiration for the community to reconnect with their cultural roots.

Social media provides an opportunity for young Cham people to actively promote and preserve their cultural heritage by raising awareness and educating their peers about the significance of their cultural values. Through online platforms, the Cham can disseminate information about their cultural heritage quickly and effectively, increasing their symbolic capital and stimulating a sense of pride in their cultural identity. Moreover, social media platforms allow the Cham community to express their views and participate in discussions about the preservation of their cultural heritage and the challenges posed by tourism development. The ability to share their thoughts and opinions on these topics through social media provides the Cham with a powerful platform to engage with the world and bring attention to their cause.

In conclusion, social media will continue to play a key role in amplifying the voices of marginalized communities, including the Cham, in their efforts to preserve their cultural heritage. Po Klaong Girai temple is a testament to the importance of cultural heritage for the Cham people and serves as a symbol of their cultural identity, one that they are determined to preserve for future generations.

Conclusion

In all these ways, the Po Klaong Girai temple plays a central role in the spiritual and social lives of the Cham people. Representations of the temple are not limited to Ninh Thuan Province but are carried by Cham people across different locations, both within Ho Chi Minh City and overseas. The annual Katé festival showcases the Cham culture's dynamic nature and highlights the community's efforts to promote and preserve their cultural heritage.

The relationship between the tangible heritage of the temple and the living heritage of the Cham people is complex and mutually constitutive. The temple's architecture is imbued with meaning as religious practices are carried out there, while these practices are meaningful as they take place in a sacred space. The temple serves as a symbol of Cham identity, cultural authenticity, and heritage preservation, reflecting the Cham community's attempts to enrich their culture and reclaim their identity.

In Ninh Thuan Province, the preservation of Cham culture is seen as a priority for developing tourism and promoting the socio-economic growth of the region and its people. Local authorities have taken steps to restore Cham temples and upgrade their infrastructure, and the Po Klaong Girai temple has been actively promoted as a tourist destination.

The conservation of living heritage is a complex process, involving authenticity, commodification, community identity, and discursive practices on social media. In the face of globalization, the Cham community is increasingly looking to affirm their cultural pride as a means of preserving their heritage. Social media provides a valuable platform for Cham people to express their sentiments and opinions about heritage preservation, both domestically and globally, and engage in discussions with the government and heritage managers.

References

Addiss, S. (1971). Music of the Cham peoples. *Asian Music, 2*(1), 32–38. https://doi.org/10.2307/833811

Baron, L. F. (2013). *The power of associations social media and social movements: Facebook in the interactions of social movement organizations.* University of Washington.

Dharma, P. (1987). Le Paɖurajga (Campa) 1802–1835. *Bulletin de l'Ecole Française d'Extrême-Orient—BEFEO*, Vol. 1–2.

Dharma, P. (2012). *Kate: Lễ tục của người Chăm Ahier hôm nay.* Retrieved June 11, 2018, from http://www.champaka.info/index.php/quandiem/quandiemtinnguong/533-kate-l-tc-

Inrasara. (2018). *Chăm sống sót, làm gì? Bảo tồn bản sắc làm gì?* Retrieved November 22, 2018, from https://www.facebook.com/photo.php?fbid=2159005530796822&set=a.747774055253317&type=3

Lafont, P. B. (2014). *The kingdom of Champa: Geography, population, history.* International Office of the Champa.

Le, L. T. T. (2015). Representation of Cham's ethnic identity through a cultural festival organized by the state. In *Interdisciplinary study in social sciences and humanities.* Vietnam National University. https://doi.org/10.13140/RG.2.1.3858.4487

Nakamura, R. (2008). The Cham Muslims in Ninh Thuan Province, Vietnam. In *Islam at the margins: The Muslims of Indochina* (CIAS Discussion Paper No. 3, pp. 7–24). https://www.cias.kyoto-u.ac.jp/files/pdf/publish/ciasdp03.pdf

Noseworthy, W. (2013). *Reviving traditions and creating futures*. International Institute for Asian Studies. The Newsletter, pp. 12–13. https://iias.asia/the-newsletter/article/reviving-traditions-and-creating-futures

Postill, J., & Pink, S. (2012). Social media ethnography: The digital researcher in a messy web. *Media International Australia*. https://doi.org/10.1177/1329878X1214500114

Sage, A. (2013). The Facebook platform and the future of social research. In *Social media, sociality, and survey research*. Wiley. https://doi.org/10.1002/9781118751534.ch4

Sakaya. (2003). *Lễ hội của ngư`ời Chăm* [The festivals of the Cham people]. NXB Van Hoa Dan Toc.

Sakaya. (2013). *Tiếp cận một số vấn đề văn hóa Champa* [Approaching some problems of Cham culture]. Tri Thuc Press.

Sedlacik, M. (2015). Social media and heritage preservation. *Present Pasts, 6*(1). https://doi.org/10.5334/pp.60

Taylor, P. (2007). *Cham Muslims of the Mekong Delta: Place and mobility in the cosmopolitan periphery*. Asian Studies Association of Australia. http://www.uhpress.hawaii.edu/p-5020-978 0824831547.aspx

Open Access This chapter is licensed under the terms of the Creative Commons Attribution 4.0 International License (http://creativecommons.org/licenses/by/4.0/), which permits use, sharing, adaptation, distribution and reproduction in any medium or format, as long as you give appropriate credit to the original author(s) and the source, provide a link to the Creative Commons license and indicate if changes were made.

The images or other third party material in this chapter are included in the chapter's Creative Commons license, unless indicated otherwise in a credit line to the material. If material is not included in the chapter's Creative Commons license and your intended use is not permitted by statutory regulation or exceeds the permitted use, you will need to obtain permission directly from the copyright holder.

Chapter 6
Examining Overlooked Living Traditions: An Analysis of the Conservation of Sacred Places in the Cham Culture of Vietnam

Introduction

In the year that followed, my grandmother and I embarked on a journey to Klaong Girai temple to participate in the Yuen Yang ritual, one of the most significant public ceremonies in the Cham culture. As we hiked up the hill, we were taken aback by a newly constructed walkway to the east that many young Indigenous Cham people were using to approach the temple. This was unexpected as Cham people had always followed the southeast route to the temple.

However, my grandmother refused to take the new path as it approached the temple from the direction of god Po Yang, and violating this sacred place would result in severe punishment by Yang. We continued to follow the traditional route to the temple, witnessing dignitaries conducting a small ritual in each direction before the main ceremony began.

This experience was a powerful reminder of the importance of cardinal directions in Cham culture and the significance of preserving traditional customs and practices. It highlighted the role of cultural heritage in shaping the identity of a community and the need to honor and respect their beliefs and traditions.

As we approached the temple, we noticed a generational divide in the Cham community, with younger members embracing change and innovation while older members remained steadfast in their adherence to traditional practices. It was a poignant reminder of the importance of striking a balance between modernization and preservation, ensuring that cultural heritage is not lost in the pursuit of progress.

Our visit to Klaong Girai temple left a lasting impression on us, underscoring the deep-seated cultural traditions and practices that have been passed down through generations of the Cham people. It reinforced the criticality of preserving these traditions and recognizing and respecting the cultural identity of Indigenous communities.

Furthermore, this story highlights the tension between traditional beliefs and the construction of a new path that conflicts with Cham philosophy regarding cardinal

© The Author(s) 2023
Q. D. Tuyen, *Heritage Conservation and Tourism Development at Cham Sacred Sites in Vietnam*, Global Vietnam: Across Time, Space and Community, https://doi.org/10.1007/978-981-99-3350-1_6

directions. It serves as a microcosm for the challenges facing the preservation and promotion of Cham heritage in Vietnam today. In light of this incident, I aimed to explore the reactions of the Cham community to the construction of the new path and to better understand the conflicts arising between tradition and modernization in sacred sites. This study will delve into the intricacies of the situation, examining the impact of the new path on the Cham community from their perspective.

The annual rituals performed by the Cham in their sacred temples, along with their religious management system, reflect the importance placed on the conservation and development of their sacred places (Tuyen & Anh, 2018). In 2011, the construction of a new pathway to the Po Klaong Girai temple from the east direction, which is considered sacred by the Cham, elicited strong reactions from the members of the Cham community. This reaction highlights the complexities surrounding the conservation and promotion of Cham heritage in the context of Vietnam's tourism industry.

The shift towards "market socialism" and increasing global economic connections, particularly with Japan and the United States, have resulted in the commodification of Indigenous culture to serve the growing tourism industry. Indigenous culture is seen as an exotic experience by tourists and is perceived as authentic only if it reflects change. As a result, the Vietnamese professional management class (Kinh) has played a role in the promotion of Indigenous culture as a tourist commodity. However, this commodification often conflicts with the traditional beliefs and values of the Cham community, as seen in the reaction to the construction of the new pathway to the Po Klaong Girai temple. Thus, the tension between preserving cultural heritage and promoting tourism is a complex issue that requires careful consideration and dialogue between various stakeholders.

In the Ninh Thuan Province of Vietnam, the priority of economic development is evident in legislative planning, often at the expense of cultural preservation initiatives. The tourism industry plays a crucial role in the province's economic growth and the preservation and promotion of Cham cultural heritage is seen as a key tourist attraction (Dop et al., 2014; Phan, 2015). Despite efforts by local authorities to preserve Cham heritage, tensions between government authorities and members of the Cham community have arisen.

This chapter will examine a particular case study in which a seemingly small event caused significant controversy within the Cham community and sheds light on the importance of respecting traditional views and meanings of Indigenous cultures and their built heritage, such as the Po Klaong Girai temple. The study will argue that the preservation of living heritage should be the primary focus in both heritage conservation and tourism development, in order to promote harmonious coexistence and enhance the effectiveness of tourism in ethnic minority sacred sites.

The Significance of Living Heritage in Heritage Conservation

The concept of living heritage has long been recognized as a crucial aspect in the definition of heritage. In fact, international organizations have acknowledged the living dimensions of heritage sites since the 1990s. In 1994, the Nara Document on Authenticity released by ICOMOS emphasized the significance of taking into account the spiritual and social values embodied in a heritage site. The document emphasized that all these values must be respected and that the tangible and intangible factors that make up a heritage site should be understood. This means that a heritage site can still be considered "authentic" even if its physical appearance has changed, as long as it retains its intangible qualities.

The protection of living heritage has been given due recognition by the international community only in recent times. While the World Heritage Convention, which was adopted in 1972, encompasses cultural and natural forms of heritage, the protection of intangible cultural heritage was not explicitly mentioned. This gap was addressed with the adoption of the 2003 Convention for the Safeguarding of Intangible Cultural Heritage (CSICH), which recognizes the need for conserving "living heritage" as a crucial component of maintaining cultural diversity. According to UNESCO (2003), living heritage includes traditions, practices, and skills that are passed down through generations, and it provides a sense of identity and continuity to the local people. This includes oral traditions, the performing arts, social practices, rituals and festive events, knowledge and practices concerning nature and the universe, and traditional craftsmanship. The preservation of living heritage not only showcases human creativity and diversity but also plays a crucial role in the preservation of cultural identity. By ensuring that the knowledge and skills embodied in the intangible cultural heritage are passed down from one generation to the next, living heritage contributes to the continuation of cultural heritage and its evolution.

The understanding and definition of heritage has long been a subject of debate among scholars and researchers. According to Smith (2006), heritage cannot be defined simply as objects or "things." Instead, she argues that heritage is created through various cultural and social activities, and it is only through these activities that value and meaning are assigned to the objects, turning them into heritage. This view challenges the conventional understanding of heritage as being solely focused on material fabric and instead emphasizes the importance of values and meanings.

Similarly, Harrington (2004) sees heritage as something that is not just about the past, but it also connects people to a distant time or place in the present. This definition highlights the central role of intangible components of heritage in the management paradigm. In line with earlier work by Byrne (1991) and others, Smith (2006) stresses the significance of values and meanings over materiality. She argues that there is no single understanding of heritage, and it should be seen as a system of values rather than just physical objects. This perspective is also reflected in the work of Harrison (2013), who views heritage as a set of values rather than a concern with materiality. The study, therefore, draws on the frameworks that emphasize the importance of understanding the meaning of heritage, as highlighted by Smith and Waterton (2009).

According to recent research by several scholars, the Asian region is distinct from the west in its material, cultural, and historical makeup (Byrne, 2012; Daly & Winter, 2012; Karlström, 2013; Silva & Chapagain, 2013; Winter, 2012). Winter (2012) suggests that there are varying historical and philosophical views on authenticity, spirituality, and historical significance, and that the ways in which cultural heritage is valued and interpreted should be considered in a culturally specific context. Chapagain (2013b) notes that Asian countries place greater emphasis on the "living heritage" aspect of cultural heritage, where the intangible aspects such as worldviews, traditions, beliefs, and everyday experiences are intertwined with the tangible elements, rather than being solely focused on physical structures.

The preservation of heritage sites in Zimbabwe often highlights the tension between external and community-based approaches to heritage conservation. This can be seen in the case of the Domboshava rock shelter, where experts focused on the tangible elements of the site such as its aesthetic and scientific value (Chirikure et al., 2010; Chirikure & Pwiti, 2008), while ignoring the perspectives and practices of the traditional owners, who valued the site for its intangible dimensions, including spiritual rituals (Chirikure et al., 2010; Chirikure & Pwiti, 2008). This disregard for the community's perspectives and practices created conflict in the management and interpretation of the site, highlighting the need for a more inclusive and culturally sensitive approach to heritage conservation.

The assessment of the value of heritage sites is never a neutral process, as it reflects the ideologies and epistemological views of those making the assessment (Byrne, 1991, p. 274). In the case of Domboshava, the focus on tangible elements of the site disregarded the spiritual significance it held for the local community, emphasizing the need to consider both the tangible and intangible dimensions of heritage in conservation efforts (Byrne, 1991, p. 274). The preservation of heritage must involve community participation and respect for the spiritual practices of Indigenous peoples to truly reflect the significance of the site for all those involved.

This emphasis on intangible cultural heritage reflects a broader trend in heritage conservation, which recognizes the significance of both tangible and intangible forms of heritage. This shift towards a more inclusive approach is necessary because intangible cultural heritage provides the context and understanding that enhances the richness of tangible heritage (Smith, 2006, p. 56). Wain (2014, p. 56) highlights the importance of conserving both tangible and intangible heritages, as intangible heritage is essential to the survival of tangible heritage. Focusing solely on tangible heritage sites may overlook the lived heritage practices of local communities, which are an integral part of heritage preservation (Weise, 2013).

In Vietnam, the Law on Cultural Heritage reflects a growing recognition of the value of cultural heritage to national development and preservation. The law has been updated to include effective management of intangible cultural heritage, reflecting the importance of considering both tangible and intangible forms of heritage. The government recognizes the role of cultural carriers as essential to the preservation of cultural heritage, and the law focuses on preserving cultural practices embraced by individuals, groups, or communities of people. By focusing on the cultural carriers, Vietnam's cultural preservation efforts are aimed at ensuring the survival and vitality of both tangible and intangible forms of heritage for future generations.

Since the 1990s, there has been an increasing interest in using tourism development as a way to mitigate the negative impacts of development and enhance the positive effects of tourism activities on society, traditional culture, and regulation and development management (Bramwell & Lane, 2012; Buckley, 2012; Sharpley, 2000). Heritage resources are viewed as valuable assets for economic development in Vietnam, leading the government to take a keen interest in preserving and promoting cultural heritage (Thien, 2017). Although heritage authorities and practitioners recognize the importance of community involvement in theory, local communities are often not given opportunities to participate in heritage management, either due to the limitations imposed by heritage management legislation or their community's traditional customs (Larsen, 2017).

In recent years, Western-style heritage management has dominated the industry, giving priority to the role of experts and relegating the role of local communities to secondary status (Byrne, 2012; Karlström, 2005; Kong, 2008; Poulios, 2014). This approach primarily focuses on the physical value of objects, buildings, and sites, rather than the beliefs and actions of people (Byrne, 2004; Giang, 2015; Silva & Chapagain, 2013; Sullivan, 2004; Wharton, 2005). This perspective has been codified in various charters and legislation, such as the Athens Charter (1931), Venice Charter (1964), and the World Heritage Convention (1972). However, there is an increasing recognition of the importance of intangible heritage elements in both local and international heritage management systems. Policies and principles that are more inclusive of intangible heritage and local communities, such as the Nara Document (1994), the updated Australian Burra Charter (2013), the Convention for the Safeguarding of Intangible Cultural Heritage (2003), and the Hoi An Protocols (2009), acknowledge the role of intangible heritage elements in local beliefs and values (Sully, 2007; Wain, 2014; Weise, 2013; Wijesuriya, 2008). The inclusion of intangible heritage elements is essential to maintain the meaning and significance of heritage sites, as living heritage elements are necessary to give materiality to heritage (Saar & Palang, 2009; Smith, 2012; Weise, 2013).

Challenges in Balancing Heritage Conservation and Tourism Development in Ninh Thuan Province

The Vietnamese government's efforts to develop tourism in Ninh Thuan Province, utilizing the rich Cham cultural heritage as a key resource, has led to the creation of many Cham cultural products for tourists. However, these products may not accurately reflect the Indigenous Cham culture, potentially misleading both Vietnamese and foreign tourists. Despite implementing policies to protect and preserve Cham temples, some negative impacts have arisen from tourism development in the region.

Some of the key issues include performances at the temple that disturb its sacred character, opening the temple's doors on taboo days, allowing inappropriate behavior that goes against Cham cultural and religious practices, intervening in traditional Cham festivals, and tolerating graffiti and billboards in the temple area. Additionally, the economic benefits from tourism are not shared with the Cham community, and the community is often neglected in decision-making processes regarding their heritage.

In this chapter, I will use the construction of new eastern pathways at the temple by state authorities as a case study to illustrate the ongoing challenges in balancing the development of tourism with the preservation of cultural heritage in Ninh Thuan Province. I will begin by providing a comprehensive overview of the heritage conservation efforts at the Cham temples in the area. Then, I will delve into how the construction of the new pathway impacted the cultural significance of the temple and created a disconnection with the living heritage.

Furthermore, I will examine why the government and other stakeholders failed to properly incorporate the perspectives and traditions of the Cham community in their decision-making processes, despite their crucial role in preserving their heritage. To conclude, I will propose practical solutions and best practices for promoting the harmonious development of tourism and cultural heritage preservation, particularly for the Cham community. This will include suggestions for involving the Cham community in decision-making, raising awareness about the significance of their cultural heritage, and implementing culturally sensitive conservation practices. The objective is to emphasize the need for preserving the cultural authenticity and significance of heritage sites, while making them accessible and appealing to tourists without compromising the traditions and well-being of local communities.

The Conservation of Cham Heritage Sites in Vietnam

Despite its cultural significance, the preservation of this temple has been largely neglected, with only individual measures taken by Vietnamese archaeologists and architects (Phuong, 2006). This is in stark contrast to the well-maintained and protected UNESCO World Heritage Site of My Son, which has received significant attention from conservation specialists.

Over three periods of restoration and conservation of Cham architecture (the French Colonial [1902–1954], the Polish-Vietnamese conservation [1975–1998], and the contemporary period [from 1999 to today]), efforts have primarily focused on preserving tangible forms of heritage by reinforcing the structure of the temples. Unfortunately, this material-oriented approach has often neglected the intangible forms of heritage that are equally important to preserving the cultural significance of these sites.

In the French colonial period, scholar Henri Parmentier was the first to conduct significant research on the architecture and sculpture of Po Klaong Girai temple. During this time, the main conservation works were limited to relocating some broken

Table 6.1 Overview of major conservation efforts at Po Klaong Girai Temple throughout history

Year	Work
1982	Reinforced broken elements with steel bars
1983	Restored and consolidated fundamental parts, a third of which were listed as severely damaged
1984	Restored the main tower by removing damaged bricks and restoring stone statues mounted inside the tower
1985	Restored almost 500 sculptural details or designs on arches, replicating original designs
1987	Restored the falling walls repaired by Polish architects

parts of the temple. In subsequent periods, the temple underwent numerous preservation and restoration efforts, particularly during the period between 1982 and 1987 under the direction of Polish experts (as outlined in Table 6.1).

While these efforts have helped to preserve the physical fabric of the temple, more comprehensive approaches are needed to ensure that both tangible and intangible forms of heritage are preserved for future generations.

In general, the conservation work at Po Klaong Girai temple has aimed to restore damaged decorative elements and bring original features back into place in a harmonious manner. Upon completion of the conservation work, the Ninh Thuan Department of Sports, Culture, and Tourism took over the maintenance and protection of the temple, attempting to prevent damage from the environment, human activity, and previous conservation efforts.

In 2005, the local government allocated 15 billion VND (US$715,000) to construct a 7.8 ha tourism area at Po Klaong Girai temple, which included a Cham exhibition, an art performance and traditional game space, and a traditional Cham house located behind the temple. The project was beneficial in terms of presenting Cham culture to tourists. Later, between 2012 and 2017, conservation and tourism development projects were implemented, with a focus on expanding the ground's site for ritual practices, consolidating the foundations, and reconstructing the exhibition area and new pathway model. However, these projects continued to neglect the cultural and spiritual significance of the tangible heritage forms. The construction of new eastern pathways at the temple by state authorities in 2012, aimed at improving accessibility for visitors, exemplifies this ongoing problem.

Understanding the Significance of Cardinal Directions in Cham Culture

According to Cham beliefs, the earth is considered a divine entity with a soul and is worshipped as Po Tanâh Raya, the earth god. Before conducting any ceremony, spiritual leaders typically perform a ritual known as Ew Tanâh Raya to invite the earth god. (Fig. 6.1 illustrates this practice.)

When performing a land worship ceremony, the Cham Ahier tradition involves paying homage to the Guardians of the Directions, also known as Yang Dar Dih/Dik. These deities are said to rule over the different directions of space. Similar to Hindu culture, directions in Cham Ahier tradition are referred to as Dih/Dik, and there are four main directions and a total of eight directions (Figs. 6.2 and 6.3).

The Cham Ahier tradition of worshiping the guardians of directions is greatly influenced by Hinduism. The east is considered the most sacred and is seen as the

Fig. 6.1 Cham Ahier priests perform a ritual invoking the earth god before the main ceremony (Courtesy by author in 2016)

Fig. 6.2 Cardinal directions of the Cham worldview (Author, 2017)

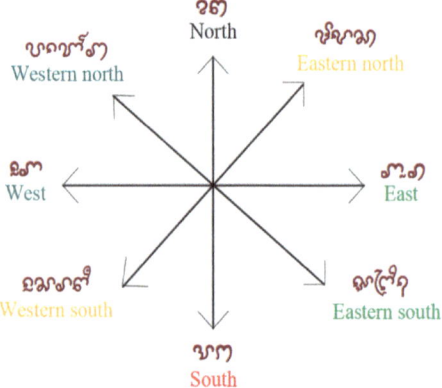

Fig. 6.3 Cardinal directions
of the Cham worldview
(Author, 2017)

starting point of cosmic movement and the direction of the gods. Ahier priests, before conducting any worship, turn to the east and offer prayers to the god Suriya. The east is considered exclusively for the gods in the divine realm, and the Cham people avoid building doorways or walking from the east side of the temple to avoid being captured by the gods. On the other hand, the west is considered less auspicious and is considered the divine direction of Islam's holy city of Mecca for Cham Awal who are influenced by Islam. The south represents the world and life, and Cham houses are often constructed facing this direction. The north, associated with demons and death, is avoided by the Cham people, and they ensure that their houses never face this direction (Table 6.2).

In Cham culture, the cardinal directions are not just a matter of orientation, but are believed to carry spiritual significance and power. Each direction has its own meaning, and this significance is reflected in the design and construction of various structures. For example, the north direction is associated with death and the afterlife,

Table 6.2 Comparison of the cardinal directions in the Cham language to Hinduism

No	English	Cham	Sanskrit
1	East	Pur	Pūrva, Prācī, Prāk, Aruna
2	West	Pay	Paścima, Pratīcī, Aparā
3	North	Ut	Uttara, Udīcī
4	South	Dak	Dakṣīṇa, Avāchip
5	Northeast	Esan	Īśānya
6	Southeast	Agrih	Āgneya
7	Northwest	Bai yap	Vāyavya
8	Southwest	Nailiti	Nairṛtya
9	Zenith	Omitted in Cham culture	Ūrdhvā
10	Nadir		Adhah

and is therefore the preferred direction for cemeteries. On the other hand, the northeast direction is associated with the mosque and the Islamic faith, while the northwest direction is associated with the common people. The east direction is considered the most sacred, as it is believed to be the realm of the gods, and therefore, it is the preferred direction for temples and shrines.

The significance of the east direction can be seen in the fact that most Cham temples are built on high hills and face east. The east direction is believed to be the realm of the yang gods, and therefore, it is considered sacred and holy. According to Cham beliefs, the east direction is not meant for human habitation and is reserved for the gods. This is why there are strict cultural norms that must be followed concerning the east direction, such as avoiding building doorways or walking from the east side of the temple. Temples that face west or south are considered special cases in Cham architecture and are believed to have unique spiritual significance (Doanh, 2002).

The importance of cardinal directions in Cham culture reflects the belief in the power and influence of the gods over daily life. These beliefs have been passed down through generations and are still deeply ingrained in Cham society today. The significance of cardinal directions in Cham culture is a testament to the enduring influence of religion and spirituality in shaping the beliefs, practices, and traditions of a community.

Cham Views on the Newly Built Pathway

The construction of a pathway to allow visitors to access a Cham temple has been met with significant opposition from the Cham community. They believe that the pathway does not align with their cultural and religious values, as it goes against the traditional beliefs about sacred sites. Physical objects and places around the temple are considered sacred and have special meanings, and the construction of a pathway facing east is viewed as a breach of these beliefs (Figs. 6.4 and 6.5).

According to the reports from many Cham interviewees, the conservation activities at the Po Klaong Girai temple have had a negative impact on their traditional spiritual beliefs and religious philosophy. They feel that the construction of an east-facing pathway for tourists goes against their traditional beliefs and practices, as the east is viewed as the starting point of the cosmic movement, the direction of time, and the divine and is reserved only for gods in the divine realm. As a result, building east-facing doorways in homes and approaching the temple from the east side are considered unacceptable and are avoided due to fear of captivity (Orang_Ka001).

Similarly, Ahier priests also shared their views, stating that the Cham philosophy about direction is highly significant to the community, both in the past and today, and that temples and homes have always been built in traditional directions. The ancestors built the temple to worship and preserve the spirituality of the gods, who come from the direction of the sun (Orang_Gu002).

Fig. 6.4 Comparison between the traditional (top image) and the newly created (bottom image) pedestrian pathways at the Po Klaong Girai temple (Ninh Thuan Museum, 2017)

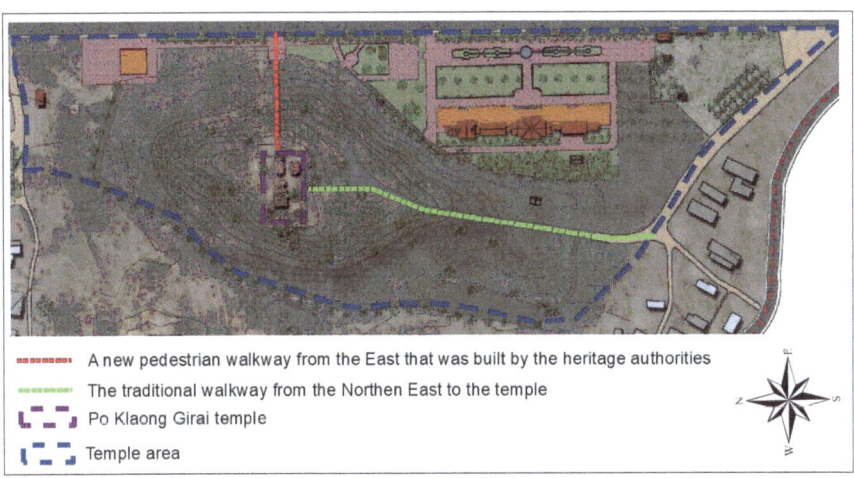

Fig. 6.5 Comparison between the traditional (top image) and the newly created (bottom image) pedestrian pathways at the Po Klaong Girai temple (Ninh Thuan Museum, 2017)

These beliefs and practices highlight the importance of cardinality in Cham culture, religion, and community, and how it influences their everyday practices at sacred sites. The creation of a new pathway to serve tourists has caused a strong reaction among the community, as it violates their traditional spiritual practices. The Cham elders have traditionally followed the southeast direction, as their ancestors did, to access and worship at the temple. This new pathway, while meant to make the site more accessible to visitors, is seen as a significant violation of Cham spirituality.

My interviews with Cham elders further highlight the issue at hand. They reported that the government had plans to build a new pathway for tourists at the temple, which was met with resistance from the community due to its contravention of Cham tradition. Meetings with heritage authorities also reflected this concern. According to one of my interviewees, the entrance from the east is referred to as "the road of gods" and is considered the road of spirits, not meant for the profane community (Orang_Ta002).

Another elder stated that although the pathway was already built and financial support was provided to preserve it, they recognized that the construction was a mistake in the conservation effort. However, they acknowledged that they did not have enough power to change what had already occurred (Orang_Ta001).

This highlights the struggle faced by the Cham community, who felt that their voices were not heard or respected during the construction of the new pathway. Despite their objections, the work continued and many Cham people now recognize that they did not have enough influence to prevent it. The situation serves as an example of how the elders' interpretation of the sacredness of Cham culture was disregarded in the face of modern development and tourism efforts. This situation highlights the issue of cultural preservation and the importance of considering local beliefs and practices when planning conservation activities at sacred sites. It also sheds light on the need for better communication and consultation with local communities to ensure that the preservation efforts are culturally appropriate and respectful.

According to the views of Cham scholars, the conservation work at the temple has been marred by frequent mistakes due to a lack of cultural understanding and inadequate involvement of the Cham community in the process. One of my interviewees expressed disappointment and stressed the importance of preserving the intangible aspects of the temple before focusing on the physical aspects. They stated, "*I was disheartened by this issue. The government did not return the right to open the temple, which created a sensitive issue for our Cham society. The first step should be preserving the spiritual aspects, and only then, we can think about preserving the physical aspects*" (Orang_Gu003).

It is evident that the Cham community needs support from the government to preserve their temples, but heritage professionals must understand and prioritize the spiritual values associated with these sites. This ensures that their conservation efforts align with Cham traditions and beliefs. The larger history of Cham cultural conservation has mostly concentrated on the physical forms of the temples, neglecting the spiritual views and practices associated with the temple (Fig. 6.6). This highlights the importance of incorporating the spiritual attitudes of the Cham community in conservation efforts. The government's support is essential in preserving the temple, but heritage professionals must prioritize the spiritual aspects of the site to ensure that their efforts align with Cham traditions. Without this understanding, the preservation of living heritage sites like Po Klaong Girai temple may fall short of its intended goals.

Fig. 6.6 Construction of a new eastern pathway in many Cham temples to accommodate tourist needs

According to the author's experience and observations, the Cham community has raised concerns about the negative impacts of preserving the Po Klaong Girai temple. However, when mistakes are made, the high-level authorities often avoid taking responsibility and instead blame subordinates and heritage officers. In interviews, the researcher noted that some responses to negative issues were vague and failed to address the root causes and find appropriate solutions. The Cham community's concerns have therefore not been adequately addressed.

It appears that the main goal of conservation at Po Klaong Girai temple is to cater to tourists rather than supporting the spiritual practices of the Cham community. Despite this, tourism at the temple has had positive effects on the local economy and has helped promote the cultural heritage of the region. However, as tourism growth can lead to significant changes in local cultures, it is important to find a way to preserve traditional rituals and cultural practices without sacrificing the authenticity of the cultural heritage. This is a common challenge not just in Vietnam but around the world.

The government, represented by the Ministry of Culture, Sports, and Tourism, acknowledges this challenge and is working to find a solution that balances tourism and cultural preservation. The goal is to maintain the original scale of festivals while still allowing the local community to be proud of their cultural heritage (Orang_Gov001).

My interviews with Cham elders help illustrate the point further: According to Orang_Ta002, the government planned to build a new pathway of the temple for tourism, but the Cham community did not agree with this decision as it went against their traditional beliefs. Despite the concern being raised in meetings with the Department of Culture, Sports, and Tourism, the government still went ahead with the construction of the pathway, ignoring the voice of the Cham community.

Orang_Ta001 also reflected on this issue during an interview with the researcher, stating that the authorities told them "the pathway was already built and costed a pretty penny so how can we remove it? And we [the state authorities] provided the Cham financial support to preserve it so this issue should not be talked again. Let's skip and ignore it." This statement shows the frustration of the Cham community, who feel that they do not have the power or voice to alter or prevent the construction of the pathway, despite acknowledging that it is a mistake in the conservation work.

These interviews help highlight the difficulties faced by the Cham community in their efforts to preserve their cultural heritage and the lack of agency they have in the decision-making process. It is clear that the government's actions in this case went against the traditional beliefs and practices of the Cham community, highlighting the importance of involving the community in the conservation efforts to ensure that the spiritual values and traditions of these sites are preserved.

It is evident from the statements made by the Cham elders (Orang_Ta002 and Orang_Ta001) that the government did not take their views into consideration when making decisions about the preservation of the Po Klaong Girai temple. Despite their objections to the construction of the new pathway, the work continued, and the government chose to ignore their criticisms. This is a prime example of the lack of agency and power that the Cham community has in decisions regarding their own cultural heritage. This raises several important questions about the role of the government in preserving cultural heritage sites. Should the state have the final say in how these sites are preserved, or should the local communities have a greater voice in the decision-making process? This highlights the tension between preserving cultural heritage sites for tourism purposes and preserving them for their spiritual and cultural significance to the local community.

In order to preserve cultural heritage sites in a manner that aligns with local traditions and beliefs, it is crucial for the government to listen to and engage with the communities who are most invested in these sites. This requires a shift in the way heritage preservation is approached, moving away from top-down decision-making and towards a more participatory approach that prioritizes local perspectives and values. In the case of the Po Klaong Girai temple, the disregard for the views of the Cham community highlights the need for more robust mechanisms to protect the cultural heritage of minority communities. Without adequate support and agency, these communities risk losing the connection to their ancestral heritage and cultural practices. The case of the Po Klaong Girai temple serves as a warning of what can happen when cultural heritage sites are not preserved in a manner that prioritizes the perspectives and values of the local community.

The construction of a new pathway in Cham temples has become a matter of concern among the Cham community and authorities. According to the authorities, Po Klaong Girai temple has become a national heritage site, and therefore, the Cham community should accept some changes to accommodate non-Cham communities. However, the Cham community has responded negatively to these changes, stating that the construction of the pathway goes against their traditions and spirituality.

In interviews with the Cham religious committee, the author discovered that there is potential for conflict between the Cham community and the government if a solution is not found that is acceptable within the Cham spiritual tradition. The new pathway does not align with Cham people's traditions and spirituality, and it was created by the government authorities who imposed their own perspective on the Cham spiritual space, contrary to the practice of Cham spirituality.

The construction of the pathway was intended to attract visitors to the temple, but it has led to tensions because of the way it violates Cham culture and spirituality. The Cham community feels that their voice has not been heard, and they were forced to accept the construction of the pathway. The custodians of the temple who the author spoke to expressed their concern that if this issue is not resolved soon, it could lead to further conflict and tensions between the Cham community and the authorities.

Discussion

Throughout the management of Po Klaong Girai temple, research has shown that conservation and tourism development projects have primarily focused on preserving the material fabric and its values. Experts have a significant influence on the conservation and management of heritage sites in Vietnam due to their institutional positionality, as noted by Smith and Waterton (2009, p. 29), who emphasize the crucial role that heritage experts play in the design, decision-making, and management of heritage. This research supports the idea that heritage experts lead the conservation efforts, while community participation remains overlooked and unrecognized.

The 2009 Vietnam Heritage Law does not explicitly mention the involvement of local communities in the definitions of intangible cultural heritage, nor does it recognize the rights of individuals and communities to participate in discussions and decisions concerning their cultural heritage (Giang, 2018). Instead, the law acknowledges only the administrative role of the state in all conservation and management activities, similar to the 2009 Hoi An Protocols, which are based on an expert-led conservation approach. As a result, it is clear that the management of Cham living heritage sites in Vietnam is primarily driven by experts, leading to limited community participation. This lack of community involvement in the conservation and management of these heritage sites may result in a misalignment with the cultural and spiritual practices of the Cham people, potentially causing tension and conflict.

The management of cultural heritage in many countries and international organizations has recently placed a greater emphasis on local cultural beliefs and practices. This shift has been reflected in the development of important heritage management documents such as the Nara Document (1994), the updated Burra Charter (2013), the CSICH (2003), and the Hoi An Protocols (2009). The Burra Charter (2013) recognizes the existence of both tangible and intangible dimensions of heritage places, where the concept of "meaning" is defined as "what a place signifies, indicates, evokes or expresses to people" (ICOMOS, 2013, p. 12) and is linked to intangible aspects such as memories and symbolic qualities. However, this trend is not being reflected in the conservation efforts at Po Klaong Girai temple. Here, conservation activities focus primarily on the preservation of the material fabric and its values, without considering the inherent meanings associated with each object at the temple. New additions to the temple are designed to cater to tourism development, rather than reflecting the cultural message of the site's creators and current users. The Vietnamese Heritage Law also fails to acknowledge the intangible meaning of relics as a basis for conservation, despite recognizing intangible cultural heritage. This supports the conclusion of Carter and Bramley (2002, p. 175) that "the values and significance of heritage resources are often acknowledged but not integrated into the management process." These findings highlight the importance of recognizing heritage as a set of values and meanings (Smith, 2006). The significance and worth of heritage are retained in the objects or places and serve as a representation of what people hold to be important and believe about their heritage (Hodder, 2014; Suprapti & Iskandar, 2020).

The presence of spiritual philosophies in the daily life of the Cham people is reflected in various aspects of their culture, including offerings, ritual spaces, directions, dress, house structures, monuments, and other elements of daily life. These philosophical meanings help to preserve Cham culture and are of great significance to the community (Sullivan, 2005). This highlights the need for heritage preservation efforts to take into consideration the cultural and spiritual beliefs of the local community, rather than relying solely on conventional approaches. The importance of recognizing and respecting each culture's particular ontologies, worldviews, and cosmologies has been emphasized in the growing body of literature on heritage management (Chapagain, 2013a; Silva & Chapagain, 2013; Winter, 2012).

Indigenous knowledge is increasingly becoming a central focus in heritage management projects around the world, particularly in the Asia-Pacific region (Andrews & Buggey, 2008; McGregor, 2004; Ross et al., 2011). Documents such as the Nara Charter (ICOMOS, 1994) and the Hoi An protocols (Engelhardt & Rogers, 2009) provide guidance for heritage management projects, taking into account the particular context and authenticity in the Asian context. The study argues that heritage experts and authorities should pay closer attention to the spiritual and cultural connections to place and space that are present across different socio-cultural contexts in Asia (Byrne, 2012; Daly & Winter, 2012; Karlström, 2005; Silva & Chapagain, 2013; Suprapti & Iskandar, 2020; Wijesuriya, 2008). Therefore, the conservation of Cham sites should be approached in a manner that takes into account Cham culture and spirituality. Further investigation into the Cham traditional philosophies and Indigenous knowledge is needed to understand how such worldviews can shape and improve conservation practices based on Cham traditions.

The growing popularity of Po Klaong Girai temple has led to a rise in tourist numbers, requiring modifications to the physical environment to accommodate the visitors. However, these modifications, such as the construction of the eastern pathway, have violated the spiritual beliefs of the Cham community, which constitutes a violation of the heritage law as outlined in Article 32[3] of the heritage law. This article states that new construction in Protection Zone I of a "special national heritage site" must not alter the authenticity of the site without considering the intangible values of the community, including their religious beliefs. Furthermore, the Hoi An Protocols, as stated in Engelhardt and Rogers (2009, p. 14), stress the importance of minimal intervention to preserve the heritage values and authenticity of the site. This study suggests that any new additions to the temple should not only be distinguishable as new but also align with the cultural and religious views of the community, and be approved only after consultation with them. The failure to consider the intangible values of the Cham community in their religious beliefs has reduced the significance and authenticity of the temple's use. A more effective conservation approach would take into account both the community's belief systems and the needs of visitors (Bui et al., 2020; Katapidi, 2021; Suntikul, 2013). This would preserve the spiritual and cultural importance of the temple while also catering to the needs of visitors.

The recognition of cultural significance and values by Indigenous communities, such as the Cham, often differs from that of heritage professionals, who tend to focus solely on the value of objects. The importance of defining the relationship between the present and the past, cultural significance, tradition, and spiritual philosophy is paramount for the Cham community, as it is for many other Indigenous groups (Settimini, 2020; Silva & Chapagain, 2013; Suprapti & Iskandar, 2020).

Heritage management should not only engage with Indigenous sites and communities but also the Indigenous knowledge and philosophies that emerge from their thoughtscapes and landscapes (Bruchac et al., 2010, p. 51). As such, the concept of authenticity in living heritage needs to be redefined according to the rationale of the Cham community, who bear and maintain their cultural heritage.

Conclusion

The Po Klaong Girai temple provides a vivid illustration of the difficulties inherent in heritage management, which must balance the needs of various stakeholders. On the one hand, the increasing popularity of the temple has generated a demand for physical modifications to accommodate an increasing number of visitors. On the other hand, it is crucial to preserve the cultural and spiritual values of the Cham community. The construction of the eastern pathway and other facilities violated the spiritual philosophy of the Cham and contravened heritage law, which calls for minimizing intervention in order to maintain the authenticity and heritage values of the site.

Scholars argue that heritage management must engage not only Indigenous sites and communities, but also the Indigenous knowledge and philosophies that underpin cultural heritage. This necessitates a reassessment of authenticity in living heritage and a redefinition of cultural significance based on the perspectives of the Cham community. The disregard of the intangible values of the community and their religious beliefs has resulted in a reduction in the significance and authenticity of the temple's use, underscoring the importance of taking into account both the community's belief systems and the external needs of visitors in heritage conservation efforts.

In conclusion, the Po Klaong Girai temple serves as a telling case study of the ongoing debates in heritage management, which seek to reconcile the interests of different groups and recognize cultural and spiritual values. Effective heritage conservation requires an appreciation of the beliefs, values, and philosophies of Indigenous communities and a willingness to work with them in preserving their cultural heritage.

References

Andrews, T., & Buggey, S. (2008). Authenticity in aboriginal cultural landscapes. *APT Bulletin, 39*(2), 63–71.

Australia ICOMOS. (2013). The Burra Charter and archaeological practice. In *The Burra Charter practice notes.*

Bramwell, B., & Lane, B. (2012). Towards innovation in sustainable tourism research? *Journal of Sustainable Tourism, 20*(1), 1–7. https://doi.org/10.1080/09669582.2011.641559

Bruchac, M. M., Hart, S. M., & Wobst, H. M. (2010). *Indigenous archaeologies: A reader on decolonization.* Archaeology and indigenous peoples series. https://doi.org/10.1016/j.watres.2007.10.044

Buckley, R. (2012). Sustainable tourism: Research and reality. *Annals of Tourism Research.* https://doi.org/10.1016/j.annals.2012.02.003

Bui, Huong T., Jones, T. E., Weaver, D. B., & Le, A. (2020). The adaptive resilience of living cultural heritage in a tourism destination. *Journal of Sustainable Tourism, 28*(7). https://doi.org/10.1080/09669582.2020.1717503

Byrne, D. (1991). Western hegemony in archaeological heritage management. *History and Anthropology, 5*(2), 269–276. https://doi.org/10.1080/02757206.1991.9960815

Byrne, D. (2004). Chartering heritage in Asia's postmodern world. *The Getty Conservation Institute Newsletter, 19*(2), 16–19.

Byrne, D. (2012). Buddhist stupas and Thai social practice. In S. Sullivan & R. Mackay (Eds.), *Archaeological sites : Conservation and management* (pp. 572–587). Getty Conservation Institute.

Carter, R. W., & Bramley, R. (2002). Defining heritage values and significance for improved resource management: An application to Australian tourism. *International Journal of Heritage Studies.*

Chapagain, N. K. (2013a). Heritage conservation in the Buddhist context. In N. K. Chapagain & K. D. Silva (Eds.), *Asian heritage management: Contexts, concerns and prospects* (pp. 49–64). Routledge.

Chapagain, N. K. (2013b). Introduction: Contexts and concerns in Asian heritage management. In K. D. Silva & N. K. Chapagain (Eds.), *Asian heritage management: Contexts, concerns, and prospects* (pp. 1–30).

Chirikure, S., Manyanga, M., Ndoro, W., & Pwiti, G. (2010). Unfulfilled promises? Heritage management and community participation at some of Africa's cultural heritage sites. *International Journal of Heritage Studies, 16*(1–2), 30–44. https://doi.org/10.1080/13527250903441739

Chirikure, S., & Pwiti, G. (2008). Community involvement in archaeology and cultural heritage management: An assessment from case studies in Southern Africa and elsewhere. *Current Anthropology, 49*(3), 467–485. https://doi.org/10.1086/588496

Daly, P. T., & Winter, T. (2012). *Routledge handbook of heritage in Asia.* Routledge.

Engelhardt, R. A., & Rogers, P. R. (2009). *Hoi An protocols for best conservation practice in Asia: Professional guidelines for assuring and preserving the authenticity of heritage sites in the context of the cultures of Asia*. UNESCO Bangkok.

Giang, N. L. (2015). Legal analysis: Current framework, challenges and opportunities. In *Understanding rights practices in the world heritage system: Lessons from the Asia Pacific* (p. 16). The Viet Nam Academy of Social Sciences & Ha Noi UNNESCO Office.

Giang, N. L. (2018). World heritage and human rights policy in Vietnam: A legal review. In P. B. Larsen (Ed.), *World heritage and human rights lessons from the Asia-Pacific and global arena*. Rougtledge.

Harrington, J. T. (2004). *Being here: Heritage, belonging and place making—A study of community and identity formation at Avebury (England), Magnetic Island (Australia) and Ayutthaya* (Thailand). James Cook University.

Harrison, R. (2013). *Heritage: Critical approaches*. Routledge.

Hodder, I. (2014). The entanglements of humans and things: A long-term view. *New Literary History*. https://doi.org/10.1353/nlh.2014.0005

ICOMOS. (1994). The Nara document on authenticity. In *Nara Conference*. https://doi.org/10.1063/1.4748569

Karlström, A. (2005). Spiritual materiality: Heritage preservation in a Buddhist world? *Journal of Social Archaeology*. https://doi.org/10.1177/1469605305057571

Karlström, A. (2013). Local heritage and the problem with conservation. In S. Brockwell, S. O'Connor, & D. Byrne (Eds.), *Transcending the culture-nature divide in cultural heritage: Views from the Asia-Pacific region* (pp. 141–156). Australian National University E-Press.

Katapidi, I. (2021). Heritage policy meets community praxis: Widening conservation approaches in the traditional villages of central Greece. *Journal of Rural Studies, 81*. https://doi.org/10.1016/j.jrurstud.2020.09.012

Kong, P. (2008). *Social quality in the conservation process of living heritage sites*. Berlageweg 1, 2628 CR Delft The Netherlands: International Forum on Urbanism (IFoU).

Larsen, P. B. (2017). *World heritage and human rights: Lessons from the Asia-Pacific and global arena*. Routledge. https://www.routledge.com/World-Heritage-and-Human-Rights-Lessons-from-the-Asia-Pacific-and-global/Larsen/p/book/9781138224223

McGregor, D. (2004). Traditional ecological knowledge and sustainable development: Towards coexistence. In M. Blaser, H. A. Ffeit, & G. McRae (Eds.), *In the way of development: Indigenous peoples, life projects and globalization* (p. 362). IDRC.

Phan, A. (2015). Phát huy giá trị văn hóa Chăm để phát triển du lịch tỉnh Ninh Thuận. *Phát Triển Kinh Tế-Xã Hội, 62*, 22–26.

Phuong, T. K. (2006). Cultural resource and heritage issues of historic Champa states: Champa origins, reconfirmed nomenclatures and preservation of sites. *SSRN Electronic Journal*. https://doi.org/10.2139/ssrn.1317157

Poulios, I. (2014). *The past in the present: A living heritage approach—Meteora, Greece*. Ubiquity Press. https://doi.org/10.5334/bak

Ross, A., Pickering Sherman, K., Snodgrass, J. G., Delcore, H. D., & Sherman, R. (2011). *Indigenous peoples and the collaborative stewardship of nature: Knowledge binds and institutional conflicts* (Vol. 320). Left Coast Press Inc. https://doi.org/10.1353/anq.2011.0046

Saar, M., & Palang, H. (2009). The dimensions of place meanings. *Living Reviews in Landscape Research*.

Settimini, E. (2020). Cultural landscapes: Exploring local people's understanding of cultural practices as "heritage." *Journal of Cultural Heritage Management and Sustainable Development, 11*(2). https://doi.org/10.1108/JCHMSD-03-2020-0042

Sharpley, R. (2000). Tourism and sustainable development: Exploring the theoretical divide. *Journal of Sustainable Tourism, 8*(1), 1–19. https://doi.org/10.1080/09669580008667346

Silva, K., & Chapagain, K. (2013). *Asian heritage management: Contexts, concerns, and prospects*. Routledge.

Smith, L. (2006). *Uses of heritage*. Routledge. https://doi.org/10.4324/9780203602263

Smith, L. (2012). *Discourses of heritage: Implications for archaeological community practice.* Nuevo Mundo Mundos Nuevos. http://nuevomundo.revues.org/64148

Smith, L., & Waterton, E. (2009). Heritage, communities and archaeology. *Duckworth Debates in Archaeology.* citeulike-article-id:9699952.

Sullivan, S. (2004). Aboriginal sites and the Burra Charter. *Historic Environment, 18*(1), 37–39.

Sullivan, S. (2005). Chapter 11: Out of the box: Isabel McBryde's radical contribution to the shaping of Australian archaeological practice. In R. Paton, I. Macfarlane, M.-J. Mountain, & A. H. Inc (Eds.), *Many exchanges: Archaeology, history, community and the work of Isabel McBryde* (Vol. Aboriginal, pp. 83–94). Aboriginal History Inc.

Sully, D. (2007). Colonising and conservation. In D. Sully (Ed.), *Decolonising conservation: Caring for Maori meeting houses outside New Zealand* (p. 273). Left Coast Press Inc.

Suntikul, W. (2013). Commodification of intangible cultural heritage in Asia. In N. K. Chapagain & K. D. Silva (Eds.), *Asian heritage management: Contexts, concerns, and prospects* (pp. 236–252). Routledge.

Suprapti, A., & Iskandar, I. (2020). Reading meaning of architectural work in a living heritage. In *IOP Conference Series: Earth and Environmental Science* (Vol. 402). https://doi.org/10.1088/1755-1315/402/1/012023

Thien, N. N. (2017). Linking preservation of intangible cultural heritage with socio-economic development in Vietnam today. *Communist Review,* 892. http://english.tapchicongsan.org.vn/Home/Culture-Society/2017/1032/Linking-preservation-of-intangible-cultural-heritage-with-socioeconomic-development-in-Vietnam-today.aspx

Tuyen, Q. D., & Anh, N. N. (2018). From the Linga-Yoni philosophy: Looking back at the connections between the Cham Ahier - Awal community through traditional rituals [Từ triết lý Linga-Yoni: Nhìn lại những kết nối giữa cộng đồng Chăm Ahier - Awal thông qua nghi lễ truyền thống]. Tạp Chí Bảo Tàng và Nhân Học, 3–4.

UNESCO. (2003). *Convention for the safeguarding of the intangible cultural heritage.* Retrieved November 15, 2017, from http://unesdoc.unesco.org/images/0013/001325/132540e.pdf

Van Doanh, N. (2002). *Champa ancient towers: Reality and legend.* Thế giới.

Van Dop, P., Anh, P. Q., & Thu, N. T. (2014). *Văn hóa phi vật thể người Chăm Ninh Thuận* [Intangible cultural heritage of the Cham people in Ninh Thuan]. NXB Nông Nghiệp TP.HCM. http://chamstudies.net/2016/02/18/van-hoa-phi-vat-the-cua-nguoi-cham-ninh-thuan/

Wain, A. (2014). Conservation of the intangible: A continuing challenge. *AICCM Bulletin, 35*(1), 52–59. https://doi.org/10.1179/bac.2014.35.1.006

Weise, K. (2013). Discourse. In K. Weise (Ed.), *Revisiting Kathmandu safeguarding living urban heritage* (pp. 1–52). UNESCO. Kathmandu Office. https://publik.tuwien.ac.at/files/publik_229747.pdf

Wharton, G. (2005). Indigenous claims and heritage conservation: An opportunity for critical dialogue. *Public Archaeology.* https://doi.org/10.1179/pua.2005.4.2-3.199

Wijesuriya, G. (2008). Values of the heritage in the religious and cultural traditions of Southern Asia. In A. Tomaszewski (Ed.), *Values and Criteria in Heritage Conservation: Proceedings of the International Conference of ICOMOS, ICCROM, Fondazione Romulado Del Bianco: Florence, March 2nd-4th 2007* (pp. 72–78). David Brown Book Company.

Winter, T. (2012). Beyond Eurocentrism? Heritage conservation and the politics of difference. *International Journal of Heritage Studies, 20*(2), 123–137. https://doi.org/10.1080/13527258.2012.736403

Open Access This chapter is licensed under the terms of the Creative Commons Attribution 4.0 International License (http://creativecommons.org/licenses/by/4.0/), which permits use, sharing, adaptation, distribution and reproduction in any medium or format, as long as you give appropriate credit to the original author(s) and the source, provide a link to the Creative Commons license and indicate if changes were made.

The images or other third party material in this chapter are included in the chapter's Creative Commons license, unless indicated otherwise in a credit line to the material. If material is not included in the chapter's Creative Commons license and your intended use is not permitted by statutory regulation or exceeds the permitted use, you will need to obtain permission directly from the copyright holder.

Chapter 7
Balancing Authenticity and Tourism Development: The Challenge of Incense at Cham Temples

Introduction

In this chapter, the focus is on the perspectives of the Cham community in Vietnam with regard to the concept of authenticity. The study, conducted between 2012 and 2017, revealed instances of the Vietnamese government officials imposing their own interpretations of authenticity on the Cham communities and their living heritage sites to meet the expectations of tourists. The tourists included both domestic and international visitors, with the majority being ethnic Vietnamese. The use of joss-stick incense at the Cham temples, which is considered taboo by the local Cham, serves as a symbol of the external imposition of cultural values and raises questions about authenticity at living heritage sites of Indigenous communities.

The research suggests that there is a need to better understand the relationship between dominant and marginalized cultural values at heritage sites and their connection to the history of cultural and spiritual practices. The Cham community members perceive the burning of joss-stick incense as a violation of their traditional customs and inauthentic from their perspective. A culturally specific definition of authenticity cannot be fully comprehended without acknowledging the broader history of threats to both tangible and intangible forms of Cham cultural heritage in Vietnam.

In light of the external imposition of cultural norms and practices, this study aimed to delve deeper into the perceptions and experiences of Cham community members regarding authenticity in living heritage sites. The questions aimed to explore the following areas: (1) the perceptions and responses of Cham community members to claims of authenticity in cultural heritage sites, (2) the factors that influence these perceptions, and (3) what can be learned from the Cham community's perspectives and experiences regarding authenticity in heritage conservation.

The study sheds light on the critical role that the beliefs, values, and philosophies of Indigenous communities play in promoting authenticity and preserving cultural heritage. By exploring the perspectives of the Cham community, this study highlights the need for a more culturally informed approach to heritage conservation and the

© The Author(s) 2023

Q. D. Tuyen, *Heritage Conservation and Tourism Development at Cham Sacred Sites in Vietnam*, Global Vietnam: Across Time, Space and Community, https://doi.org/10.1007/978-981-99-3350-1_7

importance of engaging Indigenous communities in efforts to preserve their cultural heritage (Bruchac et al., 2010; Settimini, 2020; Silva & Chapagain, 2013; Suprapti & Iskandar, 2020).

Exploring the Concept of Authenticity

The concept of authenticity has a critical impact on heritage performance within different economies, particularly in the tourism industry. Scholars have recognized the importance of the perceived authenticity of heritage sites, objects, cultural practices, and related activities, as it is a crucial factor in determining the value of a heritage tourist destination. Authenticity can be classified into four categories: (1) existential authenticity, which refers to the tourists' experience; (2) objective authenticity, inherent to the site or object; (3) staged authenticity, staged for the purpose of attracting tourists; and (4) constructive authenticity, constructed outside of the site, object, or people (Bruner, 1991; Chhabra et al., 2003; Cohen, 1988; MacCannell, 1973; Wang, 1999).

While most studies have centered on the tourists' perspectives, this study takes a different approach by examining the concept of authenticity from the local community's viewpoint, particularly in the context of tourism related to the Po Klaong Garai temple-tower complex. In this case, "living heritage" is considered authentic as it showcases the real-life activities of Cham communities and reflects the continuation of their cultural practices.

In the 1980s, tourists began seeking "living heritage" sites (Cohen, 1988, p. 373), and by the 1990s, they sought a balance between the exotic and the authentic (Tilley, 1997, p. 79). The desire for a genuine experience of real life, or how life was lived, persisted into the twenty-first century (MacCannell, 1973, 1999). With the rise of global tourism, there has been a (re)creation of cultural products to meet tourists' demands (Timothy, 2009, 2011).

Tourists often desire to experience the daily life, festivals, rituals, cuisine, and art performances of host communities, which can bring both economic benefits for the locals and an opportunity for them to assert their cultural identity (Beatrice, 2009; Davis et al., 2010; Tilley, 1997; Wang, 1999). Heritage performance can serve to preserve or reinforce cultural identity (Picard, 2008; Tilley, 1997). However, tensions may arise between those who value privacy and those who seek economic benefits, leading to the creation of a "heritage frontstage" that protects the authenticity of daily life behind the scenes (MacCannell, 1973, 1999).

According to Goffman (1959), individuals play roles in front of an audience and the norms and values of the external public shape the cultural heritage "frontstage." On the other hand, the "backstage" is a place where performers regroup, relax, and prepare, free from the judgments of the audience. Hobsbawm (1983) and Andrews and Buggey (2008) argue that cultural heritage is a dynamic and changing process, similar to Cohen's (1988) concept of "emergent authenticity," and that it constitutes a process of constructing contemporary authenticity. However, this raises the question of what happens when cultural heritage is altered by outsiders without the consent of the community. In the case of Cham communities, such changes imposed by Vietnamese authorities can evoke past experiences of cultural erasure (Bruner, 2005; Tilley, 1997; Wang, 1999). My research focuses on examining who determines the authenticity of Cham cultural heritage and how the local communities perceive authenticity in the context of tourism industry development, especially when heritage authorities attempt to commodify cultural products and heritage sites.

Exploring the Concept of Co-creation of Culture

In the realm of cultural heritage, the concept of "co-creation of culture" has been proposed as a useful approach in examining the relationship between tourists and host communities. This approach shifts the focus away from organizations as the sole actors and towards the process of joint meaning-making between organizations and people, particularly in the context of tourist experiences (Hudson et al., 2017; Ind & Coates, 2013; Ross & Saxena, 2019). According to Walmsley (2013), co-creation of culture involves three key elements: collaboration, interaction, and participation. Additionally, location and the creation of place also play an important role in shaping the meaning-making process (Miles, 2016). Simon (2010) argues that communities should play a greater role in co-creation than institutions, a viewpoint that is relevant not only to the field of museology, but also to our examination of living heritage sites. Jenkins (1996) suggests that a "participatory culture" requires engagement based on strong social connections, a shared sense of purpose, sharing of creations, and informal mentorship.

In my study, I found evidence of the conditions identified by Jenkins and Miles, but did not find that the conditions outlined by Simon for co-creation of culture were satisfied in the case of Cham cultural heritage. Specifically, Vietnamese institutions have not effectively collaborated with Cham communities, and the latter have not played a greater role in dictating the acceptable practices at heritage sites. Moreover, the existing literature on co-creation of culture does not sufficiently address the issues of Indigenous Peoples' rights or the complexities that arise when an ethnic majority, historically involved in the destruction of heritage sites, interacts with an ethnic minority, historically involved in their construction and preservation. According to the United Nations Declaration on the Rights of Indigenous Peoples (UN, 2008), respect for Indigenous Peoples' rights requires not just greater control over heritage sites on their traditionally possessed lands, but also total control. Given the current circumstances, it seems unlikely that these conditions will change in the near future.

The concept of coexistence is not a new topic in the field of cultural studies and has received significant attention from scholars. However, the existing literature has its limitations, and there is room for further exploration, especially in the context of the Cham communities in Vietnam. Tang (2015) emphasized the crucial role that coexistence plays in preventing large-scale global conflict. Nevertheless, the more pressing issue in this context is the erosion of Cham culture, which is a more immediate threat than large-scale conflict.

Banban (2018), in his research on overlaying ethno-religious communities in Qinghai, argued that the concept of "harmony in diversity" is critical in ensuring that every ethnic group has a stable identity relative to its ethnicity and important cultural traits while also being respected. In Japan, Satoru (2021) defined coexistence through three aspects of long-term interaction: the existence of different groups, interaction between them, and mutual dependence between them. In the case of Cham communities, there are examples of long-standing coexistence across different religious communities, such as the maintenance of the Ahiér-Awal relationship for centuries. The ritual attendance of Raglai peoples at the annual Katé ceremonies is another demonstration of coexistence within Cham communities. Noseworthy and Pham Huyen (2021) have suggested that shared resonances within Cham religious contexts play a role in promoting coexistence.

Despite the rhetoric of the Vietnamese state, there is no evidence of mutual dependence between different Cham communities, as seen through my fieldwork. It is possible that Vietnamese authorities may attempt to create such notions in the future, but currently, the term "coexistence" is not an accurate representation of the historical and present circumstances of the Cham communities. The question of what Vietnamese authorities could provide to members of Cham communities, and what they want, remains open-ended. My research suggests that a starting point for improving the situation would be for the Vietnamese authorities to recognize the cultural differences within Cham communities, such as the difference between burning agarwood and joss-stick incense. In conclusion, the coexistence of different cultural and religious groups is a complex and ongoing process, and there is a need for further exploration in the context of the Cham communities in Vietnam.

Cham Traditional Views on the Significance of Fire and Flames in Worship

Fire and flames hold a significant place in Cham religious traditions, serving as a means of connecting with supernatural powers, both divine and deceased. This is a common feature across many religious practices, including Easter rituals in Christianity, fire offerings in Hinduism, and burnt offerings in Buddhism. The use of fire creates meaningful symbols in religious contexts, as seen in the work of Essays (2018) and Varner (2014). In Cham traditions, two forms of fire are used in worship: candles and agarwood. Both play a crucial role in communicating with the supernatural. While Cham religions may have been influenced by Buddhist ceremonies, they do not use joss-stick incense, instead opting for a cup of charcoal to ignite agarwood or a substitute wood for worship and veneration. However, the use of substitute wood is only allowed as agarwood is becoming scarce, and joss-sticks are considered taboo and polluting.

In Cham traditions, candles are typically offered to gods and are mounted on trays, while agarwood is used exclusively by senior priests (Po Adhia). The smoke and fragrance of the agarwood serve as a conduit of communication between the seen and unseen realms, symbolizing worship and requests. This transforms mundane spaces into sacred spaces, where meditation, veneration, and worship hold meaning, and supernatural powers may grant blessings (Eliade, 1959). However, the introduction of joss-stick incense by heritage authorities as part of their infrastructure development plans around the Po Klaong Garai temple-tower complex is considered a problem by Cham perspectives. Joss-sticks are produced and sold by ethnic Vietnamese (Kinh), and are perceived as external to Cham cultural contexts. While this may not be an issue from the Vietnamese perspective of cultural heritage management, it is viewed differently by Cham communities. These views are nuanced and complex, reflecting the unique cultural and religious practices of the Cham people.

Cham Attitudes Towards the Use of Joss-Sticks in Religious Contexts

The use of joss-stick incense by tourists and heritage authorities has become a point of contention in Cham religion due to its symbolic importance in traditional burnt offerings (Fig. 7.1). Despite attempts by local authorities to find a solution, none have been satisfactory to Cham community leaders. Joss-sticks do not hold any symbolic meaning in contemporary Cham religions and are seen as an external and imported cultural practice by the ethnic Vietnamese (Kinh) community.

Interviews with a scholar and a priest reflect the tensions surrounding this issue. The scholar notes that the introduction of joss-stick incense into Cham temples disregards traditional Cham customs and harms the cultural heritage of the community. The priest asserts that while each ethnicity has the right to their own spiritual beliefs, they must be honored in the appropriate setting and not imposed on the Cham temple and its Indigenous customs.

The use of joss-sticks in Cham temples is a daily occurrence and dismisses the traditional Cham culture, leading to harm to the national heritage site and the customs of the Cham community. These views reflect the ongoing struggle to balance spiritual beliefs and cultural heritage in the context of living heritage sites.

The perspectives of key Cham community leaders towards joss-stick usage by Vietnamese (Kinh) tourists at the Po Klaong Garai temple-tower complex are negative. Despite being viewed as spiritual by the tourists, their use of joss-sticks at the temple is seen as imposing their religion on a site protected as a Cham living heritage and religious site. As per Cham beliefs, joss-sticks are only acceptable in Vietnamese Buddhist pagodas and ancestor shrines, but not at Po Klaong Garai. Cham community members emphasized the need for tourists to respect Cham practices (adat Cam) at the temple. An online survey conducted by independent scholar,

Fig. 7.1 Use of Joss-sticks by tourists at the Po Klaong Garai Temple (Courtesy by author in 2016)

Inrasara in 2016, aimed to gauge the consensus among Cham community members on this issue (Table 7.1).

The views on the use of joss-stick incense at the Po Klaong Garai temple-tower complex are diverse, with some supporting its use and others opposing it. One respondent, Orang_Ta002, expressed surprise at the option to "allow use but place outside" and shared that using joss-stick incense is against their traditional laws and goes against their efforts to preserve their heritage. This respondent emphasized that tourists visiting their temples must respect and abide by their customs. On the other hand, government officials tend to support the use of joss-stick incense, as it is used at other Cham temples. However, these sites are viewed as "dead" by Vietnamese

Table 7.1 Cham views on the use of Joss-Sticks at Po Klaong Garai Temple (Inrasara, 2016)

Contested use of Joss-Sticks by Kinh Tourists at Po Klaong Girai Temple: findings from 2016 online survey

Total	Against	Support	Allow use of incense but place the incense lamp outside
237	234	2	1
100%	98.7%	0.8%	0.5%

government officials as they do not represent contemporary Cham religious practices. Despite this, there are still significant portions of the Cham community who view these sites as "living."

Scholars and youth hold similar views on this issue, with one scholar, Orang_Ka002, noting that the Kinh cannot compare the transgressions at Po Inâ Nâgar temple with Po Klaong Girai temple. Po Klaong Girai and Po Romé temples are considered living sacred sites, with Po Klaong Girai temple recognized as a specific national heritage. The scholar emphasized that heritage managers should aim to preserve the authenticity of Cham temple culture, as the use of joss-stick incense is not part of Cham culture but rather found in Chinese and Vietnamese cultures.

This viewpoint was echoed by many young people in the community. One interviewee, Orang_De004, stated that the issue of using joss-stick incense in Cham temples is a major problem that has gotten out of hand. They said that although some Kinh people view the temples as sacred and come to pray, using joss-stick incense is not appropriate. The interviewee emphasized that the heritage manager should inform visitors not to use incense as it can lead to cultural misunderstandings, as it might give the impression that Cham culture is similar to Kinh culture. The interviewee emphasized that the use of incense should be avoided because the two cultures are different and it is important to preserve the authenticity of Cham temple culture (Figs. 7.2 and 7.3).

The issue of incense use at Cham temples has sparked a significant amount of debate and controversy within the Cham community. While some community members believe that the smoke from joss-sticks can cause damage to the temple walls, others have taken a more accepting stance towards the use of incense by Vietnamese tourists. However, this position is highly criticized within the Cham community, who feel that their religious beliefs are not being respected.

In response to these concerns, the Cham Custodial Committee organized a meeting to address the issue and agreed that incense should be allowed outside of the temple but not inside. Despite this agreement, the issue persists as local Vietnamese officials do not enforce the regulations. This has resulted in increased tensions between Cham

Fig. 7.2 Use of joss-sticks by tourists at Po Xah Inâ (Bình Thuận) (Courtesy by author in 2016)

Fig. 7.3 Use of joss-sticks by tourists at Po Inâ Nâgar (Khánh Hòa) (Courtesy by author in 2016)

custodians and Vietnamese managers, with the latter sometimes making provocative remarks about the temple being a heritage of Vietnam rather than exclusively of the Cham community.

Most Cham locals are honored with the recognition of their heritage at the national level, but they simply ask for respect of their religious beliefs. Cham scholars assert that they are rarely invited to meetings and those who are present claim that they were forced to accept the use of incense. This highlights a larger issue of cultural respect and the need for proper communication and consultation between the different stakeholders involved.

The imposition of new traditions by heritage authorities is at odds with the religious practices of the Cham community. The locals believe that conservation efforts should be aimed at supporting their community, as otherwise, the temples will gradually become Vietnamese Buddhist temples. The practice of burning joss-stick incense is an example of this trend. The question remains, what is the purpose of conservation and tourist development if the Indigenous community is not respected? According to custodians I spoke to, this situation could lead to conflict. The Cham locals believe that researchers in Cham Studies should be involved in heritage management as they possess a deep understanding of Cham culture and religion. A lead researcher from the local Cham Culture Research Center stated that: "*A better understanding of Cham culture by the heritage managers would help them comprehend the spiritual concepts of the Cham people. For the Cham community, spirituality is of great importance. Heritage management must respect this and the administrators should listen and understand the cultural meaning behind it… Regrettably, the views of the Cham Culture Research Center have not received sufficient attention* (Orang-Gov003)."

A heritage manager shared his thoughts on the issue, saying: "*In today's world, cultural exchange and integration are prevalent. Each culture should be open to embracing other cultures… However, there was a problem when a visitor hung the Buddhist swastika symbol on the statue of King Po Klaong Garai. This visitor did not understand the Cham religion and thought the symbol was beautiful. Additionally, they used incense and offered inappropriate gifts at the temple during their worship* (Orang-Gov002)."

This government official further added: "*Acculturation is happening at a fast pace. For instance, the Po [Inâ] Nagar temple is now used by the Vietnamese and has become 'Vietnamized'. This is happening to many Cham temples... The use of joss-sticks at Cham temples is a reflection of this trend. The Cham community has accepted the use of incense in their living temples and no one objects to it... we accept this practice* (Orang-Gov002)."

The statements show that the temple is no longer exclusive to the Cham community, but is also used by the Vietnamese. The responsibility of maintaining peace at the site falls on the Cham community, not the Vietnamese. This implies that the Cham must share the space with the Vietnamese. However, most Cham locals do not support the use of incense, which is in contrast to the claims made by local government officials. One of the authors, who is a member of the Cham community and specializes in Cham Studies, and who has collaborated with a former director of the local cultural office on various projects, was surprised to see that local officials did not recognize the issue as a problem. The author wrote in their notes: "*This is not acculturation. When the government allows visitors to bring their culture to another ethnic group's spiritual place, it can lead to cultural erosion. Approval of this practice can be considered assimilation. If incense use is allowed at the Po Klaong Garai temple, it will become like the Po Inâ Nâgar temple, where the Vietnamese majority community occupy and control it and perform Vietnamese religious practices at the temple. It is evident that the Cham community does not want this to happen, which is why they oppose the regulations of the local authorities* (Diary - 21 December 2016)."

The issue of assimilation is not only about the imposition of new traditions, but also about the lack of enforcement of agreements made. Conversations with authorities were often challenging due to their tendency to deflect questions and bring up unrelated topics. One example of this is the response from an official regarding the use of incense in the temples. The authorities have invited members of the Cham Council and researchers to hear their opinions, but the main concern is about maintaining the sanctity of the temple and preserving its original value. On the one hand, there is a need to accommodate tourists by providing convenient access and places to rest, but on the other hand, it should not negatively impact the religious activities and the monument. The Cham priests and elders have expressed their happiness with the restoration efforts, but they also emphasized that the restoration should not diminish the value of the temple.

In my research, Vietnamese officials were observed to have listened to the concerns expressed by members of the Cham community. However, these officials failed to take responsibility for their mistakes, instead attributing blame to subordinates and redirecting conversations to focus on new construction projects. This avoidance of negative discussions only served to exacerbate the sense of inadequacy felt by Cham locals, who felt that their concerns were not being addressed. The focus of conservation efforts has been centered on accommodating the needs of tourists, rather than considering the cultural significance of the living heritage site for the Cham community. The imposition of the use of joss-stick incense as a newly adopted tradition elicited a strongly negative reaction from the Cham people, who expressed their opposition to its usage. The strong resistance shown by the Cham people to the use of joss-stick incense as a newly adopted tradition reveals three key trends: a negative response to the incense, a lack of understanding of the Cham culture among officials and insufficient collaboration with stakeholders, and a rejection by the Cham community of assimilation into Vietnamese (Kinh) culture. This resistance to assimilation is the root of any conflict, with many Cham community members critiquing and opposing any actions perceived as an attempt to "Vietnamize" their cultural heritage. The potential long-term impact of joss-stick incense on the physical degradation of these sites remains a subject that requires further investigation.

Heritage at the Intersection of Culture and Tourism: An Analysis of Authenticity and Change at Cham Temples

Living heritage is a cultural property that is still in use by its associated community for the purpose for which it was created, and it is constantly evolving as the community changes it to suit their emerging socio-cultural and historical contexts (Wijesuriya, 2015). It is essential to understand that the Cham community owns this heritage and has the right to adapt it to their changing needs, provided that the changes are not misinterpreted or misused (Wain, 2014; Weise, 2013). This view is supported by the fact that the authenticity of living heritage is significant to contemporary communities and is considered inauthentic if imposed from outside sources (Andrews & Buggey, 2008; Clifford, 1988; Hobsbawm, 1983; Smith, 2006; Wijesuriya, 2007).

In my research, I observed that the Cham community has a strong sense of awareness about the conservation of their heritage sites and often takes the initiative to adapt to changing conditions by promoting the value of the Katé holiday as a festival, adjusting traditional costumes, adding new offerings, and even modifying elements of traditional rituals. However, they reject any innovations that go against their sense of identity, especially religious identity, as spirituality is central to defining authenticity. This highlights how authenticity is continuously evolving to create contemporary meaning (Andrews & Buggey, 2008; Clifford, 1988; Hobsbawm, 1983; Smith, 2006; Wijesuriya, 2007).

Unfortunately, external Vietnamese authorities, whether local, provincial, or national, have created their own sense of Cham authenticity for their purposes, often motivated by the desire to profit from the tourist industry. Visitors seek to experience authenticity, even if it differs from the everyday life of locals (MacCannell, 1973), and as a result, government authorities have exploited Cham communities. My research found that Vietnamese officials were observed to have listened to the concerns expressed by members of the Cham community but failed to take responsibility for their mistakes, attributing blame to subordinates, and redirecting conversations to focus on new construction projects. This avoidance of negative discussions only exacerbated the sense of inadequacy felt by the Cham community, who felt that their concerns were not being addressed. The focus of conservation efforts was centered on accommodating the needs of tourists, rather than considering the cultural significance of the living heritage site for the Cham community, as demonstrated by the imposition of the use of joss-stick incense as a newly adopted tradition, which elicited a strongly negative reaction from the Cham people, and highlights the lack of understanding of Cham culture among officials and insufficient collaboration with stakeholders. The potential long-term impact of joss-stick incense on the physical degradation of these sites remains a subject that requires further investigation.

Living heritage is a continuous process of evolution that is shaped by the needs and cultural practices of the community to whom it belongs (Wijesuriya, 2015). Cultural heritage can change over time to meet the evolving needs of the community, as long as it aligns with their beliefs and cultural identity (Poulios, 2014a; Sarah & Wijesuriya, 2014; Smith, 2006). In the case of the Cham communities in Ninh Thuận, Khánh Hòa, and Bình Thuận provinces, the authenticity of their cultural heritage is a matter of great concern, as it is being shaped by external Vietnamese authorities for the benefit of the tourist industry (MacCannell, 1973). The ceremonial performance of Rija Nâgar rituals, for example, has been criticized by members of the Cham community for being performed in an improper space and time, without regard for proper ritual orders, creating an inauthentic performance from their perspective (Weerasinghe, 2011). Similarly, the use of joss-sticks incense is seen as an imposition of Vietnamese Buddhist culture onto the Cham Ahiér culture and is only used for Vietnamese Buddhist contexts (Weerasinghe, 2011). This is a source of contention for the Cham community as it is a recent addition to their cultural heritage sites and does not align with their cultural beliefs and practices (Chirikure et al., 2010; Robert, 2016; Waterton & Watson, 2013).

The imposition of top-down cultural innovations can lead to the effective erasure and misrecognition of the cultural heritage of the Cham community (Chirikure et al., 2010; Robert, 2016; Waterton & Watson, 2013). As authenticity remains a dynamic and negotiated concept (Clifford, 1988; Cohen, 1988; Poulios, 2014b; Smith, 2006; Wijesuriya, 2007), it is important for heritage professionals and scholars to take a mediatory role, bridging the conceptual divides between the Cham community and external authorities (Weerasinghe, 2011). In short, the authenticity of Cham cultural heritage in Ninh Thuận, Khánh Hòa, and Bình Thuận provinces is under threat from external forces seeking to exploit it for tourism purposes. It is important for heritage professionals and scholars to mediate the conflicting interests and ensure that the cultural heritage of the Cham community is respected and preserved for future generations.

Examples from Southeast Asia highlight the significance of embracing a culturally relative approach in the management of heritage sites. Buddhism-based temple management practices in Thailand and Laos align with local traditions (Byrne, 2012; Karlström, 2005). The definitions of authenticity provided by heritage officials are inadequate (Lawless & Silva, 2016; Silva & Chapagain, 2013; Weise, 2013). The sites in need of preservation are not static, as they continue to be used by Cham locals, highlighting the need to view them as living heritage (Blake, 2008; Waterton, 2015). My research on the Po Klaong Garai site reveals that there are three main problems affecting its management. The first issue is the presence of invented traditions. The second issue is the imposition of policies and practices from above, without considering the needs of the local community. The third issue is the lack of consideration for the cultural context in which the site is located and the significance it holds for the local population. Previous researchers have posited that newly invented traditions or cultural products can be seen as inauthentic initially, but they can gain authenticity over time through repetition (Andrews & Buggey, 2008; Cohen, 1988; Hobsbawm, 1983). However, I argue that the newly invented traditions at Po Klaong Garai temple may be perceived as inauthentic by the Cham community because they fail to fulfill their spiritual needs or respect their cultural context.

The management of cultural heritage sites involves not just the physical objects, but also the cultural and spiritual significance of those objects for the local communities. The UNESCO Hoi An Protocols (2009) and the Burra Charter (2013) provide guidelines for the preservation and management of these sites, but they have their limitations. The Hoi An Protocols focus on the intangible and living aspects of heritage sites, but they emphasize negotiation among groups instead of traditional management systems of Indigenous communities. The Burra Charter is more useful in that it recognizes both the tangible and intangible dimensions of heritage and emphasizes cultural significance and the importance of community consultation and collaboration in management. However, it falls short in its language, which might be used to extend non-Indigenous control over Indigenous sites. The existing language of "cultural coexistence" in the Burra Charter should be recognized, respected, and encouraged, but it should not extend to new additions or practices that violate the religious worldviews of Indigenous communities. The UNDRIP outlines the importance of total control over traditional lands and sites by Indigenous religious communities.

Therefore, it is crucial to establish the relationship between the dominant and marginalized cultural values at heritage sites in accordance with the United Nations Declaration on the Rights of Indigenous Peoples (UNDRIP) and the Hoi An Protocols of UNESCO. This could be done by potentially exploring the Burra Charter for guidance on possible ways forward. However, it is important to note that these approaches must be tailored to the specific cases of these heritage sites and the history of cultural and spiritual practices at these locations.

From the perspective of many ethnic Cham people, the loss of authenticity at heritage sites is part of a larger story of Vietnamese conquest and forced assimilation that has threatened the existence of Cham culture for centuries. The discourse of authenticity must be understood in this historical context. Moreover, global concepts of co-creation of culture and coexistence may not be suitable unless they are adapted to the needs of Indigenous communities. The relationship between perceived authenticity and the impact of the tourist industry, particularly with regard to the commodification of Indigenous cultures, is well documented (Cole, 2007).

Despite this, existing literature on living heritage suggests that cultures can and should change over time (Andrews & Buggey, 2008; Byrne, 2012; Hobsbawm, 1983; Karlström, 2005; Sullivan, 1993; Wijesuriya, 2014). While some elements of Cham culture may evolve, such as contemporary adaptations of traditional dance, song, or pottery, these changes are driven by the community itself. However, changes imposed from Vietnamese contexts are viewed as inauthentic and rejected by Indigenous Cham people. The majority of the interviewees felt that these changes, imposed by government officials to meet the expectations of tourists, are part of a long history of erasure.

The development of Vietnam's market socialism still heavily relies on the tourist-based economy, which creates tensions in heritage preservation at both the national and global levels. For the Cham community members interviewed, any challenge to their cultural heritage is seen as a violation of sacred space. Hence, any future research on this topic should be community-led and aimed at precisely delineating the expectations of Indigenous communities with regard to these heritage sites, beyond simply stopping the practice of burning joss-stick incense.

A global concern that is highlighted by a local perspective is the relationship between dominant and marginalized cultural values at heritage sites. This relationship is crucial for the preservation of Indigenous cultures and their spiritual practices and must be addressed in accordance with UNDRIP and UNESCO's Hoi An Protocols. The commodification of Indigenous cultures for tourism and capital production is a major challenge faced by many Indigenous communities, including the Cham community in Vietnam, who face the threat of losing their cultural authenticity and spirituality. This challenge is not limited to Vietnam, but is faced by many Indigenous communities around the world. To address this issue, future research on heritage preservation must prioritize the needs and expectations of Indigenous communities and involve collaboration between government officials, heritage experts, and Indigenous communities to find a sustainable solution.

Conclusion

The study highlights the delicate relationship between dominant cultural values and marginalized cultural values at heritage sites in Vietnam. The Cham community, in particular, faces the challenge of preserving its cultural heritage while balancing the demands of economic development through tourism. The findings show that the imposition of a dominant cultural definition of authenticity on Indigenous heritage sites by local government officials, favoring the tourism industry, has created tensions within the Cham community. This is perceived as a violation of their customary practices and cultural heritage, leading to the loss of authenticity.

It is crucial to acknowledge that this challenge is not limited to the Cham community in Vietnam, but is a common issue faced by many Indigenous communities globally. Hence, future research on heritage preservation must prioritize the expectations and needs of Indigenous communities, rather than imposing solutions from the top down. A key consideration in this regard is the idea of living heritage, which recognizes the importance of the continuity of cultural practices and spiritual beliefs of Indigenous communities.

This study makes a contribution to the field of heritage preservation by providing insights into the perceptions of marginalized communities towards the concept of authenticity. The results can serve as a reference for future research in similar fields and as a guide for policymakers and heritage experts who work to balance the demands of economic development with the preservation of cultural heritage. Furthermore, this study opens up avenues for further research on the relationship between dominant and marginalized cultural values at heritage sites, not just in the context of the Cham community in Vietnam, but also for Indigenous communities around the world. Future research could explore alternative approaches to preserving cultural heritage that prioritize the expectations and needs of Indigenous communities, rather than imposing solutions from the top down. Additionally, more research is needed to understand the effects of tourism on the authenticity of cultural heritage and the role that government officials, heritage experts, and Indigenous communities can play in finding a solution that balances economic development with cultural preservation.

References

Andrews, T., & Buggey, S. (2008). Authenticity in aboriginal cultural landscapes. *APT Bulletin, 39*(2), 63–71.

Australia ICOMOS. (2013). *The Burra Charter and archaeological practice*. In The Burra Charter Practice Notes.

Banban, D. (2018). Harmony in diversity: An empirical study of harmonious co-existence in the multi-ethnic culture of Qinghai. *International Journal of Anthropology and Ethnology, 2*(1), 1–23. https://doi.org/10.1186/s41257-018-0010-6

Beatrice, S. (2009). Sacamefotos and Tejedoras: Frontstage performance and backstage meaning in a peruvian context. In M. Baud & J. L. Ypeij (Eds.), *Cultural tourism in Latin America: The politics of space and imagery* (pp. 117–140). Brill.

Blake, J. (2008). UNESCO's 2003 convention on intangible cultural heritage: The implications of community involvement in "safeguarding." *In Intangible Heritage*. https://doi.org/10.4324/978 0203884973

Bruchac, M. M., Hart, S. M., & Wobst, H. M. (2010). *Indigenous archaeologies: a reader on decolonization*. Archaeology and indigenous peoples series. https://doi.org/10.1016/j.watres. 2007.10.044

Bruner, E. M. (1991). Transformation of self in tourism. *Annals of Tourism Research*. https://doi. org/10.1016/0160-7383(91)90007-X

Bruner, E. M. (2005). *Culture on tour: ethnographies of travel*. The University of Chicago Press.

Byrne, D. (2012). Buddhist stupas and Thai social practice. In S. Sullivan & R. Mackay (Eds.), *Archaeological sites: Conservation and management* (pp. 572–587). Getty Conservation Institute.

Chhabra, D., Healy, R., & Sills, E. (2003). Staged authenticity and heritage tourism. *Annals of Tourism Research, 30*(3), 702–719. https://doi.org/10.1016/S0160-7383(03)00044-6

Chirikure, S., Manyanga, M., Ndoro, W., & Pwiti, G. (2010). Unfulfilled promises? Heritage management and community participation at some of Africa's cultural heritage sites. *International Journal of Heritage Studies, 16*(1–2), 30–44. https://doi.org/10.1080/135272509034 41739

Clifford, J. (1988). The predicament of culture. *Twentieth-Century Ethnography, Literature, and Art.* https://doi.org/10.2307/482934

Cohen, E. (1988). Authenticity and commoditization in tourism. *Annals of Tourism Research, 15*(3), 371–386. https://doi.org/10.1016/0160-7383(88)90028-X

Cole, S. (2007). Beyond authenticity and commodification. *Annals of Tourism Research.* https://doi.org/10.1016/j.annals.2007.05.004

Davis, P., Huang, H.-Y., & Liu, W.-C. (2010). Heritage, local communities and the safeguarding of "Spirit of Place" in Taiwan. *Museum and Society, 8*(2), 80–89. http://openarchive.icomos.org/84/1/77-LtNt-2012_.pdf

Eliade, M. (1959). *The sacred and the Profane: The nature of religion* (Vol. 77). Houghton Mifflin Harcourt. https://books.google.com/books?id=zBzzv977CLgC&pgis=1

Engelhardt, R. A., & Rogers, P. R. (2009). *Hoi An Protocols for best conservation practice in Asia: Professional guidelines for assuring and preserving the authenticity of heritage sites in the context of the cultures of Asia.* UNESCO Bangkok.

Essays, U. (2018). *The symbolism of fire in literature.* Retrieved April 15, 2019, from https://www.ukessays.com/essays/english-literature/fire-symbolism-literature.php

Goffman, E. (1959). The presentation of self in everyday life. *Teacher, 21*(5), 259. https://doi.org/10.2307/2089106

Hobsbawm, E. J. (1983). The invention of tradition. In E. J. Hobsbawm & T. O. Ranger (Eds.), *The invention of tradition* (pp. 1–14). Cambridge University Press.

Hudson, C., Sandberg, L., & Schmauch, U. (2017). The co-creation (of) culture? The case of Umeå, European capital of culture 2014. *European Planning Studies, 25*(9), 1538–1555. https://doi.org/10.1080/09654313.2017.1327032

Ind, N., & Coates, N. (2013). The meanings of co-creation. *European Business Review, 25*(1), 86–95. https://doi.org/10.1108/09555341311287754

Inrasara. (2016). *Hành hương Po Riyak.* Retrieved June 11, 2018. http://inrasara.com/2016/04/16/inrasara-hanh-huong-po-riyak/

Jenkins, R. (1996). *Social identity.* Routledge.

Karlström, A. (2005). Spiritual materiality: Heritage preservation in a Buddhist world? *Journal of Social Archaeology.* https://doi.org/10.1177/1469605305057571

Lawless, J. W., & Silva, K. D. (2016). Towards an integrative understanding of 'authenticity' of cultural heritage: An analysis of world heritage site designations in the Asian context. *Journal of Heritage Management, 1*(2), 148–159. https://doi.org/10.1177/2455929616684450

MacCannell, D. (1973). Staged authenticity: Arrangements of social space in tourist settings. *American Journal of Sociology, 79*(3), 589–603. https://doi.org/10.1086/225585

MacCannell, D. (1999). Staged authenticity. *In the Tourist.* https://doi.org/10.1016/S0160-7383(03)00044-6

Miles, A. (2016). Telling tales of participation: exploring the interplay of time and territory in cultural boundary work using participation narratives. *Cultural Trends, 25*(3). https://doi.org/10.1080/09548963.2016.1204046

Noseworthy, W. B., & Huyen, P. T. T. (2021). Shared resonances: Cham Bani conceptions of divinities in contemporary Vietnam. *Religion, 51*(3), 381–403. https://doi.org/10.1080/0048721X.2020.1860150

Picard, M. (2008). Balinese identity as tourist attraction: From 'cultural tourism' (pariwisata budaya) to 'Bali erect' (ajeg Bali). *Tourist Studies.* https://doi.org/10.1177/1468797608099246

Poulios, I. (2014a). Discussing strategy in heritage conservation: Living heritage approach as an example of strategic innovation. *Journal of Cultural Heritage Management and Sustainable Development, 4*(1), 16–34. https://doi.org/10.1108/JCHMSD-10-2012-0048

Poulios, I. (2014b). *The past in the present: A living heritage approach—Meteora.* Ubiquity Press. https://doi.org/10.5334/bak

Robert, R. (2016). Community participation in conservation of gazetted cultural heritage sites: A case study of the Agikuyu shrine at Mukurwe wa Nyagathanga. In A.-M. Deisser & M. Njuguna (Eds.), *Conservation of natural and cultural heritage in Kenya: A cross-disciplinary approach* (pp. 180–199). UCL Press.

Ross, D., & Saxena, G. (2019). Participative co-creation of archaeological heritage: Case insights on creative tourism in Alentejo, Portugal. *Annals of Tourism Research, 79*(102790), 1–14. https://doi.org/10.1016/j.annals.2019.102790

Sarah, C., & Wijesuriya, G. (2014). *People-centred approaches to the conservation of cultural heritage: Living heritage.*

Satoru, N. (2021). The role of long-distance interaction in socio-cultural changes in the Yayoi period, Japan. In E. N. Matsumoto, H. Bessho, & M. Tomji (Eds.), *Coexistence and cultural transmission in East Asia. World archaeological congress* (pp. 46–69). Left Coast Press.

Settimini, E. (2020). Cultural landscapes: Exploring local people's understanding of cultural practices as "heritage." *Journal of Cultural Heritage Management and Sustainable Development, 11*(2). https://doi.org/10.1108/JCHMSD-03-2020-0042

Silva, K., & Chapagain, K. (2013). *Asian heritage management: Contexts, concerns, and prospects.* Routledge.

Simon, N. (2010). *The participatory museum.* Museum 2.0. Museum.

Smith, L. (2006). *Uses of heritage.* Routledge. https://doi.org/10.4324/9780203602263

Sullivan, S. (1993). Cultural values and cultural imperialism. *Historic Environment, 10*(2/3), 54.

Suprapti, A., & Iskandar, I. (2020). *Reading meaning of architectural work in a living heritage.* In IOP Conference Series: Earth and Environmental Science (Vol. 402). https://doi.org/10.1088/1755-1315/402/1/012023

Tang, Y. (2015). The coexistence of cultural diversity: Sources of the value of harmony in diversity. In *Cultural interaction studies in East Asia* (pp. 285–290). https://doi.org/10.1007/978-3-662-45533-3_23

Tilley, C. (1997). Performing culture in the global village. *Critique of Anthropology, 17*(1), 67–89. https://doi.org/10.1177/0308275X9701700105

Timothy, D. (2009). *Cultural heritage and tourism in the developing world: A regional perspective.* Routledge. http://books.google.co.uk/books?id=0OLftI9psI8C

Timothy, D. (2011). *Cultural heritage and tourism: An introduction.* Channel View Publications.

United Nations. (2008). United Nations declaration on the rights of indigenous peoples. *United Nations general assembly.* http://www.un.org/esa/socdev/unpfii/en/drip.html

Varner, G. (2014). *Fire symbolism in myth and religion.* Retrieved April 15, 2019, from http://www.authorsden.com/categories/article_top.asp?catid=62&id=43114%3E

Wain, A. (2014). Conservation of the intangible: A continuing challenge. *AICCM Bulletin, 35*(1), 52–59. https://doi.org/10.1179/bac.2014.35.1.006

Walmsley, B. (2013). Co-creating theatre: Authentic engagement or inter-legitimation? *Cultural Trends, 22*(2), 108–118. https://doi.org/10.1080/09548963.2013.783176

Wang, N. (1999). Rethinking authenticity in tourism experience. *Annals of Tourism Research, 26*(2), 349–370. https://doi.org/10.1016/S0160-7383(98)00103-0

Waterton, E. (2015). Heritage and community engagement. In *The ethics of cultural heritage* (pp. 53–67). https://doi.org/10.1007/978-1-4939-1649-8_4

Waterton, E., & Watson, S. (2013). *Heritage and community engagement: Collaboration or contestation?* Taylor & Francis.

Weerasinghe, J. (2011). Living sacred heritage and 'authenticity' in South Asia. In *Heritage, memory & identity* (pp. 139–147). Sage.

Weise, K. (2013). Discourse. In K. Weise (Ed.), *Revisiting Kathmandu safeguarding living urban heritage* (pp. 1–52). UNESCO. Kathmandu Office. https://publik.tuwien.ac.at/files/publik_229747.pdf

Wijesuriya, G. (2007). Conserving living Taonga: The concept of continuity. In D. Sully (Ed.), *Decolonizing conservation: Caring for Maori meeting houses outside New Zealand (Critical cultural heritage series)* (pp. 59–69). Left Coast Press Inc.

Wijesuriya, G. (2014). Introducing people-centred approach to conservation and management of Hani Rice Terraces. In ICOMOS China (Ed.), *International workshop on the sustainable development of Honghe Hani Terraces* (pp. 23–34). Mengzi.

Wijesuriya, G. (2015). *Living heritage: A summary.* Retrieved October 20, 2016, from https://www.iccrom.org/wp-content/uploads/PCA_Annexe-1.pdf

Open Access This chapter is licensed under the terms of the Creative Commons Attribution 4.0 International License (http://creativecommons.org/licenses/by/4.0/), which permits use, sharing, adaptation, distribution and reproduction in any medium or format, as long as you give appropriate credit to the original author(s) and the source, provide a link to the Creative Commons license and indicate if changes were made.

The images or other third party material in this chapter are included in the chapter's Creative Commons license, unless indicated otherwise in a credit line to the material. If material is not included in the chapter's Creative Commons license and your intended use is not permitted by statutory regulation or exceeds the permitted use, you will need to obtain permission directly from the copyright holder.

Chapter 8
Staging Culture, Selling Authenticity: The Commodification of the Cham Community's Traditions

Introduction

The commodification of sacred spaces is becoming increasingly prevalent in the tourism industry. However, sacred spaces play a vital role in the creation and maintenance of cultural identities for local populations. The term "sacred" refers to a space that restricts access and limits behavior in a specific location (Carmichael et al., 1994; Hubert, 1994). According to Berger (2011, p. 25), the concept of "the sacred" encompasses the notion of a numinous power separate from but connected to humanity that dwells within objects and spaces. This idea of "the sacred" extends beyond moments of worship and is present in daily activities and rituals performed in these spaces. In Cham communities in Vietnam, sacred spaces such as temples and shrines are often decorated with art and smaller sacred objects that reflect the community's traditions, culture, and philosophy. Sponsel (2008) argues that rituals performed in sacred spaces are essential in demonstrating the values and traditions of Indigenous communities.

The tension between the sacred and profane at sacred spaces is a prominent issue in tourism studies. The increased impact of global capitalism has pressured many countries to reform their markets in order to gain access to the potential of capital, including the commodification of cultural products (Appadurai, 1986). As a result, cultural heritage has been promoted as a product to attract tourists for economic prosperity (Butler & Hinch, 2007; Zeppel, 2006). However, the commodification of culture, cultural activities, and sacred spaces presents challenges for local communities (Cole, 2007; Kitiarsa, 2008) as representations and meanings of sacred spaces become contested and reconstructed by various stakeholders (Bianchini, 1993; Mbaiwa, 2011; Reisinger & Steiner, 2006). Accommodating the demands of both local communities and tourists can result in tensions between them (Rutte, 2011). Tensions can manifest in three ways: competition over resources, disruption of local traditions, and erosion of spiritual values (Rutte, 2011). Additionally, if a site is perceived to have lost its spiritual value, it may also lose its value as an authentic site

© The Author(s) 2023

Q. D. Tuyen, *Heritage Conservation and Tourism Development at Cham Sacred Sites in Vietnam*, Global Vietnam: Across Time, Space and Community, https://doi.org/10.1007/978-981-99-3350-1_8

among tourists, creating a challenge in balancing the preservation of its sacred status with the benefits of involvement in the tourist industry (Brayley, 2010; Grimwood, 2009).

Scholars have paid increasing attention to the impact of tourism on religious practices, but these issues remain understudied in the context of Cham communities in Vietnam. This chapter examines the perceptions of Cham communities regarding the consumption of their "cultural products" for the tourist industry, which is controlled by Vietnamese state officials. Using the concepts of the sacred and profane, this chapter explores the tensions between the Cham communities' desire to preserve their heritage sites as authentically sacred and the expectations of Vietnamese government officials and tourists who desire a performed authenticity for the commodification of Indigenous culture. The study of these tensions provides insights into the complexities of managing sacred spaces for the benefit of both local communities and the tourist industry.

The tourist industry in Vietnam has experienced significant growth in recent years, contributing 8% to the country's GDP by 2017 (Hampton et al., 2021; Saltiel, 2014; Truong & Anh, 2016; World Bank, 2019). By 2019, Vietnam welcomed 18 million international visitors, more than double the number in 2015, with an average annual growth rate of 22.7% from 2015 to 2019 (GSO, 2020). This makes Vietnam a rapidly developing tourist economy and an emerging tourism market model for the Asia–Pacific region (UNWTO, cf. Hampton et al., 2021).

Tourism has also had a significant impact on poverty reduction in Vietnam, with policymakers making efforts to make the country a more attractive destination for international and domestic tourists (Lask & Herold, 2004; Truong, 2018; Truong & Anh, 2016). Cultural tourism, including the commodification of ethnic minority heritage, plays a significant role in Vietnam's tourist industry and is considered essential for preserving such heritage (Lask & Herold, 2004; Salemink, 2013; Saltiel, 2014).

While previous research has investigated the impact of tourism on other areas of Vietnam, such as ecotourism and gender in northern Vietnam (Tran & Walter, 2014) and tourism in the hill-station town of Sa Pa in northern Vietnam (Michaud & Turner, 2017), assessments of the impact of tourism on the ethnic minority Cham community in south-central Vietnam have not been widely circulated in English-language scholarship. The Cham community is connected to the well-known UNESCO World Heritage Site of Mỹ Sơn (UNESCO, 1999), making an understanding of their perspectives on the consumption of their cultural products for the sake of the tourist industry important.

The Champā civilization temple-tower complexes of south-central Vietnam have become valuable sources of revenue for the tourist industry, paralleling the success of the UNESCO World Heritage Site of Mỹ Sơn. The Vietnamese government profits from both the temple-tower complexes themselves and the thriving tourist markets that these sacred spaces create, as revenue from ticket sales, as well as from shops, restaurants, hotels, and transportation services, is recaptured through taxes. Major holidays, such as the New Year (Rija Nâgar) holiday at the Po Klaong Garai temple, attract throngs of tourists and represent an injection of capital into local markets.

However, the commodification of Rija Nâgar has resulted in the ceremonial religious aspects of the holiday becoming increasingly overlooked, as it is repackaged as a festival (lễ hội) for both Vietnamese audiences and international visitors. This tension between a sacred holiday (ngày lễ) and a profane festival highlights practices that contradict the religious beliefs of Indigenous communities.

By using the Po Klaong Garai temple-tower complex as a case study, we can better understand the interplay between Cham perspectives and the practices of Vietnamese government officials in the development of the tourist industry centered on Cham living heritage sites that are simultaneously sacred spaces. This study will (1) highlight how Cham cultural heritage is reproduced and transformed through cultural performances that tourists encounter, (2) examine how these embodied performances and interpretations of them are reliant upon ideologies of authenticity, and (3) investigate how performances transform heritage sites into spaces for cultural commodification and resulting ideological contestation, with an eye towards the ways that perceived inauthenticity may impact the vitality of such sites for future generations.

Through this examination, the study hopes to shed light on the complex relationship between Cham perspectives, government practices, and the development of the tourist industry centered on Cham living heritage sites.

The Interplay of Commodification and Authenticity in Tourism

Commodification of cultural heritage refers to the transformation of cultural heritage objects, activities, and spaces into commodities that can be bought and sold. The process of commodification is influenced by the perceived demand of the tourist market and the perceived authenticity of the heritage object or space (Chambers, 2009). However, the determination of value and authenticity can be subjective and can often be influenced by government officials rather than local communities.

Studies have shown that commodification can result in a reduction in the perception of authenticity, which can harm the cultural heritage object, activity, or space. For example, Johnston (2006) found that the exploitation of Maya culture in Mexico for tourism purposes has led to the damaging of sacred sites through commodification, and the desecration of these sites by inappropriate activities, which has in turn destroyed the sacred environment of Indigenous Maya communities. This process of commodification has placed the authority of government officials between Indigenous Peoples (IPs) and their sacred spaces, distancing them from their ancestral history and causing harm to the spiritual and cultural heritage of IPs.

Additionally, Hubert (1994) found that increased tourist traffic at sacred sites of IPs is often accompanied by increased inappropriate activities that desecrate these sites, further threatening the spiritual and cultural heritage of IPs. The commodification of cultural heritage objects and spaces can thus be seen as a form of cultural erasure, as it undermines the authenticity of these objects and spaces and erodes the spiritual and cultural heritage of IPs. Therefore, it is crucial to understand the implications of commodification and the impact it can have on cultural heritage, especially on sacred sites of Indigenous communities. This understanding can be used to guide the development of policies and strategies that protect the cultural heritage of Indigenous communities, and ensure the preservation of their spiritual and cultural heritage for future generations.

In an effort to mediate between local communities and tourists, state agencies may create a stage for the performance of cultural activities and rituals for tourists (Cole, 2007). While this may help to maintain a sense of cultural identity for local communities, it can also lead to a passive role for locals as agency is shifted to government officials (Cole, 2007). This, in turn, results in the commodification of local cultures to meet the demands of the tourist industry, often without input from local communities (Tilley, 1997; Timothy, 2014). The commodification of local cultures can lead to contestations between local communities, government authorities, and tourist companies (Bianchini, 1993; Mbaiwa, 2011; Reisinger & Steiner, 2006). The struggle for capital creates tension between the use of culture for community expression and the commodification of local cultures for tourist markets (Bianchini, 1993).

In some cases, government officials may even create mythical cultures to meet the expectations of the tourist industry, leading to a loss of authenticity that has no grounding in the lived realities of local communities (Koot, 2013). The tension between the need for capital and the desire to protect cultural heritage and identity can also result in internal tensions within communities (Bianchini, 1993; Reisinger & Steiner, 2006). Thus, it is crucial to understand the dynamics of commodification and authenticity in the context of cultural heritage and to consider the impact on local communities in the tourism industry.

The impact of commodification on authenticity remains a topic of ongoing debate among scholars in the field of heritage tourism. On one hand, some researchers argue that commodification does not necessarily reduce the authenticity of a culture, but rather shifts its perceived authenticity over time (Bruner, 1991). Additionally, commodification can bring income and pride to local communities (Cohen, 1988; Tilley, 1997). Cohen (1988) posits that the meaning of a commodity is not necessarily altered by its commodification and that tourist-oriented commodities can gain new meaning for locals, transforming into symbols of identity that represent local cultures to external audiences (Cole, 2007; Tilley, 1997). In these cases, cultural consumption can revitalize local communities, though the effectiveness of such revitalization depends on local communities' ability to control the production of commodities and access the capital generated from such production (Bruner, 1991; Tilley, 1997). However, the power dynamics between government officials and local communities can have an impact on the ability of local communities to generate pride through cultural displays for tourists (Bruner, 1991; Tilley, 1997). Thus, it is essential to realign these power structures in situations where conflict arises, in order to ensure the respectful treatment of sacred sites and generate a positive outcome for all involved parties.

The study of heritage tourism at sacred sites represents a distinct niche within the broader field of tourism research (Shackley, 2001; Timothy, 2014). While such tourism can provide benefits to the preservation of cultural heritage, it also carries the risk of disrupting local religious practices and diminishing the sacredness of the sites in question (Carmichael et al., 1992; Sarmiento & Hitchner, 2017). The negative effects of tourism can be exacerbated by inappropriate behavior on the part of tourists and the presence of commercial development (du Cros & McKercher, 2005). As a result, effective heritage management has become a crucial consideration in the formulation of tourism policies in Southeast Asia (du Cros & McKercher, 2005), with scholars advocating for the importance of sustainable tourism as the foundation for long-term development in the region, achieved through a collaborative effort between government and local communities (Bradford & Lee, 2004).

In sum, the impact of tourism practices on the host culture has been a topic of interest among scholars. Some researchers have expressed concerns that tourism can alter or destroy the authenticity of cultural traditions (Greenwood, 1989; Johnston, 2006; Tilley, 1997; Timothy & Nyaupane, 2009; Timothy & Prideaux, 2004), while others argue that commodification does not always have negative effects and may actually change the authenticity of cultural practices over time (Bruner, 1991; Cohen, 1988; Cole, 2007; Tilley, 1997). When local communities are given control over their heritage sites and access to the economic benefits of tourism, it can promote cultural preservation, encourage economic development, and instill pride among the locals.

The concept of authenticity in cultural heritage is often intertwined with power relations, cultural dominance, and the expertise of those who determine its value (Smith, 2006). Authenticity is associated with the idea of tradition and its perceived continuity over time, and is viewed as a crucial aspect of cultural identity (Hobsbawm, 1983). According to Andrews and Buggey (2008), authenticity is a relative and dynamic construct that is negotiated and subject to change, particularly in the context of evolving cultural traditions. Living Indigenous populations are often seen as the best judges of their cultural traditions and are therefore considered the authoritative sources for defining authenticity (Lewis & Rose, 2013; Zhu, 2012). At the same time, the materiality of cultural heritage sites may change, yet the authenticity of the site can still be maintained through spiritual and cultural practices (Weise, 2013). The function of a site also plays a significant role in determining its authenticity (Weerasinghe, 2011). In conclusion, the concept of authenticity in cultural heritage is complex and multifaceted, encompassing both material and spiritual aspects of cultural identity, and is shaped by the interplay between historical continuity, cultural evolution, and power relations.

The growth of global tourist markets has given rise to the creation and performance of cultural traditions in an effort to meet the demands of tourists (Timothy, 2009, 2011). Tourists often seek authentic cultural experiences, including observing the daily life of host communities, participating in festivals and rituals, trying local cuisine, and witnessing art performances (Beatrice, 2009). These cultural performances bring economic benefits to local communities and provide a platform for the promotion and understanding of their culture (Davis et al., 2010; Tilley, 1997; Wang, 1999). Moreover, they also offer opportunities for local communities to reinforce their traditions and cultural identity internally (Picard, 2008; Tilley, 1997). The distinction between "frontstage" and "backstage" performances introduced by

MacCannell (1973) sheds light on the negotiation process of local communities in presenting cultural performances for tourists, with the "frontstage" performance being tailored to meet the expectations of the tourist audience and the "backstage" performance being for the community and their spiritual beliefs.

However, the shaping of cultural traditions for tourist consumption can have a negative impact on the perceived authenticity of these traditions and potentially disrupt the sanctity of religious rituals (Andrews & Buggey, 2008; Hobsbawm, 1983). The imposition of external authorities, such as heritage professionals and the tourism sector, can further challenge the authenticity of these traditions (Bruner, 2005; Tilley, 1997; Wang, 1999). My research specifically focuses on the case of Cham communities in Vietnam, examining how the demands of external authorities impact the "frontstage" and subsequently, the "backstage" performance of religious rituals at the Po Klaong Garai site. While notions of authenticity are dynamic and constantly changing (Cohen, 1988; Silverman, 2016), my study contributes to the understanding of how tourism pressures can influence the viability of traditional cultural practices. To the best of my knowledge, no similar studies have been conducted in this context.

The impact of tourism on rituals and performances at religious heritage sites continues to be a topic of scholarly interest (Shepherd, 2018). Additionally, religious tourism has been acknowledged as having a unique role in such sites (Shinde, 2021). In my study, I focus specifically on non-religious tourism and the expectations and assumptions imposed by external tourists, particularly Vietnamese, and Vietnamese authorities in their efforts to cater to these tourists. This differs from a recent body of research that has explored the global phenomenon of religious tourism (Dowson, 2021; Geary & Shinde, 2021; Paganopoulos, 2021; Sołjan & Liro, 2021; Tillonen, 2021). It must be noted that the transnational nature of tourism can sometimes make it difficult to distinguish between tourists and devout believers (Zhang, 2021). Wang et al. (2020) have identified four motivational categories among tourists visiting religious sites: "fun traveler, devout believer, cultural enthusiast, and religious pragmatist," each of which may have a different impact on the site, performance of ritual, and notions of authenticity. However, these studies do not typically examine religious sites where there is a clear distinction between an ethnic majority tourist population, such as Vietnamese in my study, and an ethnic minority Indigenous religious community, such as the Cham Ahiér in my study. One exception is a recent study by Alariesto (2021), who found that tourism can be a "contaminant" at Sámi sacred sites. My study aims to contribute to the ongoing scholarly consideration of tourism at religious heritage sites by keeping the voices of Indigenous and minority communities at the forefront.

The ritual practices performed at Cham temples (bimong kalan) and shrines (danaok) are a significant aspect of living Indigenous heritage and hold a close connection to the everyday life and memory of the Cham community (palei). In recent years, temple-tower complexes and shrines have gained renewed symbolic significance for the Cham people, inspiring many youth to pursue the revival of their culture. The holidays and festivals at these sacred spaces serve to strengthen the community's understanding of their history and beliefs, as well as their sense of identity (Noseworthy, 2013). Po Klaong Garai temple is a particularly significant symbol of Cham identity that is recognized not only by Cham communities in Cambodia, but also by Cham communities in the diaspora in the United States.

The emphasis on promoting Cham culture as a commodity by the Ninh Thuận provincial government has led to the growth of the tourist industry in the region. For example, display houses showcasing Indigenous culture and "traditional handicrafts" have been constructed, and programs promoting the understanding of Cham culture have been held, all of which have attracted more tourists and generated income. However, these policies have primarily been implemented to exploit the region for economic development without consideration for the desires of the local communities. Furthermore, the Vietnamese Law on Cultural Heritage (2001) has conflated all historical, cultural, and religious sites into a single category of "cultural heritage," leading to the conversion of many sacred spaces into secular sites. These sites are recognized as "cultural sites," "national heritage sites," and "special national heritage sites," but these categories do not adequately reflect the significance of sacred spaces (Roszko, 2011). Religious ceremonies have been repackaged as "folk festivals," which have led to the intangible elements of cultural heritage being moved towards secularization and governmentalization (Cham, 2017). For example, the Po Klaong Garai temple and Cham New Year (Rija Nâgar) ceremonies have seen Indigenous values and religious practices largely ignored in the conservation and management of this heritage site, which is also a primary tourist attraction of the province.

Perceptions of Religious Practices and Rija Ceremonies Among Cham Communities

To gain a comprehensive understanding of the significance of Rija Nâgar and Po Klaong Garai, it is crucial to examine Cham views on sacred temples, rituals, and gods. Fortunately, scholars can draw on the works of Cham experts who have published in Vietnamese language, as well as the author's extensive fieldwork in Cham communities. The Cham temple-towers (bimong kalan) are considered to be among the most, if not the most, sacred locations for Cham religious communities. Although there are four different religious communities in the province, including Cham Jat (Animist), Ahiér (syncretic Hinduism with some Islamic influence), Awal-Bani (syncretic Islam with some Hindu influence), and Cham Islam (Sunni Islam), all individuals pay homage to the Po Klaong Garai temple-tower complex, which holds a special significance for the Cham Ahiér community as it was once home to the historical king of Champā who was transformed into an Ahiér god. However, it is worth noting that during Ahiér holidays, members of the Jat, Bani, and Islam communities also visit the site to show their respect.

All Cham communities believe that gods and spirits (yang) possess immense power, capable of both protection and blessings if proper ceremonies are performed. However, they also believe that if sacred spaces are disturbed, desecrated, destroyed, or not venerated properly, yang may punish the community. Thus, it is the responsibility of every individual, regardless of their religious affiliation, to protect sacred spaces and prevent profane disturbances. To preserve the sanctity of these spaces, residential areas must not be built nearby, and doors can only be opened after purification rituals have been conducted by Ahiér priests. Visitors are also expected to avoid engaging in foul language and inappropriate behavior at these sacred locations, as it would be considered an act of impurity that could result in punishment from yang.

The Cham luni-solar calendar (sakawi Cam) plays a crucial role in determining the appropriate days for religious rituals, organizing high-holidays, agricultural rituals, feasting days, and taboo days to ensure that the Awal-Bani and Ahiér religious communities can celebrate their respective holidays without conflict (Phan, 2014; Sakaya, 2016). At the temple-tower complexes in Ninh Thuận, four holidays are performed each year: Yuer Yang in the fourth month, Katé in the seventh, Cambur in the ninth, and Peh Pabah Mbeng Yang in the eleventh. If these ceremonies are conducted in the proper sequence, according to the Cham calendar, it is believed to result in good weather, abundant crops, and growth for the Cham community (Sakaya, 2003).

The Cham Ahiér belief system is characterized by a broad polytheistic outlook, with shared yang elements between both the Cham Jat and Cham Bani communities. For instance, the gods Po Yang Cek, Po Yang Tasik, and Po Tanah are worshipped by both Cham Jat and Cham Ahiér communities, as is the reverence for ancestors (Muk Kei). Additionally, the Cham Ahiér belief system shares a number of divinities with the Cham Awal-Bani belief system, which have been influenced by Islamic ideas and are referred to as "new yang" (yang biruw), such as Po Kuk Ulahuk, Po Awluah (Allah), Mohamat, and Ali. On the other hand, gods associated with Hindu influence or temple-tower complexes are considered "old yang" (yang klak) in the Cham Ahiér belief system, with examples including historical royalty who were deified, like Po Klaong Garai and Po Romé, as well as localized versions of Hindu gods like Po Yang Sibayeng and other local gods who were not royalty but were still believed to have been deified, like Po Inâ Nâgar. The distinction between yang biruw and yang klak gods is crucial in shaping the rituals of the Cham Ahiér belief system, with yang klak gods being worshipped at both temples and in household settings. They are honored during ceremonies like Katé, Cambur, Yuer Yang, and Peh Pambeng Yang at temples and Puis or Payak at households. The roots of yang klak gods, from their origins to their worship, are said to be locally based in areas now encompassing Ninh Thuận, Bình Thuận, and Khánh Hòa Provinces. At temple-tower complexes, the senior Ahiér priest (Po Adhia), the Ong Kadhar responsible for devotional hymns, and the senior priestess and spirit medium Muk Pajuw lead the rituals. In contrast, smaller ceremonies at village shrines (danaok) and households might only be presided over by the Ong Kadhar and Muk Pajuw (Table 8.1).

The beliefs and rituals of the Cham people in Panduranga, in the Ninh Thuan and Binh Thuan Provinces, are distinct from those in other regions. This is likely due to a combination of evolving religious practices and the loss of records from the northern principalities. According to Cham beliefs, there is a category of court rituals that have developed into religious ceremonies known as "rija."

Table 8.1 Classification of Cham divine systems

A perspective on the gods of Cham-Panduranga[1]

The Yang Klak (also known as Yang Bimong) is a system of gods worshipped in communal ceremonies and at temples	The Yang Biruw system represents a new perspective on gods influenced by Islamic beliefs
Po Sang	Po Auluah (Allah)
Po Ina Nagar	Nabi Mohamad
Po Bia Atakal	Po Nabi Ibrahim
Po Klaong Haluw	Po In Lak
Po Klaong Giray	Po Khar
Po Patao Binathuer	Po Mal
Po Patao At	Po Ali
Po Nit	Po Bal gana
Po Rame	Po Than–Po Thai
Po Klaong Can	Po Cah Ya
Po Klaong Kachait	Po Thun Girai
Po Girai Phaok	Po Haniim Par
Po Harum Cek	Po Tang Ahaok
Po Tang–Po Galau	Po Riyak
Po Par Thok–Po Par Mak	Po Ban Mata
Po Sai Ina	Patra Po
Cei Tathun	Patra Ligai
Cei Dalim	Po Than Mata
Cei Sit–Cei Praong	Po Rat Ina
Po Yang In	Patri Manuen
Po Dam	Pa Tri Ban So
Po Wel Palei	Po Patri Can Ni
Kai Du–Kai Dai	Po Patra Ritan
Po Nai	Po Mat Tikuk
Po Sah Bingu	Po Bana Jawet
Nai Hali Papang Mah	Po Bana Jamasier
Bia Than Can	Po Bana Jamatai
Ba Than Cih	Po bana Jali
Bia Ut	Po Mansi
Bia Chuai	Po Jalimit
Bia Nai Kon	Po Jalikam
Bai Juk	Java than Mata
Bia Binen	

The Ahiér community practices the New Year (Rija Nâgar), Day Rija (Rija Hârei), and Evening Rija (Rija Dayap) ceremonies. Meanwhile, the Awal-Bani community practices the Rija Praong ceremony. Each of these ceremonies has its own unique understanding of the Ahiér and Awal yang, and thus, it is not necessary to delve into these differences here.

---

[1] The pantheon of Ahier and Awal deities worshipped in Panduranga today is specific to that region and distinct from the worship practices in other Cham principalities. This is because either the records of worship in the northern principalities have been lost or religious practices in Panduranga have evolved separately from other regions over the course of many centuries. Hence, it would be appropriate to refer to these gods as the Panduranga gods.

It's important to note that the officiants of rija ceremonies differ from those of temple ceremonies. Only a male priest (Ong Maduer) and a female priestess (Muk Rija) are involved in rija ceremonies at the family and village levels. The Ong Maduer has no connection with the temple-tower complexes of the Ahiér religious community, while the Muk Rija is a crucial officiant for village and family-level religious ceremonies. However, during specific times, a Muk Rija and her extended family-clan network may visit the temple-tower complexes to offer prayers and offerings on behalf of community members.

In the case of the Ahiér rija ceremony, offerings such as a grilled chicken, square rice cakes, an egg, and rice wine are made to Po Bin Nâthuer, who is venerated as the synthesized head of the yang biruw system. These ceremonies are only performed at the community and family levels, not at the temple-tower complexes. It is considered taboo for Ong Maduer to perform at temple-tower complexes as it would violate the principles of Cham ethical codes (adat Cam) (see Tables 8.2 and 8.3).

During my fieldwork, I discovered that elements of Cham heritage, such as pottery wares, clothing, and decorative woven cloths and sashes, have been commodified to boost tourism. However, there has also been tension surrounding the performance of Cham religious rituals at heritage sites that are also considered sacred spaces, as these sites are being commercially exploited for the tourist industry. Specifically, I observed that the Cham New Year (Rija Nâgar) ceremony was performed at Cham temple-tower complexes for the benefit of tourists during my fieldwork, particularly during the Vietnamese Lunar New Year (Tết Nguyên Đán) in 2017. The performers were from a Cham performing arts group in Ninh Thuận Province (Đoàn Nghệ Thuật Dân Gian Chăm Ninh Thuận). However, as I have previously mentioned and will further elaborate in my findings, this use of Rija Nâgar goes against Cham cultural practices and regulations governing these religious practices (adat Cam).

Table 8.2 Classification of rituals, ritual spaces, and god systems among the Cham community

Religious Ceremony	Ritual space		God/Saint/Spirit (*Yang*) System		Chief Officiants
	Temple	Village	Old Yang, at temple-tower complexes, shrines, villages, and households (Yang Klak)	New Yang in villages and households (*Yang Biruw*)	
Katé	×	×	×		Pasaih Kadhar priest
Rija Nâgar *New year ceremony*		×	×	×	Kadhar, Maduen, Acar clerics
Other *rija* (Harei, Dayap, Praong)		×	×	×	Kadhar, Maduen, Acar clerics

Table 8.3 Classification and explanation of religious practice spaces in the Cham community for different priest systems

System of Religious Dignitaries	Religious community	Space for ritual practices		Interpretation
		Temple	Village	
Kadhar	Cham Ahiér Cham Awal	×	×	Allowed to perform rituals at Awal and Ahiér families
Pasaih	Cham Ahiér	×	×	Not allowed to perform rituals at Awal community
Maduer	Cham Ahiér Cham Awal		×	Not allowed to perform rituals at Ahiér temples
Acar	Cham Awal		×	Not allowed to perform rituals at Ahiér temples

Commodifying Sacred Heritage: The Performance of Cham Rituals at Heritage Sites

Through my interviews with members of the Cham community, I discovered that they are more wary of offering religious rituals for the purpose of entertaining tourists, compared to cultural performances such as music, dance, and song, which were widely supported. The Rija Nâgar ceremony is not typically performed at temple-tower complexes in Cham religious practices (as depicted in Fig. 8.1), and this fact was reflected in the community's skepticism towards this practice. Additionally, the dances performed during Rija Nâgar are different from those performed on regular days. However, local authorities still requested that Cham priests perform the ceremony at temples on regular days for the purpose of attracting tourists, as they believed these religious performances would be visually appealing. This request was rejected by the Council of Cham Ahiér Dignitaries, as they emphasized that exploiting rituals and customs at the temple for tourism is unacceptable. A community member stated, "The Cham people do not dare dance and play music or cook food at the temple for serving tourists because our tradition does not allow it. If we do, the gods will punish us" (Orang_Ta002).

Based on my long-form interviews with members of the Cham community, I found that the elders in the community expressed concerns about the commodification of Cham religious rituals for the purpose of tourism. One elder stated that the exploitation of these rituals at the temple has hurt the spiritual tradition and trampled on the religious heritage of the Cham people, and they cannot accept it. According to the Cham community, there are multiple consequences for violating the proper performance of a ritual in accordance with the Cham calendar. First, there is a belief that the gods will punish the community if these traditions are not upheld. Second, there is a fear that the spiritual traditions will be hurt, and if these traditions are not passed down to future generations, then the gods will punish them as well. Finally, there is a concern for the protection of religious heritage, which is theoretically protected by

Fig. 8.1   Rija Nâgar Ritual Performance for Tourists at Po Klaong Girai Temple

the Vietnamese state, but if the traditions are not upheld, then future generations will not have access to these cultural practices.

Another elder went further to suggest that the punishment from the gods may already be taking place, as many generations of Po Adhia (Cham religious leaders) at the Po Klaong Girai temple have passed away soon after being upgraded to the highest dignity in the Cham community. This elder believed that the gods punished them because the temple was open every day, and the Po Adhia did not comment or claim anything against the government. However, Po Adhia dignitaries in the Po Inâ Nâgar and Po Romé temples have lived for many years, leading the elder to believe that this may be due to the proper performance of religious rituals at these temples.

In Ninh Thuận Province, the Po Inâ Nâgar and Po Romé temples are only open for Cham Ahiér holidays and remain closed to tourists on other days. The elder of the Cham community suspects that the Po Adhia, who are responsible for upholding the rituals at Po Klaong Garai, face divine retribution for allowing the commodification of the Cham holy site for the tourist industry. According to the elder's interpretation, the lack of resistance from the Cham community is seen as an additional act that justifies the retribution. However, this interpretation places the punishment on the Cham community rather than the Vietnamese community.

The author also notes an instance where a traditional Cham ritual, the Rija Nâgar (Cham New Year), was performed by non-Cham individuals for tourists during Vietnamese Lunar New Year. The author raises concerns about the lack of knowledge and sensitivity shown by the local authority in changing the meaning, practice, and purpose of the ritual. The author wonders about the potential reactions of the Cham community to this incident.

The author's conversations with Vietnamese heritage site management staff between 2012 and 2017 revealed a significant lack of understanding of Cham religion and culture. The staff were unable to distinguish between the two major systems in Cham religion, the yang klak and yang biruw, and had limited knowledge of the history and form of Cham rituals. This lack of understanding resulted in a controversial incident where the traditional Cham New Year ritual, Rija Nâgar, was performed by non-Cham individuals during the Vietnamese Lunar New Year for the purpose of tourism.

The author cites the reactions of informed members of the Cham community to this incident, who were shocked and dismayed by this cultural appropriation and co-optation. A Cham priest expressed surprise and disappointment that the Vietnamese authorities had allowed this performance without consulting the Cham community and that they did not understand the differences between temple ceremonies and the Rija ceremony system. Another respondent characterized it as a conflict about culture and a destruction of their cultural heritage. The responses of the Cham community highlight the importance of cultural sensitivity and understanding in the management and preservation of cultural heritage sites.

It is evident that the performance of a Cham ritual in an inappropriate space has significant consequences. Our conversations with Cham Ahiér priests revealed that conducting a ritual in the wrong place is a form of cultural destruction. The Cham religious beliefs hold that such inappropriate rituals pollute the sacredness of the temple-tower complexes, potentially leading to cosmological punishments for the Cham community. This not only impacts the spiritual value of the sacred space but also undermines its significance to the Cham community. Despite the wide objections from Cham community members, it was observed that Vietnamese heritage managers continued to request Cham folk artists to perform traditional dances and music that resemble the Rija Nâgar ceremonies for tourists. Such practices not only disrespect Cham cultural norms and traditions but also perpetuate the commodification of Cham cultural heritage. The lack of understanding and sensitivity towards Cham culture and religion by Vietnamese heritage managers has become a critical issue, highlighting the importance of preserving cultural heritage in its authentic form (see Fig. 8.2).

The inappropriate performance of the Rija Nâgar ritual at the Po Klaong Garai temple caused a great deal of upset within the Cham community. According to Cham scholars and community members, heritage managers did not understand the significance of the temple as a sacred site, nor the importance of the Rija Nâgar ritual within Cham culture and philosophy. The performance of the ritual in the temple was seen as a form of cultural destruction and disrespect to the Cham community. The temple is considered sacred because it is the shrine of King Po Klaong Garai, who is revered and worshipped by all Cham people.

Young members of the Cham community expressed their anger and frustration about the situation, with some saying that they hope heritage managers learn from this experience to avoid similar situations in the future. Similarly, one community member noted that performing the Rija Nâgar ritual at the temple was part of a larger problem of lack of respect for Cham spirituality, and that it was not appropriate to

Fig. 8.2 Performance of Rija Nâgar Ritual for Tourists at the Cham Temple Complex. *Source* Author, 2017

perform such rituals at a sacred site. Instead, it would be more suitable to perform the ritual in an exhibition house.

In the Cham community, the performance of the Rija Nâgar ritual at the Po Klaong Garai temple sparked widespread public discussion and debate. The issue was particularly heated on social media networks, where Cham members from across the province and the global diaspora joined in. This "frontstage" performance resulted in a number of "backstage" controversies, which were brought to the forefront on public social media networks, further exacerbating the situation. The root cause of the tensions between Vietnamese authorities and the inappropriate organization of Cham cultural practices was largely due to a lack of understanding of Cham culture. To remedy this, Cham community members called for a greater effort from the authorities to learn about Cham culture from respected members of the community. Despite the controversy, many young Cham people expressed excitement about the temple being open to tourists, as long as it is respected as a sacred space.

Based on my interviews with members of the Cham community, there was a clear consensus regarding the performance of the Rija Nâgar ritual at temple-tower complexes, which was perceived as inappropriate and disrespectful. Community members felt that the performance was used as a commodity for tourists, and they felt explicitly coerced into participating. This resulted in a widespread public debate and controversy, which was exacerbated by the attention drawn by social media.

However, members of the Cham community were not opposed to sharing their culture with visitors and suggested alternative forms of cultural performances, dances, and music for tourists. They expressed pride in their culture and a desire to share it with visitors. To avoid such situations in the future, it is crucial for the Vietnamese heritage authorities to consult with community leaders and work in collaboration with the Cham community. This can help to avoid the exploitation of Cham religious rituals as a tourist product, which pollutes the sacred spaces in the eyes of the Cham community.

It is clear that the Vietnamese authorities had good intentions in promoting the understanding of Cham cultural heritage, but their lack of expertise in Cham culture and religion led to inappropriate actions. It is essential to understand and respect the spiritual significance of temple-tower complexes to the Cham community, and to ensure that any actions related to them are carried out in a culturally appropriate manner.

The Consequences of Commodifying Cham Cultural Authenticity

The commodification of heritage has been extensively studied in the field of cultural heritage tourism, with scholars offering contrasting perspectives on the impacts of this phenomenon. On one hand, it has been argued that commodification can lead to adverse effects on local communities (Greenwood, 1989; Johnston, 2006; Tilley, 1997; Timothy & Nyaupane, 2009). On the other hand, there is evidence to suggest that local communities may benefit from tourism and the preservation of their cultural heritage (Cohen, 1988; Cole, 2007; Tilley, 1997).

It is important to note that the outcomes of commodification are shaped by the management strategies employed by stakeholders, and that a balanced approach between development and conservation can minimize adverse effects on local communities (Bruner, 1991; Cole, 2007; Medina, 2003; Tilley, 1997). This requires a collaborative effort between tourism authorities and local communities to ensure that cultural, economic, and social life are not negatively impacted (Timothy, 2014). The results of my research on the commodification of Cham temple-tower complexes suggest that this process can have adverse effects on the Cham community. The exploitation of Cham religious rituals as a tourist product without proper consultation with the community and adequate cultural expertise led to the pollution of sacred spaces and the coercion of members into participating in culturally inappropriate performances.

The commodification of sacred space, as observed in the case of Po Klaong Garai, has the potential to significantly alter the temple's spiritual significance. According to Cham beliefs, violating taboos at the temple can lead to spiritual pollution, resulting in punishments for the Cham community, including shortened life spans for priests at the site. This degradation of the sacred nature of the temple-tower undermines its authentic use and meaning among the community, which in turn can result in a decline in cultural quality, hindering the temple's potential to generate tourism revenue. Therefore, preserving authenticity, as defined by the local community, is essential for the success of the tourism industry in Vietnam. Studies have shown that inclusive management practices, balancing development and conservation, can mitigate the adverse effects of tourism on local communities (Bruner, 1991; Cole, 2007; Medina, 2003; Tilley, 1997; Timothy, 2014; Timothy & Nyaupane, 2009). However, my research supports the idea that the commodification of heritage can have negative consequences, as seen in the case of Po Klaong Garai (Greenwood, 1989; Johnston, 2006; Tilley, 1997; Timothy & Nyaupane, 2009). It is crucial to involve voices from Indigenous communities in decision-making processes related to the development and conservation of cultural heritage sites.

The commodification of heritage, both physical and intangible, can have significant impacts on local communities and the cultural significance of sacred spaces. At Po Klaong Girai, the commodification process has led to a degradation of the temple-tower's sacred nature, causing concern among the Cham community. The temple-tower has become perceived as a recreational space and a backdrop for tourists to take photos, rather than a sacred site for religious rituals. This desecration of the site has resulted in the loss of its authenticity, as defined by the Cham community, and has the potential to decrease the potential for tourism revenue over time. These findings align with the broader academic discourse that critiques the negative impacts of the tourist industry on Indigenous communities and their cultural heritage (du Cros & McKercher, 2015; Greenwood, 1989; Johnston, 2006; Timothy & Nyaupane, 2009). The exploitation of cultural heritage for commercial purposes often leads to the destruction of sacred spaces, desecration, and the loss of their sacred environment.

The commodification of heritage, including sacred spaces, has been widely studied and has been found to result in tensions between local communities and government authorities (Bianchini, 1993; Reisinger & Steiner, 2006). This is due to the exploitation of cultural heritage for economic gain by governments and the expression of identity by local communities. The current study provides further insight into this topic by examining the case of the Cham community in Vietnam, who have experienced tensions with Vietnamese government authorities over the usage of their sacred spaces for tourist activities.

The differences in the status and agency of stakeholders have a significant impact on the goals and interests that are prioritized in development (Yang, 2007; Yang et al., 2016). In this case, the study found that Cham community members prioritized their spiritual interests and the expression of their religious identity over the priorities of provincial officials to achieve financial gains for the province. This tension highlights the importance of involving local communities in decision-making processes, as previous studies have shown that the lack of agency among Indigenous peoples and their communities often results in exploitation (Johnston, 2006; Kwon, 2017; Timothy & Nyaupane, 2009). The study also found that Cham officials have limited power to manage the temple-tower sites, and there is a desire to reverse this relationship in order to improve long-term development. In short, the commodification of heritage, including sacred spaces, has significant implications for local communities and their cultural identities. Addressing the issues arising from this process requires a more inclusive approach to development that prioritizes the needs and interests of local communities.

The performance of *Rija Nâgar* rituals at Po Klaong Garai temple-tower complex to attract tourists violates Cham religious principles. The ruptures in timing, placement, and participant structure mean that the existential purpose of the ritual is disrupted. In turn, these actions pollute the site and erode the sacred space in the eyes of local Cham community members. Hence, *Rija Nâgar* is being co-opted as a commodity, rather than performed to serve spiritual needs. Such "reconstructed authenticity" erodes perception of the ritual and space among local communities (see also: Suntikul, 2013). My research clearly showed community members disagreed with this practice but suggested performing *other* dances and music at the temple grounds, away from the sacred site, to create cultural displays for tourists. This supports Cole's (2007) argument that while cultural performances may be acceptable to promote local cultures, sacred religious rituals should not be staged or commodified for tourists' expectations. Following other studies of comparable cases (Hubert, 1994; Shepherd et al., 2012; Timothy & Olsen, 2006), the pollution and erosion of the sacred space also equates to the erosion and erasure of Indigenous culture. While MacCannell (1973) has argued that locals can use '"staged authenticity" as a resistance tool to minimize negative cultural commodification and to create equality between hosts and guests, I argue this constructed performance of "authenticity" for the purposes of economic consumption still maintains negative cultural commodification and exacerbates tensions between hosts and tourists as well as between the host community and heritage authorities, as the temple is still actively used by the Cham community for their spiritual practices.

The commodification of Rija Nâgar rituals at Po Klaong Garai temple-tower complex as a means of attracting tourists is a clear violation of Cham religious principles. The alterations in timing, placement, and participant structure undermine the purpose and significance of the ritual, resulting in the desecration of the sacred site in the eyes of the local Cham community. Rather than serving spiritual needs, Rija Nâgar has become a commodity, eroding the perception of the ritual and space among local communities. Findings from my research show that the local Cham community strongly disagrees with this practice, with some suggesting that alternative dances and music performances should be held at the temple grounds, away from the sacred site, as a means of promoting local cultures for tourists. This view aligns with Cole's (2007) argument that while cultural performances may be acceptable for promotion, sacred religious rituals should not be staged or commodified for tourists. The erosion of sacred space through commodification not only leads to the degradation of Indigenous culture, but also contributes to tensions between hosts and tourists, as well as between the host community and heritage authorities, as the temple remains an active site of spiritual practices for the Cham community.

The commodification of Rija Nâgar is not an isolated phenomenon, with similar cases of cultural commodification being studied across the Asia–Pacific region, including in Vanuatu (Tilley, 1997), Bali in Indonesia (Cole, 2007), and China (Wang, 1999). This trend extends to other Southeast Asian New Year's ceremonies, such as the Pimei New Year in Laos (Suntikul & Jachna, 2013) and among other ethnic minority communities in Vietnam. My analysis works in concert with these studies and highlights the lack of understanding among Vietnamese local authorities regarding the principles of Cham religion. They view Rija Nâgar as a mere ethnic performance to be consumed by tourists, despite the fact that members of the Cham community and the performance troop consider it inauthentic and an affront to their values. The desire for a more equal power dynamic was expressed by members of the Cham community, with some advocating for greater involvement in the decision-making process to ensure the proper respect of religious practices. To maintain the authenticity of Po Klaong Garai temple-tower complex and other heritage sites as religious sites, it is essential that the Cham community is given a greater role in the preservation and promotion of their cultural heritage.

Conclusion

The purpose of this study was to examine the perceptions of the Cham community in Vietnam regarding the commodification of their culture through the analysis of the Rija Nâgar rituals at Po Klaong Garai temple-tower complex. Through my research, I found that community members were concerned about the erosion of their sacred space and the violation of Cham religious principles. Despite their disagreements with the current practice of staging Rija Nâgar for tourists, they suggested alternative ways to showcase their culture that are less disruptive to their spiritual practices.

My research contributes to the ongoing discussion on the interconnections between Indigenous communities, government officials, and the tourist industry, and highlights the importance of community involvement in heritage tourism management. By working together with Cham communities, Vietnamese officials could present opportunities for local communities, address economic challenges, and contribute to the preservation of Cham traditional culture.

In conclusion, the role that ethnic and Indigenous communities play in heritage tourism is crucial and should not be ignored. By recognizing the values of living heritage and involving communities in decision-making processes, we can promote sustainable and culturally respectful tourism practices. This not only contributes to the preservation of local cultures, but also to the global understanding of Vietnam as a multicultural society. In line with the emerging policy of the Vietnamese government, it is essential to build a national brand for the tourist sector that prioritizes sustainable development and community involvement.

References

Alariesto, E. (2021). The conflict of sacred and contaminant: The impurifying effects of tourism in Sámi sacred sites. *Matkailututkimus, 17*(1), 64–70. https://doi.org/10.33351/mt.109699

Andrews, T., & Buggey, S. (2008). Authenticity in aboriginal cultural landscapes. *APT Bulletin, 39*(2), 63–71.

Appadurai, A. (1986). *The social life of things.* Cambridge University Press. https://doi.org/10.1017/CBO9780511819582

Beatrice, S. (2009). Sacamefotos and Tejedoras: Frontstage performance and backstage meaning in a Peruvian context. In M. Baud & J. L. Ypeij (Eds.), *Cultural tourism in Latin America : The politics of space and imagery* (pp. 117–140). Brill.

Berger, P. L. (2011). *The sacred canopy: Elements of a sociological theory of religion.* Open Road Integrated Media.

Bianchini, F. (1993). Culture, conflict and cities: Issues and prospects for the 1990's. In M. Parkinson & F. Bianchini (Eds.), *Cultural policy and urban regeneration: The West European experience* (pp. 199–231). Manchester University Press.

Bradford, M., & Lee, E. (2004). *Tourism and cultural heritage in Southeast Asia.* SEAMEO-SPAFA.

Brayley, R. E. (2010). Managing sacred sites for tourism: A case study of visitor facilities in Palmyra, New York. *Tourism: An International Interdisciplinary Journal, 58*(3), 289–300. http://hrcak.srce.hr/62781?lang=en

Bruner, E. M. (1991). Transformation of self in tourism. *Annals of Tourism Research.* https://doi.org/10.1016/0160-7383(91)90007-X

Bruner, E. M. (2005). *Culture on tour: Ethnographies of travel.* The University of Chicago Press.

Butler, R., & Hinch, T. (2007). *Tourism and indigenous peoples: Issues and implications* (Vol. 8). Butterworth-Heinemann. https://doi.org/10.1080/14724040902786641

Carmichael, D. L., Hubert, J., Reeves, B., & Schanche, A. (1992). *Sacred sites, sacred places.* Routledge.

Carmichael, D. L., Hubert, J., Reeves, B., & Schanche, A. (1994). *Sacred sites, sacred places. One world archaeology series 23.* Routledge.

Cham, N. T. P. (2017). A number of trends in folk festival celebration today. *Vietnam Social Sciences, 2*(178), 72–84.

Chambers, E. (2009). Can the Anthropology of tourism make us better travelers? In J. M. T. Wallace (Ed.), *Tourism and applied anthropologists: Linking theory and practice* (Napa Bulletin 23) (pp. 27–44). Wiley-Blackwell. https://doi.org/10.1002/9781444307412.ch1

Cohen, E. (1988). Authenticity and commoditization in tourism. *Annals of Tourism Research, 15*(3), 371–386. https://doi.org/10.1016/0160-7383(88)90028-X

Cole, S. (2007). Beyond authenticity and commodification. *Annals of Tourism Research.* https://doi.org/10.1016/j.annals.2007.05.004

Davis, P., Huang, H.-Y., & Liu, W.-C. (2010). Heritage, local communities and the safeguarding of "Spirit of Place" in Taiwan. *Museum and Society, 8*(2), 80–89. http://openarchive.icomos.org/84/1/77-LtNt-2012_.pdf

Dowson, R. (2021). 'Biker revs' on pilgrimage: Motorbiking vicars visiting sacred sites. *Religions, 12*(3). https://doi.org/10.3390/rel12030148

du Cros, H., & McKercher, B. (2005). Relationship between tourism and cultural heritage management: Evidence from Hong Kong. *Tourism Management, 26*(4), 539–548. https://doi.org/10.1016/j.tourman.2004.02.018

du Cros, H., & McKercher, B. (2015). *Cultural tourism* (2nd ed.). Routledge.

Geary, D., & Shinde, K. (2021). Buddhist pilgrimage and the ritual ecology of sacred sites in the Indo-Gangetic region. *Religions, 12*(6). https://doi.org/10.3390/rel12060385

Greenwood, D. (1989). Culture by the pound: An anthropological perspective on tourism as cultural commodification. In V. Smith (Ed.), *Hosts and guests: The anthropology of tourism* (2nd ed., Vol. 2, pp. 171–185). University of Pennsylvania Press.

Grimwood, B. (2009). Is the sacred for sale? Tourism and indigenous peoples. *Journal of Ecotourism, 8*(February 2015), 217–220. https://doi.org/10.1080/14724040902786625

GSO. (2020). *Socio-economic situation in the first quarter of 2020.* Ha Noi. https://www.gso.gov.vn/default.aspx?tabid=621&ItemID=19558

Hampton, M. P., Jeyacheya, J., Long, P. H., Group, F. S., Tung, L. T., Canavan, B., … Bafadhal, A. S. (2021). Tourism development in Vietnam: New strategy for a sustainable pathway. *Annals of Tourism Research, 37*(2). https://doi.org/10.1080/00220388.2017.1296572

Hobsbawm. (1983). The invention of tradition. In E. J. Hobsbawm & T. O. Ranger (Eds.), *The invention of tradition* (pp. 1–14). Cambridge University Press.

Hubert, J. (1994). Sacred beliefs and beliefs in sacredness. In D. L. Carmichael, J. Hubert, B. Reeves, & A. Schanche (Eds.), *Sacred sites, sacred places* (pp. 1–19). Routledge.

Johnston, A. M. (2006). *Is the sacred for sale: Tourism and Indigenous peoples.* Routledge.

Kitiarsa, P. (2008). *Religious commodifications in Asia.* Race Class (Vol. 48). Routledge. https://doi.org/10.1177/030639680604800116

Koot, S. P. (2013). *Dwelling in tourism: Power and myth amongst Bushmen in Southern Africa* (A. S. Centre Collection, Ed.). African Studies Centre.

Kwon, H. (2017). Villagers' agency in the intangible cultural heritage designation of a Korean village ritual. *International Journal of Heritage Studies, 23*(3), 200–214. https://doi.org/10.1080/13527258.2016.1261920

Lask, T., & Herold, S. (2004). An observation station for culture and tourism in Vietnam: A forum for world heritage and public participation. *Current Issues in Tourism, 7*(4–5), 399–411.

MacCannell, D. (1973). Staged authenticity: Arrangements of social space in tourist settings. *American Journal of Sociology, 79*(3), 589–603. https://doi.org/10.1086/225585

Lewis, D., & Rose, D. (2013). The shape of the dreaming: The cultural significance of Victoria River rock art. In R. Mackay & S. Sullivan (Eds.), *Archaeological sites: Conservation and management* (pp. 607–614). Getty Conservation Institute.

Mbaiwa, J. (2011). Cultural commodification and tourism: The Goo-Moremi community, Central Botswana. *Tijdschrift Voor Economische En Sociale Geografie, 102*(3), 290–301. https://doi.org/10.1111/j.1467-9663.2011.00664.x

Medina, L. K. (2003). Commoditizing culture: Tourism and Maya identity. *Annals of Tourism Research, 30*(2), 353–368. https://doi.org/10.1016/S0160-7383(02)00099-3

Michaud, J., & Turner, S. (2017). Reaching new heights. State legibility in Sa Pa, a Vietnam hill station. *Annals of Tourism Research, 66.* https://doi.org/10.1016/j.annals.2017.05.014

National Assembly Vietnam. Law on Cultural Heritage, Pub. L. No. Law#28/2001/QH10, 23. (2001). *Vietnam.* http://www.unesco.org/culture/natlaws/media/pdf/vietnam/vn_law_cltal_her itage_engtof.pdf

Noseworthy, W. (2013). Reviving traditions and creating futures | International Institute for Asian Studies. *The Newsletter,* pp. 12–13. https://iias.asia/the-newsletter/article/reviving-traditions-and-creating-futures

Paganopoulos, M. (2021). Contested authenticity anthropological perspectives of pilgrimage tourism on Mount Athos. *Religions, 12*(4). https://doi.org/10.3390/rel12040229

Phan, T. (2014). Bảo tồn và phát huy nét đẹp văn hóa truyền thống qua lễ tục Ếw muk kei, Lễ hội Katé – Ramâwan và Lễ hội Rija Nâgar. In T. Phan (Ed.), *Những vấn đề văn hoá – xã hội người Chăm ngày nay* (pp. 5–31). TP. NXB Trẻ.

Picard, M. (2008). Balinese identity as tourist attraction: From 'cultural tourism' (pariwisata budaya) to 'Bali erect' (ajeg Bali). *Tourist Studies.* https://doi.org/10.1177/1468797608099246

Reisinger, Y., & Steiner, C. J. (2006). Reconceptualizing object authenticity. *Annals of Tourism Research, 33*(1), 65–86. https://doi.org/10.1016/J.ANNALS.2005.04.003

Roszko, E. (2011). *Spirited dialogues: Contestations over the religious landscape in Central Vietnam's Littoral Society.* Martin-Luther-Universität Halle-Wittenberg. https://d-nb.info/102 5352424/34

Rutte, C. (2011). The sacred commons: Conflicts and solutions of resource management in sacred natural sites. *Biological Conservation, 144*(10), 2387–2394. https://doi.org/10.1016/j.biocon.2011.06.017

Sakaya. (2003). *The festivals of the Cham people* [Lễ hội của người Chăm]. NXB Van Hoa Dan Toc.

Sakaya. (2016). *Lịch pháp của người Chăm* [Cham calendar]. Tri Thuc Press.

Salemink, O. (2013). Appropriating culture: The politics of intangible cultural heritage in Vietnam. In H.-T. M. Sidel (Ed.), *State, society and the market in contemporary Vietnam: Property, power and values* (pp. 158–180). Routledge. https://doi.org/10.4324/9780203098318

Saltiel, L. (2014). Cultural governance and development in Vietnam. *University of Pennsylvania Journal of International Law, 35*(3), 893–915. https://scholarship.law.upenn.edu/jil/vol35/iss3/6

Sarmiento, F. O., & Hitchner, S. (2017). *Indigeneity and the sacred: Indigenous revival and the conservation of sacred natural sites in the Americas* (1st ed.). Berghahn Books.

Shackley, M. (2001). Sacred world heritage sites: Balancing meaning with management. *Tourism Recreation Research, 26*(1), 5–10.

Shepherd, R. (2018). When sacred space becomes a heritage place: Pilgrimage, worship, and tourism in contemporary China. *International Journal of Religious Tourism and Pilgrimage*. https://doi.org/10.21427/D7TM64

Shepherd, R., Yu, L., & Huimin, G. (2012). Tourism, heritage, and sacred space: Wutai Shan, China. *Journal of Heritage Tourism, 7*(2), 145–161. https://doi.org/10.1080/1743873X.2011.637630

Shinde, K. (2021). Sacred sites, rituals, and performances in the ecosystem of religious tourism. *Religions*. https://doi.org/10.3390/rel12070523

Silverman, H. (2016). Heritage and authenticity. In E. Waterton & S. Watson (Eds.), *The Palgrave handbook of contemporary heritage research* (pp. 69–88). Palgrave Macmillan. https://doi.org/10.1057/9781137293565_5

Smith, L. (2006). *Uses of heritage*. Routledge. https://doi.org/10.4324/9780203602263

Sołjan, I., & Liro, J. (2021). Religious tourism's impact on city space: Service zones around sanctuaries. *Religions, 12*(3), 1–14. https://doi.org/10.3390/rel12030165

Sponsel, L. E. (2008). *Sacred places and biodiversity conservation*. Retrieved January 4, 2016, from http://www.eoearth.org/view/article/155815/

Suntikul, W. (2013). Commodification of intangible cultural heritage in Asia. In N. K. C. Kapila D. Silva (Ed.), *Asian heritage management: Contexts, concerns, and prospects* (pp. 236–252). Rougtledge.

Suntikul, W., & Jachna, T. (2013). Contestation and negotiation of heritage conservation in Luang Prabang, Laos. *Tourism Management, 38*, 57–68. https://doi.org/10.1016/j.tourman.2013.02.005

Tilley, C. (1997). Performing culture in the global village. *Critique of Anthropology, 17*(1), 67–89. https://doi.org/10.1177/0308275X9701700105

Tillonen, M. (2021). Constructing and contesting the shrine: Tourist performances at Seimei Shrine. Kyoto. *Religions, 12*(1), 1–20. https://doi.org/10.3390/rel12010019

Timothy, D. (2009). *Cultural heritage and tourism in the developing world: A regional perspective*. Routledge. Retrieved from http://books.google.co.uk/books?id=0OLftI9psI8C

Timothy, D. (2011). *Cultural heritage and tourism: An introduction*. Channel View Publications.

Timothy, D. J. (2014). Contemporary cultural heritage and tourism: Development issues and emerging trends. *Public Archaeology, 13*(1–3), 30–47. https://doi.org/10.1179/1465518714Z.00000000052

Timothy, D. J., & Nyaupane, G. P. (2009). *Cultural heritage and tourism in the developing world: A regional perspective*. Routledge. https://doi.org/10.4324/9780203877753

Timothy, D., & Olsen, D. (2006). *Tourism, religion and spiritual journeys*. Routledge.

Timothy, D. J., & Prideaux, B. (2004). Issues in heritage and culture in the Asia pacific region. *Asia Pacific Journal of Tourism Research*. https://doi.org/10.1080/1094166042000290628

Tran, L., & Walter, P. (2014). Ecotourism, gender and development in northern Vietnam. *Annals of Tourism Research, 44*, 116–130. https://doi.org/10.1016/j.annals.2013.09.005

Truong, V. D. (2018). Tourism, poverty alleviation, and the informal economy: the street vendors of Hanoi, Vietnam. *Tourism Recreation Research, 43*(1). https://doi.org/10.1080/02508281.2017.1370568

Truong, D. Van, & Anh, L. (2016). The evolution of tourism policy in Vietnam, 1960–2015. In C. M. Hall & Stephen J. Page (Eds.), *The Routledge handbook of tourism in Asia* (pp. 191–204). Routledge. https://doi.org/10.4324/9781315768250

UNESCO. (1999). *My son sanctuary—UNESCO World Heritage Centre*. Retrieved February 23, 2016, from http://whc.unesco.org/en/list/949

Wang, K. Y., Kasim, A., & Yu, J. (2020). Religious festival marketing: Distinguishing between devout believers and tourists. *Religions, 11*(8). https://doi.org/10.3390/rel11080413

Wang, N. (1999). Rethinking authenticity in tourism experience. *Annals of Tourism Research, 26*(2), 349–370. https://doi.org/10.1016/S0160-7383(98)00103-0

Weerasinghe, J. (2011). Living sacred heritage and 'authenticity' in South Asia. In *Heritage, memory & identity* (pp. 139–147). Sage.

Weise, K. (2013). Discourse. In K. Weise (Ed.), *Revisiting Kathmandu safeguarding living urban heritage* (pp. 1–52). UNESCO. Kathmandu Office. https://publik.tuwien.ac.at/files/publik_229747.pdf

World Bank. (2019). *Vietnam's economy expanded by 6.8 percent in 2019 but reforms are needed to unleash the potential of capital markets*. https://www.worldbank.org/en/news/press-release/2019/12/17/vietnams-economy-expanded-by-68-percent-in-2019-but-reforms-are-needed-to-unleash-the-potential-of-capital-markets

Yang, J., Zhang, L., & Ryan, C. (2016). *Social conflict and harmony*. Emerald Group Publishing Limited.

Yang, L. (2007). *Planning for ethnic tourism: Case studies from Xishuangbanna, Yunnan, China*. University of Waterloo.

Zeppel, H. (2006). Indigenous ecotourism: Sustainable development and management (Ecotourism Series, 3). *CABI*. https://doi.org/10.1016/b978-0-7506-6446-2.50025-9

Zhang, Y. (2021). Transnational religious tourism in modern china and the transformation of the cult of Mazu. *Religions, 12*(3). https://doi.org/10.3390/rel12030221

Zhu, Y. (2012). Performing heritage: Rethinking authenticity in tourism. *Annals of Tourism Research, 39*(3), 1495–1513. https://doi.org/10.1016/j.annals.2012.04.003

Open Access This chapter is licensed under the terms of the Creative Commons Attribution 4.0 International License (http://creativecommons.org/licenses/by/4.0/), which permits use, sharing, adaptation, distribution and reproduction in any medium or format, as long as you give appropriate credit to the original author(s) and the source, provide a link to the Creative Commons license and indicate if changes were made.

The images or other third party material in this chapter are included in the chapter's Creative Commons license, unless indicated otherwise in a credit line to the material. If material is not included in the chapter's Creative Commons license and your intended use is not permitted by statutory regulation or exceeds the permitted use, you will need to obtain permission directly from the copyright holder.

Chapter 9
Navigating the Balance Between Revenue Generation and Conservation at a Cham Living Sacred Heritage Site: Priestly Views and Challenges

Introduction

Tourism Benefit-Sharing (TBS) has gained significant attention in the past two decades as a means of providing economic opportunities and preserving natural protected areas (PAs) and cultural heritage sites globally (Akbar & Yang, 2021; Xu et al., 2009). TBS fosters relationships between local communities and authorities, providing an important factor in creating sustainable destinations and contributing to the 17 SDGs (Carius & Job, 2019; Imanishimwe et al., 2018). Effective benefit-sharing, as described in this study, involves local authorities fairly distributing the economic benefits from tourism revenue to Indigenous communities, which enhances their social and economic environment and encourages mutual relationships (Balmford et al., 2009).

Revenue generated from tourism development of PAs has the potential to provide economic benefits, introduce local culture, promote economic diversification, improve the quality of social services, and enhance local infrastructure (Melita & Mendlinger, 2013; Tumusiime & Vedeld, 2012). However, despite extensive research on TBS, debates on the most effective forms of PA conservation persist (Archabald & Naughton-Treves, 2001; Queiros & Mearns, 2019; Spenceley et al., 2017). Local communities play a crucial role in identifying and evaluating the value of TBS, despite varying stakeholder perceptions (Tumusiime & Vedeld, 2012). Hence, there is a pressing need for win–win TBS policies that maintain the sustainable development of PAs (Benjaminsen & Svarstad, 2010; Mukanjari et al., 2013; Spenceley et al., 2017; Tumusiime & Vedeld, 2012).

TBS has been widely studied in the context of national parks around the world (Makame & Boon, 2017; Munanura et al., 2016), but less research has focused on TBS at cultural heritage sites, particularly living heritage sites, which play a crucial role in preserving the cultural heritage of Indigenous communities. Literature suggests that TBS is an important way to explore the economic impacts of tourism on local communities (Mbaiwa & Stronza, 2010; Xu et al., 2009). However, most studies

© The Author(s) 2023
Q. D. Tuyen, *Heritage Conservation and Tourism Development at Cham Sacred Sites in Vietnam*, Global Vietnam: Across Time, Space and Community,
https://doi.org/10.1007/978-981-99-3350-1_9

have been conducted in African countries, leaving other regions, such as Southeast Asian countries, largely overlooked. This research fills this gap by focusing on TBS in the context of ethnic and cultural heritage in Vietnam.

Studies on TBS have investigated perspectives of various stakeholders, including authorities, PA management boards, and local communities (Bruyere et al., 2009; Carius & Job, 2019; MacKenzie, 2012; Weisse & Ross, 2017). However, in-depth studies on different target groups within the local community, especially those engaged in conservation of living heritage, seem to be scarce. Moreover, previous studies have emphasized tourism revenue allocation but have not clarified the distribution of tourism revenue among host communities and who in the community should receive it (Mbaiwa & Stronza, 2010; Snyman & Bricker, 2019). In the Vietnamese context, there have been studies on the living heritage of the Kinh majority group, such as Huong Pham's (2015) examination of the economic impact of tourism on local people in Hoi An Ancient Town. However, the living heritage of minority communities has not received the same level of attention.

Tourism plays a significant role in driving Vietnam's transformation into a developed nation (Saltiel, 2014). One of the key components of this growth is the promotion and preservation of ethnic minority heritage, which attracts a significant number of tourists to the country (Lask & Herold, 2004; Salemink, 2013; Saltiel, 2014; Truong, 2013). The government of Vietnam has recognized the importance of ethnic minority heritage and has issued several policies and guidelines aimed at promoting socio-cultural and social development for ethnic minorities, including the Cham people of Ninh Thuận (Lask & Herold, 2004). The preservation of the Cham cultural heritage is crucial not only for the promotion of tourism but also for the overall development of the country and its people.

As the focus of this study, the Cham people in Ninh Thuận boast an abundant cultural heritage, including over 70 festivals and ceremonies that are still performed annually with the participation of the Cham community and guidance from religious dignitaries (Sakaya, 2003). The Cham's traditional approaches to the stewardship of sacred sites have been officially recognized and promoted by the government since 2012, with representatives from the Ahier Cham community serving as consultants on cultural and religious issues concerning the Cham community.

This rich cultural heritage, particularly the temple-tower architecture system found throughout the Central region and in Ninh Thuận Province, has become a major tourist attraction and product in Vietnam. In 2019, Ninh Thuận welcomed 2.35 million visitors, a 7.3% increase from the previous year, with 100,000 being international arrivals (an annual increase of 25%) and 2.25 million being domestic arrivals (an annual increase of 6.6%) (Sở VH-TT-DL, 2020).

While the rise in tourism has brought positive economic benefits to the region, it has also led to concerns over the allocation of economic benefits from the Cham cultural heritage sites and the satisfaction of the Cham people as the owners and guardians of this cultural heritage. This chapter seeks to address these concerns by exploring the challenges faced by Cham dignitaries in maintaining their cultural heritage through TBS, and examining their perspectives on TBS and its impact on their cultural heritage. This study aims to contribute to the understanding of how equitable TBS can be developed at a living heritage site, where the financial benefits from the commodification of minority culture can be used to support local communities and the custodians of Indigenous heritage.

The contribution of this research is substantial in several key aspects. Firstly, it brings to light the difficulties faced by Cham dignitaries in safeguarding the cultural heritage of the Cham community in Ninh Thuận. Secondly, it explores the views of the Cham dignitaries on TBS and its impact on their cultural heritage. Additionally, it provides an in-depth understanding of the distribution of economic benefits from Cham cultural heritage sites and the satisfaction of the Cham community with TBS. Furthermore, this research contributes to the broader knowledge base on the significance of TBS in the preservation and promotion of cultural heritage. The findings can serve as a useful reference for policymakers and practitioners when developing equitable TBS programs, especially in the context of living heritage sites. The study emphasizes the importance of inclusive and culturally appropriate TBS programs that prioritize the involvement and benefit of local communities, including Indigenous people, by taking into account the challenges faced by the Cham dignitaries and their perspectives. Furthermore, the insights gained from this study can also inform the creation of sustainable and socially responsible cultural tourism programs. By highlighting the challenges faced by the Cham dignitaries, this research can steer future research in the field of cultural heritage preservation and promote best practices for equitable TBS. Overall, this study provides valuable insights into the challenges and opportunities faced by the Cham community in preserving their cultural heritage and the role of TBS in supporting these efforts.

Traditional Custodianship and Cultural Heritage Preservation

The preservation of cultural heritage has been a topic of great concern in the contemporary era. Western heritage management practices have widely impacted many nations, and although these approaches have had a significant impact, they have often neglected the vital role that traditional custodianship systems play in protecting and preserving a community's heritage in the long term. Despite the recognition of the crucial role that traditional custodianship systems play in heritage management, these systems have often been overlooked in regions such as Asia and Africa (Chirikure et al., 2010; Ndoro & Wijesuriya, 2015).

However, this perspective has been challenged by several case studies in Africa that demonstrate the significance of traditional custodianship systems in heritage management (Abungu, 2015; Waterton, 2010). These studies highlight the importance of incorporating traditional management systems into the management of cultural heritage and have been recognized by UNESCO (2013) as a key component in the management of cultural heritage.

Unfortunately, some researchers have found that there is a lack of consultation with local communities in the management of cultural heritage in Africa in practice, as these communities are not considered to be conservation experts (Abungu, 2015; Waterton, 2010). This overlooks the vital role that traditional custodianship systems play in protecting and managing cultural heritage over the long term (Chirikure et al., 2010; Ndoro & Wijesuriya, 2015). However, there is a growing recognition of the significance of traditional custodianship systems in managing cultural heritage, and their role is increasingly being acknowledged and integrated into heritage management practices (Abungu, 2015; UNESCO, 2013).

To effectively preserve cultural heritage, it is crucial to recognize the value of traditional custodianship systems and to involve local communities in the management and protection of their cultural heritage (Chirikure et al., 2010; Ndoro & Wijesuriya, 2015). By doing so, we can ensure that cultural heritage is not only preserved, but also sustained and passed down from generation to generation (Abungu, 2015; UNESCO, 2013). The integration of traditional management systems into heritage management practices will also ensure that the heritage reflects the values and traditions of the local communities and that their voices are heard in the decision-making process (Weise, 2013). In short, the recognition of the importance of traditional custodianship systems and the involvement of local communities in the management of cultural heritage are critical components in ensuring the preservation and sustainability of cultural heritage (Abungu, 2015; Chirikure et al., 2010; Ndoro & Wijesuriya, 2015; UNESCO, 2013; Weise, 2013).

Traditional custodianship systems play a key role in the preservation and management of cultural heritage within communities. These systems are often rooted in customary laws that govern the use of sacred sites and protect them from violations (Abungu & Githitho, 2012; Harris, 1991; Shen et al., 2012). The regulations and principles established by these traditional systems help to minimize negative impacts on heritage sites and are a significant aspect of the local community's connection to the landscape and its resources (Smith & Turk, 2013). However, the significance of traditional custodianship systems is often disregarded in heritage conservation and development, leading to the creation of a form of heritage that goes against local views and traditions, thereby reducing the cultural significance of the heritage being preserved (Byrne, 2012). This is due in part to the fact that these systems are often overlooked in heritage management practices (Bwasiri, 2011).

To address this issue, scholars have recommended integrating local customary systems within Western conservation models as the most effective approach to cultural heritage management (Bwasiri, 2011; Smith & Turk, 2013). This approach enables the exploration of the social concerns and needs of the local community, which is a crucial consideration, particularly in the case of the Cham community studied in this research. By considering the perspectives and needs of the Cham community, the government can effectively manage the Cham temples for the benefit of the Cham people, while preserving the cultural heritage and its traditional values.

The preservation of cultural heritage requires a holistic approach that takes into account the perspectives and needs of the local community who are connected to the heritage site (Weise, 2013). A top-down approach to heritage management, such as limiting access to cultural heritage resources for local communities, can have negative consequences for their livelihoods and traditional ways of life (Fletcher et al., 2007; Miura, 2005). Miura (2005) suggests that heritage sites should be protected by incorporating the values held by the living population, as they are the ones who will be responsible for passing down these values to future generations.

Moreover, imposing heritage management without taking into account the desires of the community and providing a functional and sustainable system will result in the loss of authenticity, as argued by Weise (2013). In order to preserve cultural heritage, it is necessary to consider both the tangible and intangible aspects of heritage, as well as the social concerns of the local community. Decision-making in heritage management should be guided by the living heritage and the perspectives of the community who holds the heritage, as this will ensure that the heritage is maintained in a culturally appropriate and sustainable manner (Weise, 2013).

Tourism Benefit-Sharing: The Importance of Involving Local Communities

The literature review section on Tourism Benefit-Sharing (TBS) has focused on exploring the relationship between protected areas (PAs) that have become tourism destinations and the allocation of benefits to local communities. TBS has emerged as a crucial component of sustainable tourism development in protected areas, providing finance for conservation activities and infrastructure development (Mbaiwa & Stronza, 2010; Spenceley et al., 2017). In recent years, scholars have become interested in integrating heritage conservation and tourism development (Munanura et al., 2016), recognizing that benefits derived from tourism can bring tangible and intangible benefits to local communities.

Tangible benefits include the creation of jobs, direct income, and improved infrastructure, while intangible benefits include capacity building, skills training, and cultural development (Spenceley et al., 2017). The key to effective TBS is a mutual understanding between the government and local communities, where the government provides welfare opportunities and the local communities maintain conservation and sustainable development (Bebbington, 1999; Makame & Boon, 2017; Spenceley et al., 2017). This relationship can be further strengthened by providing social and cultural capital, as well as living support and substantive opportunities to encourage community engagement in heritage conservation (Bebbington, 1999; Gautam, 2009). Local communities should also have equal social and economic support and opportunities to achieve sustainable livelihoods (Norton & Foster, 2001; Spenceley et al., 2017).

However, there have been cases where TBS has not been fair to local communities, with only a small part of tourism revenue being shared with a small number of direct beneficiaries in the community (Schnegg & Kiaka, 2018). Benefits are often leaked externally to foreign travel agencies, provincial or central businesses, or other organizations (Ahebwa et al., 2012; Sandbrook, 2010). To ensure that economic benefits are directly shared with the local community, it is important to establish access rights and sharing mechanisms for the host community (Kiss, 2004; Lapeyre, 2011; Wunder, 2000). For example, in Rwanda, 5% of the annual income from tourism revenue is dedicated to promoting local community livelihoods, demonstrating that TBS can improve lives and sustainably preserve heritage (Munanura et al., 2016).

The concept of Tourism-based Sustainability (TBS) has been a topic of interest among scholars and researchers due to its complexity and difficulty in implementation. This is highlighted in the studies conducted by Adams et al. (2004) and Snyman and Bricker (2019) which indicate the multifaceted nature of TBS. To address the challenges of TBS, local authorities must adopt a comprehensive approach that considers the interests of all stakeholders (Benjaminsen & Svarstad, 2010). One way of enhancing the success of TBS is through community empowerment. This involves encouraging communities to take an active role in tourism activities, such as through joint ventures or other cooperative management models (Baghai et al., 2018). This is further emphasized by Heslinga et al. (2019) who stress the significance of community empowerment in overcoming participation barriers in TBS.

Furthermore, a study by Li (2006) on community participation in decision-making in Sichuan, China found that communities still benefit from tourism development even when their participation in decision-making is weak. This highlights the importance of community involvement in TBS, as it not only benefits the community but also contributes to the overall success of TBS initiatives. Li (2006) argues that community participation is not a final goal in itself, but rather a means to achieving community involvement in tourism activities.

The literature on Tourism-based Sustainability (TBS) has mainly focused on collaborations between Indigenous communities and governments (Chirikure et al., 2010; Smith & Waterton, 2009; Waterton, 2015) and Indigenous custodian systems (Jones, 2007; Ndoro, 2004; Sharma, 2013; Smith & Turk, 2013). However, despite this extensive research, the social conditions of the Indigenous custodians, who play a central role in Indigenous custodianship, have often been overlooked. This is particularly problematic in the case of the Ahiér priests, who serve as Cham custodians, and are vital for effectively managing living Cham heritage sites to achieve sustainability. The Ahiér priests bring the Po Klaong Girai temple and Cham culture to life.

This research highlights the importance of understanding the social conditions of Cham custodians in the context of TBS. Snyman and Bricker (2019) argue that identifying the needs and problems of the community's institutional system is necessary to comprehend the effectiveness of TBS. Moreover, MacKenzie (2012) and Strickland-Munro and Moore (2013) emphasize that understanding the needs of Indigenous communities and stakeholders in TBS is a critical foundation for achieving sustainable development goals.

In conclusion, the literature highlights the importance of considering the social conditions of Indigenous custodians in TBS. It is necessary to understand the community's institutional system and the needs of Indigenous communities and stakeholders for effective TBS and sustainable development.

Study Background and Context

The Cham are a distinct ethnic group in Vietnam, originating from the central region and known for their long-standing history and rich cultural traditions. Their contributions to Vietnamese culture are especially evident in their beliefs and customs, which are reflected in traditional festivals and ancient beliefs.

The Cham communities are still predominantly concentrated in certain provinces in South Central and Southern Vietnam, with the oldest settlements located in Ninh Thuận Province. According to the General Statistics Office, there were 178,948 Cham people in Vietnam in 2019, with 82,532 residing in Ninh Thuận Province alone. The Cham culture is alive and vibrant in Ninh Thuận, with vibrant colors evident in writing, costumes, architectural art, sculptures, and traditional crafts. The preservation of Cham matriarchal customs is noteworthy (Biên et al., 1989, 1991; Sakaya, 2003), and many forms of Cham cultural heritage have been recognized by the Vietnamese state (Table 9.1).

The Po Klaong Girai temple is a revered site for the Cham community where they come to worship their wise king and participate in various spiritual activities. The temple is famous for hosting cultural, religious, and traditional festivals throughout the year, particularly the Kate festival which takes place in the seventh month of the Cham calendar. This event attracts tourists from all over the world to the temple, making it a significant cultural and economic asset for Ninh Thuận Province.

As a part of its tourism development strategy, local authorities in Ninh Thuận Province have identified the importance of Cham culture and have taken measures to conserve and promote Cham temples and craft villages as key tourist attractions. These efforts have not only brought economic benefits to the region but also helped some Cham people living in craft villages. Nevertheless, the preservation and promotion of Cham cultural heritage through tourism development should be approached with caution, as this may result in the degradation of the heritage and the exploitation of local communities.

Table 9.1 International and national recognition of Cham cultural heritage in Ninh Thuận province

No	Cultural heritage	Type of recognition	Year
1	New Year's ritual of the Cham people in Binh Nghia village	National Intangible Cultural Heritage	2021
2	Kate Festival of the Cham ethnic people in Ninh Thuận province	National Intangible Cultural Heritage	2017
3	Traditional pottery art of the Cham people in Bau Truc village	National Intangible Cultural Heritage	2017
		UNESCO's List of Intangible Cultural Heritage in Need of Urgent Safeguarding	2022
4	Po Klaong Garai temple	Special National Monument	2016
5	Hoa Lai temple	Special National Monument	2016
6	Po Rome temple	National Architectural Monument	1992

Table 9.2 Number of visitors to the Po Klaong Girai temple and revenue generated

Year	Visitors	Domestics	Foreigners	Revenue in VND	Revenue in US dollars
2015	5556	5289	267	83,340,000	378,800
2016	6138	5536	582	92,070,000	418,500
2017	104,335	100,605	3,395	1,570,025,000	71,365,000
2018	140,000	135,780	4,220	2,060,000,000	93,636,000
2019	134,000	133,550	450	2,350,000,000	102,367,000

Notes Data compiled by officers from Ninh Thuận Department of Culture, Sports, and Tourism reports. Exchange rate: 1 USD = 22,000 VND

The Po Klaong Girai temple has gained recognition as a popular tourist destination in Ninh Thuận Province, and its entrance ticket sales have had a positive impact on local government budgets (Table 9.2). The temple's tourism revenue has experienced a significant increase, particularly from 2017 onwards. Despite the fact that the revenue from tourism is not a major contributor to the province's overall revenue, it holds great importance for the Cham community as it provides the necessary financial support for the preservation of their cultural heritage.

Challenges in Preserving Indigenous Cultural Traditions

The two major challenges identified were related to education and finances. Additionally, a widely held belief was that the Ahiér priests, as the primary custodians of heritage sites such as the Po Klaong Girai temple, should play a crucial role in preserving and promoting Cham culture through their extensive knowledge of traditional customs, religion, literature, and history.

Financial Challenges: Loss of Agricultural Assets

Traditionally, the Cham community allocated fields and buffaloes to priests and other individuals who dedicated their lives to spiritual activities. This provided stable income and allowed the priests to spend their time researching books, the Cham calendar, and other traditions, forming a community of intellectuals who held extensive knowledge of Cham culture, language, and history (Noseworthy, 2017). These individuals were highly respected by the community and were considered crucial for the preservation of Cham culture. However, after the reunification of Vietnam in 1975, the nationalization of farming assets had a significant impact on the Cham community. Many custodians lost their farming assets, and their main source of income became community contributions during ritual activities, while fields were only an additional source of income.

According to Orang005, the Po Klaong rice fields were hired by the Cham community for ritual activities and were a crucial source of income for the custodians. They could devote all their time to the community without disturbing the economy. On the other hand, Orang001 experienced a loss of their buffaloes and rice fields and had to resort to manual labor to make a living. This loss of agricultural assets made life significantly harder for the Cham community.

The declining number of Cham custodians is a significant challenge facing the preservation of Cham culture. The traditional practice of only allowing custodians' children to follow this line of work limits the pool of potential custodians, putting added pressure on the existing community of priests. The passing of Ahier religious priests not only means the loss of their experiences and deep understanding of Cham tradition, cultural rules, and the yearly calendar, but also creates a significant threat to the sustainability of the priest system itself. In the most populated Cham village, Hamu Tanran, it is becoming increasingly difficult to find a Basaih priest for important rituals such as cremation ceremonies. Villagers must often search for priests in other villages or even travel to Palei Kraong in Binh Thuận Province. This lack of continuity in the community is causing great concern for the future of traditional Cham activities and the survival of Cham culture as a whole.

During my fieldwork, I had the opportunity to engage with many Cham priests and gain a deeper understanding of their struggles and aspirations. These priests are not just performers, but they also play the role of instrument makers, historians, and keepers of Cham culture, tradition, and history. Although there are a few officially recognized artists and drum players, custodians like Ong Maduen and Kadhar, who make ginang and kanyi instruments and are responsible for preserving traditional knowledge for future generations, are often overlooked.

The priests face many challenges in their daily lives, such as the difficulty of earning a living, a lack of interest in their line of work, and unequal recognition of their contributions. As Kadhar, one of the custodians, stated, "I am not just an instrument player, I keep all the hymns about the lives of Cham Kings, and I have documents on ancient Cham traditions passed down from my ancestors. I will transfer them to the next generation, but there is no benefit. While the ginang player may be recognized as an artist, custodians like me who play more important roles in preserving traditional values and knowledge receive no recognition."

The conservation of living heritage sites is not limited to protecting temples and monuments. It involves preserving the spiritual life and cultural heritage of the Cham people, which is deeply intertwined with the knowledge and practices of the priests. Hence, adequate support for these custodians is critical to ensure the survival of Cham culture. Unfortunately, following agricultural land ownership reforms in Vietnam, many priests have been forced to pursue alternative means of earning a livelihood, leading to a disconnect between the present and the past, and a discontinuity in Cham heritage. The absence of new priests and the financial difficulties faced by the community have resulted in the disappearance of some public rituals, highlighting the need for greater support for the preservation of living heritage sites.

Low Levels of Public Education

The second challenge faced by the Cham community is the low levels of public education. Historically, the Cham people used their native language in all aspects of their lives, including the study of Cham texts that taught about geography, history, and customs. Young priests received specialized training at the homes of their Gurus, rather than in the public education system. However, this form of education was disrupted after 1975, leaving many without a proper high school or higher education. Those who did attend public schools were not necessarily priests, and many struggled to follow the curriculum, eventually dropping out to work in family businesses. This has resulted in a limited understanding of social history and contemporary society for many within the Cham community.

Orang008 shared that their father encouraged them to strive for higher education and pursue a career as a doctor, teacher, or in a similar field, rather than becoming a custodian. However, they found it difficult to keep up with the curriculum and eventually left school to work in agriculture. On the other hand, some custodians were able to finish high school, which made their transition to working on the Bramanism committee much easier. These individuals have a greater sense of confidence in communicating and working with the local government. Additionally, Orang001 spoke about their experience of dropping out of school due to difficult family circumstances, but eventually finishing high school. They explained that the lack of education for many within the community leads to a shyness in discussing traditional customs in Vietnamese when working with the local government. However, as a result of their education, they feel more confident in their ability to read and write Vietnamese and to work on paperwork for the committee when reporting to the local government. They believe that higher levels of education would benefit the entire community, providing them with a greater understanding of society's issues.

The poor education received by custodians through the public education system, combined with frequent misunderstandings, has made their work challenging and hindered their ability to express their opinions in meetings with local government. Only a few priests have basic reading and writing skills and have never even left their villages. Life is difficult for them as most of their time is spent earning a living, leaving little time for other interests. This has resulted in many grammatical errors when writing reports and public announcements in Vietnamese, as noted by Orang020.

Due to their limitations in managing cultural heritage, some retired intellectuals from the community may work with the committee. These individuals have higher levels of education and experience in working with the government. According to members of the Cham community, poorly educated priests are not aware of their responsibilities and positions within the Cham society and spiritual world. Despite the high intellectual standard of the Cham community, the low level of Vietnamese public education among most Cham priests leads to them being underappreciated and not respected by Cham intellectuals and the wider community. As stated by a Cham elder, Orang009: "*Some young and fresh priests do not even know the religious norms of daily life. How can they be spiritual leaders of the Cham Ahier community? They have not only a low level of public education but also a lack of understanding of the Cham language and ancient manuscripts."*

Junior priests have reported feeling that society only values doctors, engineers, and government officers and not priests who preserve cultural values. This has led to feelings of depression, low confidence, and even mental health issues, as expressed by Orang010: *"I feel sad sometimes because my friends do not really respect my position as a priest. However, I still want to continue being a priest, following my family tradition. Today, there are no young people taking up this responsibility, so who will serve spiritual ceremonies for the community in the future?"*

Both priests and the Cham community believe that financial support for training custodians to acquire knowledge about society and technology is needed. This would help them to better understand their position within the Cham community, be more confident in their work, and be better equipped to work effectively with the local government.

Investigating the Cham Community's Standpoint on Sharing the Revenue from Tourism Benefits

According to the interviews, the Cham community is not benefiting equitably from the economic benefits of tourism. Despite being the traditional custodians and owners of their heritage, they do not receive financial compensation in the same manner as government employees. The interviewees expressed their disappointment with the current state of affairs, where the income generated from entrance fees is not shared with the Cham community. They believe that this money should be used to support traditional ceremonies and restore those that have been lost due to insufficient funding.

One interviewee (Orang004) stated that the government is taking money from the Cham's heritage without sharing the benefits with the custodians. Another (Orang001) added that the small amount of money provided to the Cham community from the entrance ticket sales is unreasonable. Similarly, several interviewees (Orang002, Orang007) expressed frustration over the government keeping all of the money from ticket sales, without giving any to the Cham community.

The negative sentiments and testimonials from elders and priests are driven by the economic hardships they face in their daily lives. Despite the increase in popularity of the area as a tourist destination, generating significant revenue, the funds are not being used to support the traditional Cham custodians. Instead, they are being used for employees working at the temples and other local officials. The interviewees believe that a part of this revenue should be shared with the custodians so that they can perform spiritual activities and protect their community heritage.

Several interviewees reported feeling ownership over Cham cultural heritage, and as a result, believe they should be entitled to receive a portion of the tourism revenue generated by these sites. This is in light of the fact that the current distribution of funds only goes towards paying heritage staff and not the Cham priests, who are essential in preserving and conserving the heritage.

One interviewee, Orang026, stated, *"It's difficult for us as we work daily for the community without receiving any payment. Meanwhile, the revenue generated from tourism at the Cham temples is not being distributed to us."* Another interviewee, Orang029, shared, *"At the very least, they should give us half of the tourism revenue so that the dignitaries can dedicate themselves to performing and preserving the rituals at the temple."*

The lack of financial support for Cham priests has led to the disappearance of many traditions and cultural practices. Orang005 shared, "I have had to discontinue two major festivals, Pakap Halau Kraong and Palao Kasah, due to the lack of funds. These festivals bring unity to the Cham community and promote cultural values. If I had the resources, I would call for the community to come together to revive these ceremonies. I still have records of how to perform them, but many of the custodians who knew how to celebrate have passed away, and their knowledge has been lost."

Cham elders are advocating for a more equitable distribution of the tourism revenue in order to better preserve and promote their cultural heritage. Muk Pajuw, a female medium, stated, *"I wasn't aware of this issue until I saw the lack of funds for worship ceremonies. I've seen dignitaries calling for support from the Cham community. If there is a significant amount of ticket sales, they should allocate some of it towards the community."*

According to Interviewee 04, sharing 20–30% of the tourism benefits with the Cham priests would help preserve the Cham culture and support those who maintain it. They would be grateful for this gesture.

Interviewee 14 stated that they have spoken to the authorities many times about the unfair distribution of tourism benefits, but their concerns have been ignored. The local government has many sources of revenue, but the revenue from tourism at the Cham temple is small in comparison. However, for the Cham people, it is a large amount that is important for preserving their cultural heritage. Sharing this revenue would show the state's concern for ethnic minorities. Similarly, Interviewee 14 shared that the Cham people are not mentioned in the decisions made regarding the distribution of tourism revenue. 60% of the revenue is kept for staff salaries and renovations at the temple, while 40% is deducted for the state budget, leaving nothing for the Cham community. This is viewed as inequality and injustice.

The majority of the interviewees believe that the tourism revenue at the Cham temple is not fairly shared with the Cham people. They believe that if the state and local authorities shared the economic benefits, it would demonstrate concern for ethnic minorities in Vietnam.

Revenue Sharing Expectations of the Cham Community from Tourism

In addition to the lack of support for their physical well-being, the traditional temple guardians and primary custodians of the sacred temples in Ninh Thuận Province also face financial difficulties. Despite the efforts they have put into protecting Cham cultural heritage for generations, they are not adequately compensated for their work, and many are struggling to make ends meet.

During my fieldwork, I met with senior priests who shared their financial and health concerns with me. Despite the critical role they play in maintaining Cham cultural heritage, they receive little support from the government, and their ability to continue performing their duties is in jeopardy. One priest, Orang006, expressed his desire for basic health care and insurance. He stated, "It is great if the government gives us support for a medical check-up. I would be very happy about that. I am old now, and I do not have money for a health check-up. Neither do other custodians. I am old with many health issues. Where can I get money for these check-ups? I have been expecting health insurance from the government, but there has been no response on that."

Members of the committee responsible for the stewardship of the sacred temples have also proposed this support but have met with little response from the local government. Orang003, a member of the committee, shared, "*I have proposed it many times as senior priests are facing health issues. They have devoted their lives to the community, so they should receive a payback for their old age. However, the local government refused the proposal and explained that other religions might ask for the same healthcare support.*"

The situation highlights the need for greater support and recognition of the important role played by these traditional temple guardians and primary custodians in maintaining Cham cultural heritage. With the harsh environmental conditions and lack of financial and healthcare support, it is uncertain who will continue their work in the future.

This situation has led to a major concern for the well-being of the priests, especially the older ones, who are already facing health issues. The harsh weather conditions can exacerbate their existing health problems and make it difficult for them to perform their duties effectively (Fig. 9.1). Moreover, the lack of support from the government, in terms of providing basic health care and insurance, adds to the priests' difficulties and raises the question of who will take over their duties in the future.

In this context, it is crucial for the local government to consider the well-being of the priests and provide them with adequate support, including basic health care and insurance, to help them carry out their duties and preserve the cultural heritage of the Cham people. The priests have dedicated their lives to the community, and it is only fair for the government to recognize their contributions and provide them with the support they deserve. Failure to do so could result in a loss of Cham cultural heritage, as younger generations may not be willing or able to continue the work of their elders.

Fig. 9.1 Elder priests performing rituals under the intense heat of the tropical sun

During my fieldwork, I interviewed several individuals who expressed their views on the relationship between the local government and the Cham community in regard to tourism revenue. Many of these respondents believed that, as the authorities benefit from tourism at Cham temples, the government has a responsibility to provide support to the priests. One interviewee, Orang018, suggested that priests should receive a monthly salary so they could concentrate on their religious duties, or be hired as official tour guides at the temples. They explained that this would allow them to earn money to support their families while also introducing Cham culture in an accurate and honest way.

Orang005, who worked in the Balamon Dignitaries Council, shared their under-standing of the economic difficulties faced by the Cham community, including the loss of fields for their livelihoods. They argued that the government should provide financial support to the priests to allow them to maintain the temples and share their knowledge with visitors.

Other interviewees, such as Orang17 and Orang024, emphasized the importance of using tourism revenue to improve the education and knowledge of young Cham priests. They believed that this would help them better contribute to the conservation and promotion of Cham culture. Orang024 explained that without the preservation of Cham heritage, there would be no tourism development and profit.

In short, many of the interviewees believed that the local government should use tourism revenue to support the Cham community, including providing financial support for priests, creating job opportunities for them as tour guides, and improving the education of young priests for better preservation of Cham culture. Some respondents argued that priests should receive a monthly salary, so they can focus on their duties and others felt that tourism revenue should be used to provide financial support for their daily lives and re-train them in heritage conservation. The overall sentiment was that tourism revenue is crucial for the Cham community, and should be used to promote and maintain their culture.

Achieving Fair Distribution of Tourism Revenues for Heritage Stewards

This chapter explores the difficulties faced by traditional Cham custodians in their efforts to conserve their cultural heritage and their views on the distribution of tourism benefits at their living heritage sites in Vietnam. The study reveals that the benefits of tourism are not fairly distributed among the Cham community, with most of the revenue going to the state and government staff. The economic hardships faced by the Cham priests, including limited educational opportunities and lack of financial support, put pressure on them to seek alternative sources of income, thus compromising their cultural and religious obligations. The unequal distribution of tourism revenues is a major barrier to successful and sustainable heritage conservation in the Cham community.

The role of Ahier priests in preserving Cham cultural heritage cannot be overstated, particularly in regard to the Cham living temples in Ninh Thuận Province. As the overseers of religious activities and teachers of Cham culture, these priests have maintained the manuscripts and passed on the knowledge of the Cham community's history, astronomy, law, customs, literature, and the legacies of its kings (Abdul, 2013). However, previous studies (Mbaiwa & Stronza, 2010; Xu et al., 2009) on the economic benefits of tourism development for local communities have failed to consider the specific needs and challenges faced by those who play a crucial role in preserving Indigenous culture. This study confirms the significance of maintaining cultural heritage and highlights how the everyday concerns of the Ahier priests need to be taken into account in the management of heritage sites.

Given the crucial role that Ahier priests play in leading spiritual practices and cultural events at the temples, I argue that the management of living heritage sites should not only consider the values held by the living community, but also the social concerns of these priests. Jigyasu (2015) also argues that the management of living heritage sites must take into account the contemporary context and the immediate socio-economic challenges faced by local communities in light of damages to the heritage (Kong, 2008). The findings of this study are consistent with Ahebwa's (2012) findings that such challenges must be recognized and managed when implementing TBS as a policy for sustainable tourism.

The findings of my research highlight the increasing recognition of Ahier priests by government authorities in the conservation and development activities at the Po Klaong Girai temple. This shift towards collaboration with Cham communities in co-managing their living heritage sites is commendable, but the socio-economic conditions of the Cham Ahier priests still require attention. Despite the priests being instrumental in preserving their cultural heritage, they do not receive any economic benefits from the heritage sites, which hinders their ability to preserve the resources and work effectively with the local government. This lack of recognition and financial support for the priests is not unique to Cham people. Many studies have shown that tourism can exacerbate inequality and inhibit the participation of local communities in the distribution of benefits (Archabald & Naughton-Treves, 2001; Heslinga et al., 2019; Spenceley et al., 2017; Tumusiime & Sjaastad, 2014). This can lead to conflict between the financial beneficiaries of tourism and the cultural owners of the heritage, as seen with the Cham Ahier priests. The failure to address this conflict can have negative impacts on the economic, cultural, social, and political lives of stakeholders (Jamal & Stronza, 2009).

This study adds to the body of literature (Queiros & Mearns, 2019; Tumusiime & Sjaastad, 2014; Walpole & Goodwin, 2001) that demonstrates the importance of sharing tourism benefits fairly and recognizing the importance of local communities in the conservation of heritage sites. The Ahier priests, who play a central role in maintaining the spiritual activities and cultural events at the temple, require financial support for their livelihoods, education, and health care. Providing this support through TBS is necessary to foster their participation in the conservation of Cham living heritage sites and overcome their economic and educational challenges. The findings from this research align with studies that highlight the unequal distribution of benefits from tourism (Huong, 2015; Miura, 2005). In the case of the Po Klaong Girai temple, it is clear that the local Cham community is not receiving the same economic benefits from the temple that other communities, such as those near Angkor Wat and Hoi An, are receiving from their respective heritage sites. Unlike these communities, the livelihoods of the Cham people are not tied to the landscape around the temple, but rather to the resources they need to maintain their cultural traditions. This unequal distribution of benefits can lead to conflicts between the financial beneficiaries of tourism and the cultural owners of heritage sites, as has been demonstrated in several studies (Jamal & Stronza, 2009; Queiros & Mearns, 2019; Tumusiime & Sjaastad, 2014; Walpole & Goodwin, 2001). In the case of the Cham people, this conflict is exacerbated by the lack of recognition of the socio-economic conditions of the Ahier priests, who face significant economic and educational difficulties that pose a threat to the sustainability of their living heritage sites.

To mitigate these challenges and ensure the preservation of the Cham living heritage, it is necessary for the local government to provide the necessary support to the Ahier priests, including financial support for their livelihoods, education, and health care. This support is critical to overcome the economic and educational difficulties facing the Ahier priests, and to foster and encourage their participation in the conservation of the Cham living heritage sites (Kong, 2008). Failure to provide this support could result in the loss of vitality and outstanding universal values associated with these sacred temples, highlighting the need for prompt action.

My research reveals a distinct case of benefit-sharing ambiguity in the laws, policies, and mechanisms of the Vietnamese government, particularly with regard to the Heritage Legislation of Vietnam. Despite the law stipulating the sharing of economic benefits to the local community (as noted in studies by Heslinga et al. in 2019 and Scheyvens in 2002), the Heritage Legislation of Vietnam fails to consider the rights, justice, and economic benefits for those who are responsible for maintaining the cultural heritage. Although the Hoi An Protocols mention the importance of cultural resources for "sustained and equitable social and economic development" (Engelhardt & Rogers, 2009, p. 2), there is a need for clearer language to define what is meant by "sustained" and "equitable," especially in the context of rapid socioeconomic transformation affecting Indigenous communities. This lack of consideration for the social aspects of local communities, as highlighted by Kong (2008, p. 14), contributes to ineffective management of living heritage sites, as noted by Weise (2013).

Weise (2013) highlights the importance of considering the needs of local communities in the relationship between heritage sites and their surrounding communities. The living heritage of these communities, including their traditional practices, must be valued and protected. The cultural richness of heritage sites, such as the Po Klaong Girai temple, is derived not only from its architectural design, but also from the spiritual and ritual practices that give the site its "life force." This is why it is crucial to ensure that the local communities who maintain and practice their living heritage at these sites also benefit from their preservation and conservation. As Miura (2008) points out, conserving heritage without considering the daily needs of the living population can result in a "frozen past." Given the significance of Cham heritage in Ninh Thuận Province, it is imperative that the benefits of its conservation are shared by all stakeholders, including the local community. The need for community participation in heritage conservation is emphasized by Kong (2008), who argues that effective management of living heritage sites must consider the social considerations of local communities. This can be achieved through providing institutional and financial support that is equitable and respectful of local traditions. Only by taking these steps can we ensure sustainable development and effective conservation of the living heritage of the Cham community.

My research findings highlight the ongoing struggles of the Cham community in terms of their involvement and benefit-sharing in the Tourism Based Services (TBS) at their living heritage site. Despite their crucial role in preserving the heritage, the Cham dignitaries have expressed their disappointment and frustration over the lack of recognition and profit-sharing from the tourism industry. My study sheds light on the perspectives and experiences of the core communities who are directly involved in preserving the living heritage site. Previous studies have emphasized the importance of community participation and benefit-sharing in TBS (Makame & Boon, 2017; Munanura et al., 2016; Snyman & Bricker, 2019). However, this research highlights the need for further examination on TBS and its impact on the social and economic well-being of local communities. It is crucial to ensure that the distribution of tourism benefits is equitable and that the local communities are not detached from their living heritage sites. This study therefore calls for further research to address these pressing concerns and ensure the sustainability of both the heritage sites and the communities that hold them dear.

This study sheds light on the pressing issue of benefit-sharing for the Cham community in the context of TBS at their living heritage site. It highlights the importance of involving the community, particularly the cultural carriers, in the preservation and promotion of their living heritage. As pointed out by Jamal and Stronza (2009) and Lindberg (1991), the community's participation and contribution are crucial for successful heritage conservation and sustainable development. The findings of this study are consistent with those of previous studies on TBS, such as those by Makame and Boon (2017), Munanura et al. (2016), and Snyman and Bricker (2019). These studies emphasize the negative impact of unfair TBS on tourism development and heritage conservation. Snyman and Bricker (2019) also underscore the importance of community attitudes and willingness to contribute to conservation efforts. However, the current heritage and tourism laws in Vietnam overlook the rights, justice, and economic benefits of the community, who are the creators and bearers of cultural heritage. This study aligns with the findings of Lapeyre (2011) and Tumusiime and Vedeld (2012), who argue that tourism development must critically consider the real benefits for the environment and the host community. It calls for a reexamination of these laws and policies to ensure that the benefits of tourism development at cultural heritage sites are shared fairly and equitably with the local communities.

Conclusion

This research sheds light on the challenges faced by the Cham community in preserving and promoting their cultural heritage through TBS at their living sacred sites in Ninh Thuận Province, Vietnam. The study highlights that the Cham people face significant economic and educational barriers that hinder the preservation and development of their cultural heritage. Moreover, the community has expressed their dissatisfaction with the unequal distribution of tourism benefits, which raises questions about the fairness towards the owners and bearers of cultural heritage.

While previous research has focused on TBS in protected areas in Africa, this study emphasizes the importance of considering the perspectives of Indigenous and ethnic communities in living heritage sites. The participation of the host community is critical in preserving cultural heritage and promoting sustainable tourism development. Listening to the voices of Indigenous and ethnic people who play a crucial role in preserving cultural heritage is crucial to address the challenges faced in preserving and promoting heritage values.

This research offers evidence for improving heritage management practices by proposing tourism development policies that promote equality and justice among stakeholders, especially minority and disadvantaged groups. It serves as a valuable lesson for sustainable heritage management in living heritage sites in other ethnic minority areas in Vietnam and around the world.

References

Abdul, M. E. (2013). *Nager Cam and the priests of prowess: A history of resilience.* University of Hawaii at Manoa.

Abungu, G. O. (2015). UNESCO, the World Heritage convention, and Africa: The practice and the practitioners. In W. Logan, M. N. Craith, & U. Kockel (Eds.), *A companion to heritage studies* (pp. 373–391). Wiley-Blackwell.

Abungu, G. O., & Githitho, A. (2012). Homelands of the Mijikenda people: Sacred Mijikenda Kaya Forests, Kenya. In A. Galla (Ed.), World Heritage benefits beyond borders (pp. 147–157). Cambridge University Press. https://doi.org/10.1017/CBO9781139567657

Adams, W. M., Aveling, R., Brockington, D., Dickson, B., Elliott, J., Hutton, J., Roe, D., Vira, B., & Wolmer, W. (2004). Biodiversity conservation and the eradication of poverty. *Science, 306*(5699), 1146–1149. https://doi.org/10.1126/science.1097920

Ahebwa, W. M., van der Duim, R., & Sandbrook, C. (2012). Tourism revenue sharing policy at Bwindi Impenetrable National Park, Uganda: A policy arrangements approach. *Journal of Sustainable Tourism, 20*(3), 377–394. https://doi.org/10.1080/09669582.2011.622768

Akbar, I., & Yang, Z. (2021). The influence of tourism revenue sharing constraints on sustainable tourism development: A study of Aksu-Jabagly nature reserve, Kazakhstan. *Asian Geographer, 39*(2), 133–153. https://doi.org/10.1080/10225706.2021.1894462

Archabald, K., & Naughton-Treves, L. (2001). Tourism revenue-sharing around national parks in Western Uganda: Early efforts to identify and reward local communities. *Environmental Conservation.* https://doi.org/10.1017/S0376892901000145

Baghai, M., Miller, J. R. B., Blanken, L. J., Dublin, H. T., Fitzgerald, K. H., Gandiwa, P., Laurenson, K., Milanzi, J., Nelson, A., & Lindsey, P. (2018). Models for the collaborative management of Africa's protected areas. *Biological Conservation, 218*, 73–82. https://doi.org/10.1016/j.biocon.2017.11.025

Balmford, A., Beresford, J., Green, J., Naidoo, R., Walpole, M., & Manica, A. (2009). A global perspective on trends in nature-based tourism. *PLoS Biology, 7*(6). https://doi.org/10.1371/journal.pbio.1000144

Bebbington, A. (1999). Capitals and capabilities: A framework for analyzing peasant viability, rural livelihoods and poverty. *World Development.* https://doi.org/10.1016/S0305-750X(99)00104-7

Benjaminsen, T. A., & Svarstad, H. (2010). The death of an elephant: Conservation discourses versus practices in Africa. *Forum for Development Studies, 37*(3), 385–408. https://doi.org/10.1080/08039410.2010.516406

Biên, P. X., An, P., & Van Dop, P. (1989). *The Cham people in Thuan Hai Province* [Người Chăm ở Thuận Hải]. Văn hoá Thông tin Thuận Hải.

Biên, P. X., An, P., & Van Dop, P. (1991). *The Cham culture* [Văn hoá Chăm]. KHXH.

Bruyere, B. L., Beh, A. W., & Lelengula, G. (2009). Differences in perceptions of communication, tourism benefits, and management issues in a protected area of rural Kenya. *Environmental Management, 43*(1), 49–59. https://doi.org/10.1007/s00267-008-9190-7

Bwasiri, E. (2011). The implications of the management of Indigenous living heritage: The case study of the Mongomi Wa Kolo rock paintings World Heritage Site, Central Tanzania. *The South African Archaeological Bulletin, 66*(193), 60–66.

Byrne, D. (2012). Buddhist stupas and Thai Social Practice. In S. Sullivan & R. Mackay (Eds.), *Archaeological sites: Conservation and management* (pp. 572–587). Getty Conservation Institute.

Carius, F., & Job, H. (2019). Community involvement and tourism revenue sharing as contributing factors to the UN Sustainable Development Goals in Jozani–Chwaka Bay National Park and Biosphere Reserve, Zanzibar. *Journal of Sustainable Tourism, 27*(6), 826–846. https://doi.org/10.1080/09669582.2018.1560457

Chirikure, S., Manyanga, M., Ndoro, W., & Pwiti, G. (2010). Unfulfilled promises? Heritage management and community participation at some of Africa's cultural heritage sites. *International Journal of Heritage Studies, 16*(1–2), 30–44. https://doi.org/10.1080/135272509034 41739

Engelhardt, R. A., & Rogers, P. R. (2009). *Hoi An protocols for best conservation practice in Asia: Professional guidelines for assuring and preserving the authenticity of heritage sites in the context of the cultures of Asia.* UNESCO Bangkok.

Fletcher, R., Johnson, I., Bruce, E., & Khun-Neay, K. (2007). Living with heritage: Site monitoring and heritage values in Greater Angkor and the Angkor World Heritage Site. *Cambodia. World Archaeology, 39*(3), 385–405. https://doi.org/10.1080/00438240701465001

Gautam, A. P. (2009). Equity and livelihoods in Nepal's community forestry. *International Journal of Social Forestry, 2*(2), 101–122.

Harris, R. B. (1991). Conservation prospects for musk deer and other wildlife in southern Qinghai, China. *Mountain Research and Development, 11*(4), 353–358. https://doi.org/10.1016/0006-3207(93)90773-T

Heslinga, J., Groote, P., & Vanclay, F. (2019). Strengthening governance processes to improve benefit-sharing from tourism in protected areas by using stakeholder analysis. *Journal of Sustainable Tourism, 27*(6), 773–787. https://doi.org/10.1080/09669582.2017.1408635

Huong, P. T. T. (2015). Living heritage, community participation and sustainability: Redefining development strategies in Hoi An Ancient Town World Heritage property, Viet Nam. In W. L. Sophia Labadi (Ed.), Urban heritage, development and sustainability international frameworks, national and local governance (pp. 274–290). Routledge.

Imanishimwe, A., Niyonzima, T., & Nsabimana, D. (2018). Contribution of community conservation and ecotourism projects on improving livelihoods and sustainable biodiversity conservation in and around Nyungwe National Park (NNP). *Journal of Tourism & Hospitality, 7*(4). https://doi.org/10.4172/2167-0269.1000363

Jamal, T., & Stronza, A. (2009). Collaboration theory and tourism practice in protected areas: Stakeholders, structuring and sustainability. *Journal of Sustainable Tourism.* https://doi.org/10.1080/09669580802495741

Jigyasu, R. (2015). The intangible dimension of urban heritage. In F. Bandarin & R. van Oers (Eds.), *Reconnecting the city* (pp. 130–159). Wiley. https://doi.org/10.1002/9781118383940

Jones, E. R. (2007). Three management challenges for protection of aboriginal cultural heritage in a Tasmanian multiple-use conservation area. *Australian Geographer, 38*(1), 93–112.

Kiss, A. (2004). Is community-based ecotourism a good use of biodiversity conservation funds? *Trends in Ecology and Evolution.* https://doi.org/10.1016/j.tree.2004.03.010

Kong, P. (2008). *Social quality in the conservation process of living heritage sites.* International Forum on Urbanism (IFoU).

Lapeyre, R. (2011). The Grootberg lodge partnership in Namibia: Towards poverty alleviation and empowerment for long-term sustainability? *Current Issues in Tourism, 14*(3), 221–234. https://doi.org/10.1080/13683500.2011.555521

Lask, T., & Herold, S. (2004). An observation station for culture and tourism in Vietnam: A forum for World Heritage and public participation. *Current Issues in Tourism, 7*(4–5), 399–411.

Li, W. (2006). Community decisionmaking participation in development. *Annals of Tourism Research, 33*(1), 132–143. https://doi.org/10.1016/j.annals.2005.07.003

Lindberg, K. (1991). Policies for maximizing nature tourism's ecological and economic benefits. In *International conservation financing project working paper* (p. 37). World Resources Institute (WRI).

MacKenzie, C. A. (2012). Trenches like fences make good neighbours: Revenue sharing around Kibale National Park, Uganda. *Journal for Nature Conservation, 20*(2), 92–100. https://doi.org/10.1016/j.jnc.2011.08.006

Makame, M. K., & Boon, E. K. (2017). Sustainable tourism and benefit-sharing in Zanzibar: The case of Kiwengwa-Pongwe forest reserve. *Journal of Human Ecology, 24*(2), 93–109. https://doi.org/10.1080/09709274.2008.11906105

Mbaiwa, J. E., & Stronza, A. L. (2010). The effects of tourism development on rural livelihoods in the Okavango Delta, Botswana. *Journal of Sustainable Tourism, 18*(5), 635–656. https://doi.org/10.1080/09669581003653500

Melita, A. W., & Mendlinger, S. (2013). The impact of tourism revenue on the local communities' livelihood: A case study of Ngorongoro conservation area, Tanzania. *Journal of Service Science and Management, 6*(1), 117–126. https://doi.org/10.4236/jssm.2013.61012

Miura, K. (2005). Conservation of a 'living heritage site': A contradiction in terms? A case study of Angkor World Heritage Site. *Conservation and Management of Archaeological Sites, 7*(1), 3–18. https://doi.org/10.1179/135050305793137602

Miura, K. (2008). The need for anthropological approaches to conservation and management of living heritage sites: A case study of Angkor, Cambodia. In I. C. Glover, P. D. Sharrock, & A. B. Elisabeth (Eds.), *Interpreting Southeast Asia's past: Monument, image and text* (pp. 377–390). NUS Press Pte Ltd. https://muse.jhu.edu/chapter/883481

Mukanjari, S., Bednar-Friedl, B., Muchapondwa, E., & Zikhali, P. (2013). Evaluating the prospects of benefit sharing schemes in protecting mountain gorillas in Central Africa. *Natural Resource Modeling, 26*(4), 455–479. https://doi.org/10.1111/nrm.12010

Munanura, I. E., Backman, K. F., Hallo, J. C., & Powell, R. B. (2016). Perceptions of tourism revenue sharing impacts on Volcanoes National Park, Rwanda: A sustainable livelihoods framework. *Journal of Sustainable Tourism.* https://doi.org/10.1080/09669582.2016.1145228

Ndoro, W. (2004). Traditional and customary heritage systems: Nostalgia or reality? The implications of managing heritage sites in Africa. In R. Smeets, C. Westrick, & E. de Merode (Eds.), *Linking universal and local values: Managing a sustainable future for World Heritage* (pp. 81–84). UNESCO World Heritage Centre.

Ndoro, W., & Wijesuriya, G. (2015). Heritage management and conservation: From Colonisation to Globalisation. In L. Meskell (Ed.), *Global heritage: A reader* (pp. 131–149). Wiley-Blackwell.

Norton, A., & Foster, M. (2001). *The potential of using sustainable livelihoods approaches in poverty reduction strategy papers* (No. 148). ISBN: 85003 528 7.

Noseworthy, W. (2017). Khik Agama Cam: Caring for Cham religions in Mainland Southeast Asia, 1651–1969. University of Wiscosin-Madison.

Queiros, D., & Mearns, K. (2019). Khanyayo village and Mkhambathi Nature Reserve, South Africa: A pragmatic qualitative investigation into attitudes towards a protected area. *Journal of Sustainable Tourism, 27*(6), 750–772. https://doi.org/10.1080/09669582.2018.1436177

Sakaya. (2003). *The festivals of the Cham people* [Lễ hội của người Chăm]. NXB Van Hoa Dan Toc.

Salemink, O. (2013). Appropriating culture: The politics of intangible cultural heritage in Vietnam. In H.-T. Ho Tai. & M. Sidel (Eds.), *State, society and the market in contemporary Vietnam: Property, power and values* (pp. 158–180). Routledge. https://doi.org/10.4324/9780203098318

Saltiel, L. (2014). Cultural governance and development in Vietnam. *University of Pennsylvania Journal of International Law, 35*(3), 893–915. https://scholarship.law.upenn.edu/jil/vol35/iss3/6

Sandbrook, C. G. (2010). Putting leakage in its place: The significance of retained tourism revenue in the local context in rural Uganda. *Journal of International Development, 22*(1), 124–136. https://doi.org/10.1002/jid.1507

Scheyvens, R. (2002). *Tourism for development: Empowering communities.* Themes in Tourism Series (Vol. 27). https://doi.org/10.1016/j.tourman.2005.07.013

Schnegg, M., & Kiaka, R. D. (2018). Subsidized elephants: Community-based resource governance and environmental (in)justice in Namibia. *Geoforum, 93,* 105–115. https://doi.org/10.1016/j.geo forum.2018.05.010

Sharma, T. (2013). A community-based approach to heritage management from Ladakh, India. In K. D. Silva & N. K. Chapagain (Eds.), *Asian heritage management: Contexts, concerns, and prospects* (pp. 271–284). Routledge.

Shen, X., Lu, Z., Li, S., & Chen, N. (2012). Tibetan sacred sites: Understanding the traditional management system and its role in modern conservation. *Ecology and Society, 17*(2). https://doi.org/10.5751/ES-04785-170213

Smith, A., & Turk, C. (2013). Customary systems of management and World Heritage in the Pacific Islands. In S. Brockwell, S. O'Connor, & D. Byrne (Eds.), *Transcending the culture–nature divide in cultural heritage: Views from the Asia-Pacific Region* (pp. 23–34). ANU E Press.

Smith, L., & Waterton, E. (2009). *Heritage, communities and archaeology. Duckworth Debates in Archaeology.* Bloomsbury Academic.

Snyman, S., & Bricker, K. S. (2019). Living on the edge: Benefit-sharing from protected area tourism. *Journal of Sustainable Tourism, 27*(6), 705–719. https://doi.org/10.1080/09669582. 2019.1615496

Sở VH-TT-DL. (2020). *Ninh Thuan tourism activity in 2019* [Hoạt động du lịch năm 2019].

Spenceley, A., Snyman, S., & Rylance, A. (2017). Revenue sharing from tourism in terrestrial African protected areas. *Journal of Sustainable Tourism.* https://doi.org/10.1080/09669582. 2017.1401632

Strickland-Munro, J., & Moore, S. (2013). Indigenous involvement and benefits from tourism in protected areas: A study of Purnululu National Park and Warmun Community, Australia. *Journal of Sustainable Tourism, 21*(1), 26–41. https://doi.org/10.1080/09669582.2012.680466

Truong, V. D. (2013). Tourism policy development in Vietnam: A pro-poor perspective. *Journal of Policy Research in Tourism, Leisure and Events, 5*(1), 28–45. https://doi.org/10.1080/19407963. 2012.760224

Tumusiime, D. M., & Sjaastad, E. (2014). Conservation and development: Justice, inequality, and attitudes around Bwindi Impenetrable National Park. *Journal of Development Studies, 50*(2), 204–225. https://doi.org/10.1080/00220388.2013.841886

Tumusiime, D. M., & Vedeld, P. (2012). False promise or false premise? Using tourism revenue sharing to promote conservation and poverty reduction in Uganda. *Conservation and Society, 10*(1), 15–28. https://doi.org/10.4103/0972-4923.92189

UNESCO. (2013). *Operational guidelines for the implementation of the World Heritage Convention.* Operational Guidelines for the Implementation of the World Heritage Convention.

Walpole, M. J., & Goodwin, H. J. (2001). Local attitudes towards conservation and tourism around Komodo National Park, Indonesia. *Environmental Conservation, 28*(2), 160–166. https://doi. org/10.1017/S0376892901000169

Waterton, E. (2010). *Politics, policy and the discourses of heritage in Britain.* Palgrave Macmillan.

Waterton, E. (2015). Heritage and community engagement. In *The ethics of cultural heritage* (pp. 53–67). Palgrave Macmillan. https://doi.org/10.1007/978-1-4939-1649-8_4

Weise, K. (2013). Discourse. In K. Weise (Ed.), *Revisiting Kathmandu safeguarding living urban heritage* (pp. 1–52). UNESCO. Kathmandu Office. https://publik.tuwien.ac.at/files/publik_229 747.pdf

Weisse, A., & Ross, A. (2017). Managing a contested cultural heritage place on K'gari (Fraser Island), Queensland, Australia. *Archaeology in Oceania, 52*(3), 149–160. https://doi.org/10. 1002/arco.5130

Wunder, S. (2000). Ecotourism and economic incentives—An empirical approach. *Ecological Economics.* https://doi.org/10.1016/S0921-8009(99)00119-6

Xu, J., Lü, Y., Chen, L., & Liu, Y. (2009). Contribution of tourism development to protected area management: Local stakeholder perspectives. *International Journal of Sustainable Development and World Ecology, 16*(1), 30–36. https://doi.org/10.1080/13504500902757189

Open Access This chapter is licensed under the terms of the Creative Commons Attribution 4.0 International License (http://creativecommons.org/licenses/by/4.0/), which permits use, sharing, adaptation, distribution and reproduction in any medium or format, as long as you give appropriate credit to the original author(s) and the source, provide a link to the Creative Commons license and indicate if changes were made.

The images or other third party material in this chapter are included in the chapter's Creative Commons license, unless indicated otherwise in a credit line to the material. If material is not included in the chapter's Creative Commons license and your intended use is not permitted by statutory regulation or exceeds the permitted use, you will need to obtain permission directly from the copyright holder.

Conclusion: Towards a Sustainable Future—Navigating the Cham Living Heritage in Tourism's Landscape

Introduction

While the work for this research project has been completed, my commitments to my community, both personally and professionally, are lifelong endeavors and a journey upon which I remain (*Jalan daok nao*). I strive to continue helping the Cham community in Vietnam and elsewhere around the world, as well as other ethnic minority communities in Southeast Asia, regarding heritage conservation, sustainable tourism development, and their active participation in these processes. The preservation and promotion of Indigenous heritage is a continual effort, not just a one-time event or a result of legislative actions. As Vietnam and other areas continue to evolve economically and culturally, it's vital for marginalized communities to have allies and advocates across various socio-economic and linguistic groups. This research is a step in that direction. The following sections aim to present the study's conclusions and contributions, including the potential impact on policy, limitations of the study, and suggestions for future research.

Contributions of this Research

This book adds in-depth knowledge of living heritage in the context of Vietnam's national heritage management. My study indexes a paradigm shift from focusing on tangible heritage to more seriously engaging with intangible heritage and focusing more on human lives and local communities. At the heart of heritage conservation is people. This study also adds to current academic debates on heritage conservation and management that are largely influenced by Western models, standards, and practices for both defining and conserving heritage. The necessary inclusion of Indigenous communities only helps to broaden the theoretical and methodological

© The Editor(s) (if applicable) and The Author(s) 2023
Q. D. Tuyen, *Heritage Conservation and Tourism Development at Cham Sacred Sites in Vietnam*, Global Vietnam: Across Time, Space and Community,
https://doi.org/10.1007/978-981-99-3350-1

horizons of heritage management fields beyond such limitations. The Cham community in Vietnam offers one such perspective from Southeast Asia, where religious philosophies, cultural practices, and the social relations within the community help to define the objectives and approaches towards conserving the past in the present, while also embracing the future.

As discussed above, the literature on living heritage shows that, for most communities, heritage can change over time. In fact, Hobsbawm (1983), Sullivan (1993), Karlström (2005), Andrews and Buggey (2008), Byrne (2012), Wijesuriya (2014), and many others argue that traditions should change as living descendants of those who created the heritage bring their narrative(s) of heritage into contexts of modernity. In the case of Cham experiences analyzed in this study, however, change more often comes from outside. In other words, this situation does not describe the reproduction and transformation of heritage in a rapidly changing world, but rather that there is frequently imposed change, from above, from government officials, who want to change traditions to meet tourist expectations and thereby commodify Cham heritage in ways that are directly beneficial for the government and tour operators. For Cham communities, this is a challenge to the authenticity of their heritage and a diminution in the significance of the physical elements of the place (especially the temple), as well as the intangible elements of Cham beliefs and spiritual practices. External pressures that derive from tourism in the context of Vietnam's development present perhaps the greatest challenges to the successes of conserving Cham heritage. Nevertheless, the most effective solutions begin with the internal dynamics of local people within the Cham community.

Specifically, cultural tradition, Indigenous knowledge, and cultural identity must be acknowledged and foregrounded in heritage management planning stages and the development of tourism at cultural sites. For Cham heritage, there is a need to consider the range of Cham perceptions through a recognition of the multivocal perceptions and understandings about sacred sites. In the broader context of Vietnam, the heritage conservation of ethnic minority groups also needs to take a similarly multivocalic approach in considering local perceptions and beliefs in order to determine the most appropriate strategies for sustainable heritage management. In tandem with Indigenous voices at the heart of conservation, the economic benefits and other capital generated in association with heritage management needs to take a similarly inclusive approach. In many countries, tourism has become a driving force to generate income and economic benefits. However, there continue to be many documented negative impacts on host communities in both socio-economic and cultural ways. There should be a clear legal framework for heritage sites, including guidelines for communities, at both the provincial and national levels, especially for supporting heritage livelihoods, specifically equitable benefit-sharing, and creating a role for local communities to co-manage heritage effectively. The negative impacts of heritage conservation and heritage tourism development on living heritage sites have been recognized by heritage authorities and scholars in the past (Baillie, 2007; Cole, 2006; Daly & Winter, 2012; Huong, 2015; Suntikul & Jachna, 2013). However, although community participation in heritage management is increasingly recognized (Byrd,

2007; Cole, 2006; Larsen, 2018; Smith & Waterton, 2009), local voices and perceptions remain marginalized. The Cham community of Vietnam are eager to ensure the longevity of their traditions, rituals, religions, language, and arts, and inclusive approaches to management appear to be aptly complimentary for this context.

Social media presents a valuable opportunity for marginalized communities to voice their perspectives and advocate for the preservation of their cultural heritage. Despite the lack of a direct communication channel between these communities and the government, new forms of media have the potential to facilitate meaningful dialogue and drive social change. To fully harness the potential of social media in the context of heritage conservation, future research could partner with local communities to establish centralized platforms for preserving their cultural heritage through direct communication channels. Currently, the traditional means of information dissemination through heritage management authorities and institutions are often inaccessible to community members. However, freely accessible social networking platforms offer a more efficient and effective way to disseminate information and raise awareness about the values, traditions, and cultural heritage of these communities, which are often threatened.

Additionally, it is essential to recognize the role of the community in heritage conservation by incorporating their perspectives and experiences into the laws and policies that govern heritage management. As noted in this research, the Cham temple is a significant spiritual and cultural site for the Cham community, and their religious beliefs and practices are an integral part of the temple's heritage. However, the current heritage law does not adequately reflect this importance, leading to a narrow understanding of what constitutes heritage and how it should be managed. To rectify this situation, the heritage law should be revised to include the classification of spiritual heritage, and specific regulations should be developed to support the participation of ethnic minority groups in heritage management. This would allow for the meaningful engagement of communities in the preservation of their cultural heritage and promote the sustainability of heritage management practices.

This book makes a valuable contribution to the field of cultural heritage management in Vietnam by focusing on the heritage of the ethnic Cham community. Despite previous literature on heritage conservation and tourism development in Vietnam having focused on the Kinh majority community's heritage (Huong, 2015; Logan, 2009), very few studies have paid attention to heritage conservation and tourism development in ethnic minority communities apart from studies by Larsen (2015, 2018) on Indigenous communities in Quang Binh Province and Salemink (2006, 2013, 2016) on Uplanders.

The book investigates the relationship between heritage conservation and tourism development in the context of sacred spaces in the Cham community and provides an in-depth case study to demonstrate the challenges faced by the Cham in maintaining their cultural heritage in a rapidly changing Vietnam. In addition, the author criticizes several sections of Vietnamese heritage law in several chapters, highlighting the important issue that the role of the community in everyday heritage conservation practices has not been recognized. The author's case study of the sacred temple of the Cham provides concrete evidence of the need to supplement the cultural heritage classification to account for spiritual heritage, as well as separate regulations for ethnic minority communities in their living heritage sites.

Internationally, literature on Cham studies has mostly focused on the tangibility of heritage, such as archaeology, architecture, and arts, and largely ignores the intangible cultural heritage and lives of the Cham community. This book bridges the knowledge gap in the context of Cham cultural heritage in Vietnam, from the perspectives of an Indigenous community. It provides an in-depth case study of tourism development related to the sacred spaces of the Cham ethnic minority group in Vietnam, and explores the relationship between heritage conservation and tourism development in sacred spaces.

Furthermore, I investigate the central question of whether tourism is a good opportunity for economic development to preserve cultural heritage, or whether it brings the possibility of cultural erosion of Indigenous and ethnic people. Through this work, I introduce a new context of living heritage and sacred spaces among Indigenous people and explore the challenges between conservation and development in the specific context of Vietnam, demonstrating various challenges faced by the Cham community in maintaining their cultural heritage amidst rapidly changing Vietnam.

Limitations to the Research

There are several limitations to this research that should be acknowledged. Firstly, this research is a single case study focusing on the perceptions of the Cham community on the issues of heritage conservation and tourism development in Ninh Thuan Province. This means that the findings are not necessarily applicable to other experiences of the Cham community in different regions of Vietnam or to other ethnic minority groups. Each group may have its own unique sociohistorical context and dynamic local politics that shape their heritage experiences. Therefore, this study should be considered as a starting point towards the greater inclusion of local communities and their experiences in cultural heritage management and tourism development.

Another limitation is that the study mainly focused on the views of people from within the Cham community and the heritage authorities who manage their cultural sites. There is a need to examine the perspectives of other stakeholders such as tourists, local authorities, and business owners who are also involved in the development of tourism at Cham sacred sites. These stakeholders may have different attitudes, beliefs, and behaviors that can significantly impact the development of tourism and the conservation of Cham cultural heritage. The study would have benefited from a broader examination of these perspectives to gain a more complete understanding of the challenges and opportunities in heritage management and tourism development.

Finally, the study faced significant challenges in translating and interpreting terms of Cham culture and philosophy. As a Cham author with over 15 years of experience in researching Cham cultural heritage, the author still encountered difficulties in accurately translating and interpreting Cham terms. This is because each term is closely connected to the depth and connotation of Cham cultural philosophy, making it diffi-cult to translate and interpret accurately. Despite consulting with foreign experts, many of the terms remain complex and confusing, leading to limitations in the study. In conclusion, these limitations should be kept in mind when interpreting the findings of this research.

The study of heritage conservation and tourism development in relation to local communities and ethnic minorities has been gaining momentum in recent years. In light of this, it is essential to examine the role of the community in the implemen-tation of World Heritage Conventions and its relationship to human rights (Blake, 2011, 2015; Disko, 2015; Langfield et al., 2010; Larsen, 2017; Logan, 2012, 2015). This is particularly relevant for Indigenous communities worldwide, as the rights of communities living in and around heritage sites may be affected in either positive or negative ways, depending on the state authorities' approach to this issue.

One of the main challenges in this field is to encourage effective, ongoing collab-oration between government authorities and local communities. Although granting local communities the right to have a voice in heritage management practices is a step in the right direction, it does not guarantee equitable outcomes in the long term. Therefore, it is crucial to identify and understand the obstacles that have led to ineffective collaboration between these two groups and what future obstacles may arise (Larsen, 2017). In the context of the Cham heritage in Ninh Thuan Province, Vietnam, tensions have arisen between the Cham community and heritage authorities. However, this does not mean that there is no potential for more beneficial and produc-tive engagements in the future. Hence, research that aims to monitor the balance and potential imbalances between stakeholders is crucial for places like Vietnam undergoing rapid modernization. Furthermore, a more in-depth understanding of the barriers to community participation and the potential for equitable collaboration would help to determine how best to balance the interests of local communities and government authorities for the long-term preservation and management of Cham heritage sites (Blake, 2011).

Additionally, the examination of the ways in which tourism development has impacted local communities could be a valuable area of research. How does the devel-opment of tourist sites impact the cultural practices and beliefs of local communities, and how does this impact the cultural heritage of these groups? Does the increase in tourism lead to a loss of cultural heritage or does it provide an opportunity for cultural revitalization? This type of research would provide an opportunity to gain insight into the impact of tourism development on the preservation of cultural heritage and its importance to local communities. It would also provide a deeper understanding of the challenges and opportunities for sustainable heritage management in the context of tourism development.

Furthermore, the issue of cultural appropriation and commodification of heritage also deserves attention in the context of Cham heritage management and tourism development. The development of tourism sites may result in the commercializa-tion of cultural heritage, which can lead to a loss of cultural significance. Research that examines the impact of cultural commodification and commercialization on the preservation of cultural heritage and its significance to local communities could provide important insights into the ways in which tourism development affects the cultural heritage of these groups.

In conclusion, there is a wealth of potential research to be conducted in the field of Cham heritage management and tourism development, which could provide valuable insights into the ways in which local communities can effectively participate in the preservation of their cultural heritage. These insights could help to promote sustainable heritage management and support the human rights of local communities, as well as contribute to the development of more equitable and sustainable tourism practices.

Concluding Remarks

Heritage is a living entity, and in the context of preservation, there are challenges and risks associated with cultural survival. Humans and the communities in which they live provide the essential keys for the futures of Indigenous cultural and religious traditions. Heritage has a heart, and that heart is made up of the communities that embody heritage in all of its various forms. With the case of the sacred temple of the Cham people, the heritage conservation and impacts of tourism have brought many negative issues for the Cham community. For many people in the Cham community, modernization and tourism development are inevitable, but changes at the temple are viewed as more negative than positive. Such changes have impacted cultural identity and understandings of authenticity in ways that inspire Cham people to respond harshly to those issues at sacred sites. The promotion of cultural heritage is seen as means to awaken and revitalize cultural identity among younger generations, and to counter the long-standing history of degradation and destruction of the Champā civilization. It is assumed that challenges and risks at sacred sites will continue to happen, but the enduring strength of ethnic identity and cultural consciousness will be imperative elements for the ongoing protection of Cham sacred space, especially as Vietnam continues to change in different socio-economic ways. This research project has been an opportunity to convey the voices of the Cham community for both researchers and others who are interested in the history of Champā or the heritage of the Cham people. Cham voices reflect a heart that is still beating in a rapidly globalizing world, and it is a heart looking to be nurtured in strength and stamina so as to bring the heritage of ancestors into a prosperous and enduring future. As I embarked on the task of writing this book, I was driven by a desire to offer a unique and comprehensive perspective on the conservation and promotion of Cham heritage in Central Vietnam. My approach was distinct in that it consolidated the various aspects of conservation and development that were previously addressed in separate published works, allowing for a more nuanced understanding of the challenges facing the Cham community in preserving their heritage.

Through the course of the book, I take the reader on a journey through the various issues and challenges facing the Cham people. I highlight the criticality of recognizing and preserving traditional beliefs and practices in shaping the cultural identity of Indigenous communities. Through a series of insightful analyses, I demonstrate the importance of Indigenous living heritage in safeguarding heritage for future generations, underscoring the need for more culturally sensitive approaches to heritage conservation and management.

The book's contribution lies in its ability to provide a comprehensive overview of the Cham people's heritage value and the challenges they face in preserving it. By consolidating different perspectives into one volume, it offers a more complete picture of the issues surrounding the conservation and promotion of Cham heritage. In doing so, it serves as an essential resource for anyone interested in the preservation and promotion of cultural heritage, particularly in the context of Indigenous living heritage.

Glossary

List of Glossary of Terms

	English	Vietnamese
1	Vietnam Cultural Heritage Association	Hội Di Sản Văn Hóa Việt Nam
2	The National Council of Cultural Heritage	Hội đồng Di sản Văn hoá Quốc gia
3	The Department of Culture, Sports and Tourism	Sở Văn hoá, Thể thao và Du lịch
4	The Ministry of Culture, Sports and Tourism	Bộ Văn hoá, Thể thao và Du lịch
5	The Museum Conservation Department	Cục Bảo tồn Bảo tàng
6	Cham Cultural Research Center	Trung tâm Nghiên cứu Văn hoá Chăm
7	National Assembly of the Socialist Republic of Vietnam	Quốc hội nước Cộng hoà Xã hội Chủ nghĩa Việt Nam
8	The Law on Cultural Heritage	Luật Di sản Văn hoá
9	General Statistics Office	Tổng cục Thống kê
10	Ninh Thuan Council for Brahman Dignitaries	Hội đồng Chức sắc Chăm Balamon tỉnh Ninh Thuận

© The Editor(s) (if applicable) and The Author(s) 2023
Q. D. Tuyen, *Heritage Conservation and Tourism Development at Cham Sacred Sites in Vietnam*, Global Vietnam: Across Time, Space and Community,
https://doi.org/10.1007/978-981-99-3350-1

List of Glossary of Cham Terms

Frequently used local terms		
	Term	Explanation
1	Ahier	Ahier is a form of localized Hinduism that has its own unique beliefs and practices. The dignitaries within the Ahier religion are classified into a hierarchical order, starting from the lowest rank of Basaih Ndung Akaok (Beginner) to the highest rank of Po Adhia. In ascending order, the other ranks are Basaih Liah, Basaih Pahuak, and Basaih Tapah (On Bac). Po Adhia holds the highest status in both the religious and social spheres of the Ahier community
2	Awal	"Awal" is a form of localized Islam and its dignitaries are classified in ascending order of rank as Acar (Beginner), Madin (responsible for leading the call to prayers), Katip (readers), Imâm, and Po Gru, the highest level of authority in the Awal religion and community
3	Kadhar	Kadhar plays a vital role in the traditional spiritual and cultural practices of the community. As an official musician, he is responsible for providing musical accompaniment and singing hymns and praises to the gods during religious rituals, both at temples and within families. The use of the traditional *kanyi* instrument adds to the rich and vibrant atmosphere of these events, and the skill of the Kadhar in playing it is greatly valued and respected
4	Po Adhia	Po Adhia is a highly respected and influential figure within the Ahier community, elected from among the dignitaries of Po Tapah. This esteemed position is responsible for overseeing religious activities, including presiding over rituals and determining the dates for significant events such as weddings, funerals, and house blessings. Po Adhia serves as the spiritual leader of the Ahier community, making important decisions and delegating tasks to ensure that all cultural and religious activities are carried out in accordance with Ahier traditions

(continued)

(continued)

Frequently used local terms

	Term	Explanation
5	Muk Pajuw	Muk Pajuw is a female medium who serves as the primary representative of the gods in the Ahier community. She is responsible for inviting the gods to participate in religious ceremonies, preparing offerings for these ceremonies, and dancing to celebrate their success. Muk Pajuw plays a crucial role in connecting the community to the gods and ensuring the success of religious activities
6	Ong Camânei	The Ong Camânei, also known as "the temple guard," plays a crucial role in the maintenance and protection of the Ahier community's spiritual heritage. This person is responsible for overseeing the upkeep of temples and safeguarding the sacred utensils used in rituals. In addition, they assist the Po Adhia, the head of the Ahier priestly hierarchy, during ceremonies by keeping the offerings for the gods. The Ong Camânei is essential in ensuring the preservation of the tangible aspects of the Ahier community's religious practices
7	Ong Maduen	Ong Maduen is a ceremonial official who presides over various important events in the Cham community, such as the Rija ceremony, both at the family and village levels. He is not affiliated with the Ahier temples and serves a distinct role within the community
8	Muk Rija	Muk Rija is a female spiritual figure who acts as a vessel for the spirits of Cham deities and spirits in possession ceremonies. Her role is separate from guiding and supporting ceremonies at temples, but she is involved in bringing offerings to the temples for community or family rituals, often alongside her family members
9	Ong Ka-ing	Ong Ka-ing, also known as the male dancer, is a member of the lower religious elite in the Cham hierarchy. He is primarily responsible for performing in Rija Harei and Rija Nâgar ceremonies, which are held within villages and families. According to Abdul (2013), his role is limited to these specific ceremonies and he does not play a larger role in the broader religious and spiritual activities within the Cham community

(continued)

(continued)

Frequently used local terms		
	Term	Explanation
10	The Katé	The Katé is a significant cultural and religious celebration in the Cham community, held annually on July 1st according to the Cham calendar. It is a time for reflection and honoring Cham kings, national heroes, and ancestors, as well as for asking for blessings from the gods. The festival seeks to secure a bountiful harvest, good weather conditions, and fertility, as well as peace and prosperity for the people. It is a celebration that brings the community together in unity, reminding everyone of their rich cultural heritage and the importance of preserving it

References

Andrews, T., & Buggey, S. (2008). Authenticity in aboriginal cultural landscapes. *APT Bulletin, 39*(2), 63–71.

Baillie, B. (2007). Conservation of the sacred at Angkor Wat: Further reflections on living heritage. *Conservation and Management of Archaeological Sites, 8*(3), 123–131. https://doi.org/10.1179/175355206x265788

Blake, J. (2011). Taking a human rights approach to cultural heritage protection. *Heritage & Society, 4*(2), 199–238. https://doi.org/10.1179/hso.2011.4.2.199

Blake, J. (2015). *International Cultural Heritage Law*. OUP Oxford.

Byrd, E. T. (2007). Stakeholders in sustainable tourism development and their roles: Applying stakeholder theory to sustainable tourism development. *Tourism Review, 62*(2), 6–13. https://doi.org/10.1108/16605370780000309

Byrne, D. (2012). Buddhist stupas and Thai social practice. In S. Sullivan & R. Mackay (Eds.), *Archaeological sites: Conservation and management* (pp. 572–587). Getty Conservation Institute.

Cole, S. (2006). Cultural tourism, community participation and empowerment. In M. Smith & M. Robinson (Eds.), *Cultural tourism in a changing world: Politics, participation and (re) presentation* (pp. 89–103). Multilingual Matters Ltd.

Daly, P. T., & Winter, T. (2012). *Routledge handbook of heritage in Asia*. Routledge.

Disko, S. (2015). Indigenous peoples' rights and the world heritage convention. In W. Logan, M. Nic Craith, & U. Kockel (Eds.), *A Companion to Heritage Studies* (p. 624). Wiley. http://eu.wiley.com/WileyCDA/WileyTitle/productCd-1118486668.html

Hobsbawm. (1983). The invention of tradition. In E. J. Hobsbawm & T. O. Ranger (Eds.), *The invention of tradition* (pp. 1–14). Cambridge University Press.

Huong, P. T. T. (2015). Living heritage, community participation and sustainability: Redefining development strategies in Hoi An Ancient Town World Heritage property, Viet Nam. In W. L. Sophia Labadi (Ed.), *Urban heritage, development and sustainability international frameworks, national and local governance* (pp. 274–290). Rougtledge.

Karlström, A. (2005). Spiritual materiality: Heritage preservation in a Buddhist world? *Journal of Social Archaeology*. https://doi.org/10.1177/1469605305057571

Langfield, M., Logan, W., & Nic Craith, M. (2010). Cultural diversity, heritage and human rights: Intersections in theory and practice. *Key Issues in Cultural Heritage*. https://doi.org/10.4324/9780203863015

Larsen, P. B. (2015). Some preliminary issues and lessons from Phong Nha Ke Bang, Vietnam. In *Understanding community participation and rights-based approaches in world heritage* (p. 13). The Viet Nam Academy of Social Sciences & Ha Noi UNNESCO Office.

© The Editor(s) (if applicable) and The Author(s) 2023   231
Q. D. Tuyen, *Heritage Conservation and Tourism Development at Cham Sacred Sites in Vietnam*, Global Vietnam: Across Time, Space and Community,
https://doi.org/10.1007/978-981-99-3350-1

Larsen, P. B. (2017). *World Heritage and human rights: Lessons from the Asia-Pacific and global arena*. Routledge. https://www.routledge.com/World-Heritage-and-Human-Rights-Lessons-from-the-Asia-Pacific-and-global/Larsen/p/book/9781138224223

Larsen, P. B. (2018). World Heritage and Ethnic Minority Rights in Phong Nha Ke Bang, Vietnam: Cosmopolitan Assemblages in Neoliberal Times. In P. B. Larsen (Ed.), *World Heritage and Human Rights Lessons from the Asia-Pacific and global arena*. Rougtledge.

Logan, W. (2009). Hanoi, Vietnam: Representing power in and of the nation. *City, 13*(1), 87–94. https://doi.org/10.1080/13604810902726251

Logan, W. (2012). Cultural diversity, cultural heritage and human rights: Towards heritage management as human rights-based cultural practice. *International Journal of Heritage Studies, 18*(3), 231–244. https://doi.org/10.1080/13527258.2011.637573

Logan, W. (2015). Community participation in World Heritage sites in Australia and Vietnam. In *Understanding Community Participation and Rights-Based Approaches in World Heritage*. The Viet Nam Academy of Social Sciences & Ha Noi UNNESCO Office.

Salemink, O. (2006). Changing rights and wrongs: The transnational construction of indigenous and human rights among Vietnam's Central Highlanders. *Focaal, 2006*(47), 32–47. https://doi.org/10.3167/092012906780646514

Salemink, O. (2013). Appropriating culture: The politics of intangible cultural heritage in Vietnam. In H.-T. H. T. M. Sidel (Ed.), *State, society and the market in contemporary Vietnam: Property, power and values* (pp. 158–180). Routledge. https://doi.org/10.4324/9780203098318

Salemink, O. (2016). Described, inscribed, written off: Heritagisation as (dis)connection. In P. Taylor (Ed.), *Connected and disconnected in Vietnam: Remarking social relations in a post-socialist nation* (pp. 311–345). ANU Press.

Smith, L., & Waterton, E. (2009). *Heritage, communities and archaeology*. Duckworth Debates in Archaeology. https://doi.org/10.1080/00665983.2009.11078253

Sullivan, S. (1993). Cultural values and cultural imperialism. *Historic Environment, 10*(2/3), 54.

Suntikul, W., & Jachna, T. (2013). Contestation and negotiation of heritage conservation in Luang Prabang, Laos. *Tourism Management, 38*, 57–68. https://doi.org/10.1016/j.tourman.2013.02.005

Wijesuriya, G. (2014). Introducing people-centred approach to conservation and management of Hani Rice Terraces. In ICOMOS China (Ed.), *International Workshop on The Sustainable Development of Honghe Hani Terraces* (pp. 23–34). Mengzi.

Uncited References

Adams, M. J. (2014). Pukulpa pitjama Ananguku ngurakutu - Welcome to Anangu land: World Heritage at Uluru-Kata Tjuta National Park Pukulpa pitjama Ananguku ngurakutu - Welcome to Anangu land. World Heritage Sites and Indigenous Peoples' Rights.

Akagawa, N. (2014). Heritage conservation and Japan's cultural diplomacy: Heritage, national identity and national interest. *Heritage Conservation and Japan's Cultural Diplomacy: Heritage, National Identity and National Interest*. https://doi.org/10.4324/9781315886664

Boisselier, J. (1963). La statuaire du Champa: recherches sur les cultes et l'iconographie. École française d'Extrême-Orient; dépositaire: Adrien-Maisonneuve.

Bui, Huong T., Jones, T. E., Weaver, D. B., & Le, A. (2020). The adaptive resilience of living cultural heritage in a tourism destination. *Journal of Sustainable Tourism, 28*(7). https://doi.org/10.1080/09669582.2020.1717503

Bui, H. T., & Lee, T. (2015). Commodification and politicization of heritage: Implications for heritage tourism at the imperial citadel of Thang Long, Hanoi (Vietnam). *Current Research on Southeast Asia, 8*(2), 187–202.

Cadge, W. (2017). The sacred canopy: Elements of a sociological theory of religion. *Journal of the American Academy of Religion*. Open Road Integrated Media. https://doi.org/10.1093/jaa rel/lfx076

Claudia, R. (2011). The sacred commons: Conflicts and solutions of resource management in sacred natural sites. *Biological Conservation, 144*(10), 2387–2394. https://doi.org/10.1016/j.biocon. 2011.06.017

de la Torre, M. (2013). Values and heritage conservation. *Heritage & Society, 6*(2), 155–166. https://doi.org/10.1179/2159032X13Z.00000000011

Denzin, N., & Lincoln, Y. (2005). *The Sage handbook of qualitative research*. Sage Publications.

Dharma, P., Lafont, P.-B., & Nara, V. (1977). Catalogue des manuscrits Cam des bibliothèques françaises (EFEO). *de l'Ecole Francaise Extreme-Orient*, Vol. CXIV.

Dung, N. K. (n.d.). Intangible Cultural Heritage Safeguarding System in Vietnam. Retrieved February 15, 2018, from https://ich.unesco.org/doc/src/00174-EN.pdf

Finot, L. (1901). La Religion des Chams d'après les monuments, étude suivie d'un Inventaire sommaire des monuments Chams de l'Annam. *Bulletin De L'ecole Française D'extrême-Orient, 1*(1), 12–33. https://doi.org/10.3406/befeo.1901.950

Finot, L. (1909). Notes d'épigraphie XII. Nouvelles inscriptions de Pô Klaun Garai. *Bulletin de l'Ecole française d'Extrême-Orient, 9*(1), 205–209. https://doi.org/10.3406/befeo.1909.1930

Giang, N. L. (2018). World heritage and human rights policy in Vietnam: A legal review. In P. B. Larsen (Ed.), *World Heritage and Human Rights Lessons from the Asia-Pacific and global arena*. Rougtledge.

GSO. (2019). Results of the entire 2019 Census [Kết quả toàn bộ Tổng điều tra dân số 19/12/2019. Trung tâm Tư liệu và Dịch vụ Thống kê, Tổng cục Thống kê]. Ha Noi.

Haley, U., & Haley, G. (1998). Investing in sustainable tourism in Vietnam: Implications for governmental policy. *The Journal of Viet Nam Studies, 1*(1), 8–32.

IUCN, & UNESCO. (2005). Declaration on the Role of Sacred Natural Sites and Cultural Landscapes in the Conservation of Biological and Cultural Diversity. In International Symposium "Conserving Cultural and Biological Diversity: The Role of Sacred Natural Sites and Cultural Landscapes." Tokyo, Japan. https://www.un.org/esa/socdev/unpfii/documents/tokyo_final_dec laration_en.pdf

Lan, L. T. H. & D. (2005). Bước đầu tìm hiểu các hệ lịch của người Chăm. In Đời sống văn hóa xã hội người Chăm thành phố Hồ Chí Minh. Văn hóa dân tộc.

Merlan, F. (2009). Indigeneity: Global and local. *Current Anthropology*. https://doi.org/10.1086/597667

Mod, M. (1978). Đặc điểm gia đình, thân tộc và xã hội của đồng bào Chàm. In *Những vấn đề dân tộc học ở miền Nam Việt Nam* (Vollume II). Nxb KHXH.

Nakamura, R. (1999). *Cham in Vietnam: Dynamics of ethnicity*. Univeristy of Wangshinton.

Nakamura, R. (2000). The coming of Islam to Champa. *Journal of the Malaysian Branch of the Royal Asiatic Society, LXXIII*, 58.

Pike, K. (1954). *Language in relation to a unified theory of the structure of human behaviour*, 1. Summer Institute of Linguistics.

Smith, L., & Akagawa, N. (2009). Intangible heritage. UK National Commission for UNESCO 2006 Annual Conference Report. https://doi.org/10.4324/9780203884973

Tien, N. H., Minh, H. T. T., & Dan, P. V. (2019). Branding building for Vietnam higher education industry-reality and solutions. *International Journal of Research in Marketing Management and Sales, 1*(2), 118–123. ISSN 2663-3337

Timothy, D. (2014). Contemporary cultural heritage and tourism: Development issues and emerging trends. *Public Archaeology, 13*(1–3), 30–47. https://doi.org/10.1179/1465518714Z.000000 00052

Trinh, B. Van. (2018). Áo dài phụ nữ Chăm trong lễ và hội [Traditional Cham cloth in rituals and festivals]. Retrieved November 20, 2018, from https://www.facebook.com/permalink.php? story_fbid=692289794480087&id=100010972178674

Tung, L. T. (2020). Tourism develpopment in Vietnam: New strategy for a sustainable pathway. *GeoJournal of Tourism and Geosites, 31*(3), 1174–1179. https://doi.org/10.30892/gtg.313 32-555

Var, T. (1994). Tourism industry in Vietnam. *Annals of Tourism Research, 21*(2), 420–422. https://doi.org/10.1016/0160-7383(94)90064-7

Viya, T. (2018). Tradition and non-tradition [Truyền thống và phi truyền thống]. https://www.fac ebook.com/travigia/posts/23009945234619525?__tn__=K-R

Walter, N. (2021). Narrative approach to living heritage. *Protection of Cultural Heritage, (10).* https://doi.org/10.35784/odk.2443

Wild, R., McLeod, C., & Valentine, P. (2008). Sacred Natural Sites. Guidelines for Protected Area Managers. *Best Practice Protected Area Guidelines* (Vol. 16). IUCN. https://doi.org/10.2305/IUCN.CH.2008.PAG.16.en

Zeppel, H. (1997). Maori tourism in New Zealand. *Tourism Management, 18*(7), 475–478. https://doi.org/10.1016/S0261-5177(97)84399-3